BUILDING THE AMERICAN COMMUNITY

This book is a history of the development of the twentieth century American school curriculum. The curriculum developed, so the book argues, out of the efforts of a number of educators who identified themselves professionally with the field of curriculum to reconcile the gap between liberal-democratic values and the realities of urban, industrial life. In effect, then, these educators were doing nothing more than were other early twentieth century American intellectuals in other walks of life who were concerned about the disruptive effect of America's transition from a rural, agarian to an urban, industrial society. The reconciliation these educators, as well as most American intellectuals, sought was one that would preserve the historic values of rural, agarian America, the values of liberty and equality, in an urban, industrial society. They talked about this effort as that of a search for community. The curriculum, then, became for these educators who founded the field of curriculum, an instrument for restoring a sense of community to modern American society. In talking about the search for community, these founding theorists of the curriculum field embraced a central organizing concept from the field of sociology, that of social control. They saw the curriculum as an instrument of social control for restoring a sense of community to urban, industrial America. The book traces how curriculum theorists from 1900 to the mid-1950s first conceptualized the curriculum as an instrument of social control and how educators in one city, Minneapolis, sought to actually use the curriculum as such an instrument.

Building the American Community

The School Curriculum and the Search for Social Control

Studies in Curriculum History 4

Building the American Community

The School Curriculum and the Search for Social Control

Barry M. Franklin
Kennesaw College

The Falmer Press
(A member of the Taylor & Francis Group)
London and Philadelphia

UK   The Falmer Press, Falmer House, Barcombe, Lewes, East Sussex, BN8 5DL

USA   The Falmer Press, Taylor & Francis Inc., 242 Cherry Street, Philadelphia, PA 19106-1906

First published 1986

Library of Congress Cataloging in Publication Data

Franklin, Barry M.
  Building the American community.

  (Studies in curriculum history;)
  Includes index.
  1. Public schools—United States—Curricula—
Philosophy. 2. Social control. 3. Curriculum planning
—Minnesota—Minneapolis—Case studies. I. Title.
II. Series.
LB1570.F677 1985 375'.001'09776579 85-12853
ISBN 1-85000-076-X (pbk.)
ISBN 1-85000-075-1

Jacket illustration by Kerry Freedman

Jacket design by Caroline Archer

Typeset in 11/13 Garamond by
Imago Publishing Ltd, Thame, Oxon

Printed in Great Britain by Taylor & Francis (Printers) Ltd, Basingstoke

Contents

To Lynn, Nathan, and Jeremy

Foreword

In *Building the American Community* Barry Franklin seems preeminently concerned to break down the polarized positions which have emerged around the concept of social control. His concern throughout is less with the simplifications of political posturing than with the complexities of curriculum policy and action. He is with Cohen in condemning a 'one-dimensional understanding of the development of American education as the result of a conspiracy of evil men plotting evil deeds for sinister ends.' Whilst he argues that we cannot adequately understand American educational policy or practice unless we take account of the concept of social control, he adds:

> In this respect, I should note that the use of the term, social control, is not synonymous with embracing a radical politics. As I will show in this volume, American educators of both liberal and conservative political persuasions were to be found during this century invoking the idea of social control.

The elucidation of the complexity of curriculum is further illustrated in Franklin's final chapter. Franklin has been a leading advocate of a version of curriculum history undertaken by curriculum specialists precisely so as to illuminate the complexity of 'internal' curriculum process. Chapter 6 indicates that the translation of curriculum ideas and rhetoric into curriculum practice must follow a tortuous route. Above all he draws our attention to the 'local mediating factors' involved in the day to day operation of the Minneapolis schools. He argues 'if what we have found about the relationship between curriculum theory and practice in Minneapolis is true for other school systems, we will need to revise our understanding of that relationship.'

Quite so, and one can immediately grasp the relevance of this contention for other national educational systems. However, the distinctiveness of Franklin's study must also be appreciated, deriving as it does from the differing modalities of control and operation in the US system. The centrality given to curriculum thought reflects the assumed centrality of curriculum thinkers in influencing curriculum action. Hence the major part of the volume focuses on the examination of 'the recommendations and proposals emanating throughout this century from the writings of those individuals who held university teaching positions in schools of education and identified themselves professionally with curriculum as a field of work and study.' Franklin believes that 'although the ideas proposed by those who teach and write about curriculum in the university do not tell us exactly what was happening in schools throughout this century, they do provide a picture on a national scope of the general shape and direction the school curriculum was taking.'

In England and Wales such a contention would be far less sustainable. Here we should be more concerned to scrutinize examination syllabuses, HMI and DES reports than curriculum specialists' writings. These would provide a closer indication of the general shape and direction of the school curriculum than, say, the writings of Peters, Hirst, Stenhouse, Bantock or Lawton. To say this is merely to indicate that curriculum history will need to take different forms in different national and indeed local locations; the forms of curriculum history will then need to respect the modalities of control and operation of the local and national milieux.

Interestingly Franklin draws our attention to a further distinction between American and English curriculum history. In the USA a different conception of the curriculum has arisen, moving away from the stress on academic disciplines and mental faculties towards a curriculum which is more complex but also more disparate and locally oriented. Here he introduces the importance of the curriculum specialists' notion, albeit idealized, of the community. 'The rural roots of this new class of intellectuals led them to see American democracy as being embodied in the values and attitudes of the small town.' More recently, however, he judges that after the publication of *A Nation at Risk* there may be a return to academic disciplines and a stress on mental faculties.

Above all Franklin's study exemplifies the kind of work which the series *Studies in Curriculum History* seeks to showcase. Two primary justifications were given in the first volume. First, such work will improve our knowledge of the school curriculum. Historical studies can elucidate the changing human process behind the definition and promotion of school subjects. Employing this strategy shifts the emphasis from questions of the intrinsic and philosophic value of subjects, from their existence as objective realities, to the motives and activities immanent and inherent in their construction and maintenance. Further, historical scrutiny offers insights into the existence of patterns and recurring constraints: why, for instance, certain 'traditions' in the school curriculum survive and others disappear. Whilst historical studies do not, as their major intention, seek to prove particular theories, nonetheless they may use and contribute to theory.

Secondly, at the level of school practice historical studies can aid analysis. Such studies might even help to explain the emergence and maintenance of anti-research traditions among teachers. Partly teachers' antipathy derives from the point Shipman makes about the curriculum project with which he was involved: 'The end product of the project was determined in the field, in contact with the school, not on the drawing board . . . in the end it was what worked that survived.' But the autonomy of the teacher, his capacity for active reinterpretation should not be overestimated, for major constraints do exist. Hence, Shipman's judgment in a sense misses the point: only what is prepared on the drawing board goes into the school and therefore *has a chance* to be interpreted and to survive. Exploring the editing process which takes place on the drawing board of history with respect to the school curriculum is more than static historicism. By understanding this process we can define a range of constraints that are immanent in the teachers' work.

Ivor Goodson
Series Editor
July 1985

Preface

No issue, I think, has been more central to the discussions, debates, and conflicts that have accompanied the historical development of American public education than has the question of the social role that schooling should fulfill among a people committed to what I call a liberal democratic ethic. From the very beginning, Americans have sought with a special passion the realization of two values. First, they have committed themselves to the proposition that individuals, acting alone or in groups, should be able to pursue their various public and private interests free from arbitrary restraint. Second, they have dedicated themselves to the belief that individuals should enjoy equal access to those opportunities and resources needed to pursue these interests with a reasonable chance of success. Taken together, these two beliefs, one to liberty and the other to equality, constitute a liberal democratic ethic that characterizes, I believe, what America, its people, and its institutions, is all about.

One fruitful way of thinking about the history of American public education is as the effort of individuals to use one institution, the schools, to create a social and political climate to allow this liberal-democratic ethic to flourish. We can, in other words, look at the major events that have occurred in our educational history, the struggle for the common school, the extension of compulsory schooling, and the conflict over school segregation, to name but a few, as instances of this endeavor to use the schools to enhance liberal democratic values.

The purpose of this volume is to examine one of the most important instances of this use of the schools during the twentieth century, the attempt of professional educators from about 1900 to the mid-1950s to design a curriculum appropriate for preparing youth for life in an urban, industrial society. Key to this effort was the emergence during this period of the curriculum field, both as an academic discipline within the university and as an occupational role within the public schools. It was those educators within the university and the public schools who identified themselves professionally with the field of curriculum who assumed the leadership in this effort to fit the schools and its course of study to the demands of urbanization and industrialization and in so doing to champion liberal democratic values.

In trying to develop a curriculum appropriate for the conditions of twentieth century life, these first curriculum workers found it necessary to borrow and use ideas that many American intellectuals were then using to talk about urbanization and industrialization. Two of these ideas, social control and community, would prove most important in their work. If the schools and its curriculum were to promote a liberal democratic ethic, they would, these educators argued, have to assume a very special social role. They would have to become an instrument of social control for restoring a sense of community to twentieth century American society. In this volume, I will explore what American intellectuals, including those within the field of curriculum, meant when they invoked the ideas of social control and community. I will trace these two ideas from their appearance in our early twentieth century intellectual thought, through their adoption by the formative theorists of the curriculum field, to their use by educators in one urban school system, the Minneapolis Public Schools, in the selection and organization of the actual school curriculum.

Acknowledgements

In writing this volume, I have benefited from the wise comments and thoughtful criticisms of a number of colleagues and friends. I am indebted to those who were willing to read drafts of the various chapters. I am equally indebted to those whose conversations with me about the ideas contained in this volume helped shape my argument. They include Carl Chrislock, Millard Clements, Cathy Cornbleth, Tom Hawkins, Diane Pike, Paul Ringel, Jose Rosario, Sheldon Rosenstock, William Sutton and Jane White. Four individuals from the University of Wisconsin, Madison, once teachers and now friends, deserve special mention. They are Michael Apple, Herbert Kliebard, John Palmer and Thomas Popkewitz. Although they would no doubt interpret the history of the curriculum differently than I, they each, in their own way, helped me clarify my thinking about the social purpose of the curriculum.

I am indebted to the following libraries and institutions for granting me access to the manuscript collections used in this essay and to their staffs for assisting me in my research: University of Chicago Library (George Herbert Mead papers and Ralph Tyler papers), University of Illinois, Chicago Library (papers of the Immigrants' Protective League), Minneapolis Public Schools, Information Service Center (general files of the Minneapolis Public Schools), Ohio State University Library (W.W. Charters papers), State Historical Society of Wisconsin (Edward A. Ross papers) and the University of Wyoming, American Heritage Center (Hollis Caswell Collection).

At critical points in the preparation of this essay, I received financial support that enabled me to devote full-time to research and writing. For this assistance I am indebted to the Committee on Faculty Development at Augsburg College, the Division of College and University Services of the American Lutheran Church, and the Midwest Faculty Seminar Program of the University of Chicago.

Lynn, my wife, deserves a special note of thanks. Not only did she cover for me, so to speak, in our shared domestic responsibilities so that I could sneak away to carry out my research, she was an important participant in the research itself. It was her reading of the Mead papers that uncovered what was my most useful resource in understanding Mead, his unpublished manuscript on the effects of industrialization which I cite in chapter 3.

Portions of this essay represent expanded and rewritten versions of articles that have appeared elsewhere. The segment of chapter 3 that deals with Thorndike was based on a paper entitled 'Curriculum thought and social meaning: Edward L. Thorndike and the curriculum field', which appeared in *Educational Theory*, Volume 26, summer, 1976. Chapter 6 is an expanded version of a paper entitled 'The social efficiency movement reconsidered: Curriculum change in Minneapolis, 1917–1950', which appeared in *Curriculum Inquiry*, Volume 12, spring, 1982.

1 Curriculum, Community, and Social Control: An Introductory Framework

During the last two decades, no idea has probably been more popular among scholars in their efforts to explain the nature and purpose of American education than has been that of social control. Embued with a critical spirit and a left-of-center, if not radical, political ideology, many educational scholars during the 1960s and 1970s found in the idea of social control the answer to what they saw as the central educational question of the day, the historic failure of American public schools to live up to their promise of promoting individual opportunity and building a more equal society. Using the idea of social control, these scholars could explain this failure by arguing that in truth American education was never designed to achieve egalitarian ends but rather to regulate the poor and ethnic minorities in order to preserve the interests of those within society who monopolized political and economic power. Not since the 1920s when the concept of social control enjoyed a dominant position in the social sciences, much as did the idea of equilibrium in the 1940s and 1950s and as does the idea of conflict today, have educational thinkers appeared more interested in invoking the idea of social control in their writings.[1]

Despite the use which educational scholars during the last two decades have made of the term 'social control' they have shown little interest in its meaning. The reason for this has to do, I believe, with the way they have used this concept. Rarely, if ever, did these educators define what they meant by social control. Instead, they tended to use the term as a label to refer to those individuals and groups and those educational practices which they believed have stood in the way of egalitarian reform.

The lack of conceptual clarity that surrounds our use of the concept of social control has recently led some educators to question the continued value of the term. The educational historian Sol Cohen, for example, has suggested that the term, social control, offers an under-standing of educational ideas and practices which is 'a dead end as far as historical usefulness is concerned'. Cohen's position seems to be that our use of the term as a label of opprobrium leads us to a one-dimensional understanding of the development of American education as the result of a conspiracy of evil men plotting evil deeds for sinister ends. Existing social control interpretations, Cohen suggests, offer a view of the American public school as an agency so single-mindedly dedicated to repressive, inegalitarian ends that change and reform are hopeless.[2]

Some who share Cohen's criticism have been concerned that invoking the idea of social control is tantamount to embracing a radical political position. As a consequence, they have abandoned the term in favor of what appears to be less ideological explanatory categories.[3] Others, who appear less worried about exposing radical political learnings, have moved what seems to be even further to the left and adopted, as a replacement for the idea of social control, the concept of hegemony as defined by the Italian Marxist Antonio Gramsci.[4]

I find neither alternative, abandoning the idea of social control nor embracing the notion of hegemony, particularly inviting. Social control is more than a label which contemporary educators have used to characterize the workings of American schools. It is one of the concepts which those individuals who established and gave shape to our educa-tional system during the first years of this century used to describe their work. One of the distinctive features of these individuals has been their use of the idea of social control, not simply as a label but as a seemingly 'scientific' concept replete with assumptions about the nature of the social order and the role of individuals within that order. I do not think that we can adequately understand American educational thought or practice during this century unless we are willing to take into account the concept of social control. In this respect, I should note that the use of the term, social control, is not synonymous with embracing a radical politics. As I will show in this volume, American educators of both liberal and conservative political persuasions were to be found during this century invoking the idea of social control.

As for the second alternative, I do not find anything in the notion of hegemony that advances our understanding of American education. To claim, as did Gramsci, that it is a sense of willing acquiescence that pervades and captures, so to speak, all aspects of social reality that enables one class to dominate all others, reduces everything in social life to one complete and total sameness.[5]

The concept of hegemony does, I think, play violence with our ability to understand the nature of American culture. It is a concept that tends to flatten our view of our historical experience by attenuating everything into a monolithic effort at class domination. All the richness, variety, and difference that make up American culture are reduced to an all-embracing, single-minded, and sinister purpose.

Now Gramsci's use of hegemony may suggest the kind of social order that this devoted follower of Lenin would have liked to impose on twentieth-century Europe. It may even have been the kind of order he believed, writing from Mussolini's jail, to exist in the Italy of his day. It is not, however, an appropriate concept for making sense of American society. It reflects a profoundly totalitarian view of social life that does not take into account the kind of pluralism that exists in our economic and political relationships.

II

In this volume, then, I will use the concept of social control as an explicit explanatory construct for examining the development of twentieth-century American education. Specifically, I will use a social control interpretation to account for the shape and direction that one segment of the American educational enterprise, the school curriculum, has taken during the course of this century.

The majority of this volume will examine the recommendations and proposals emanating throughout this century from the writings of those individuals who held university teaching positions in schools of education and who identified themselves professionally with curriculum as a field of work and study. In the last chapter of the volume, however, I will shift the emphasis and consider the efforts of school people to incorporate these recommendations and proposals into the actual curriculum of one major, urban school system, the Minneapolis Public Schools.

There has been, I should note, no immediate or one-to-one correspondence during this century between the proposals exposed by university curriculum scholars and the actual practices that have occurred in the schools. What curriculum ideas have during this century found their way into the schools as well as the precise forms these ideas have taken when translated into school practice has hinged, I believe, on the influence of a myriad of local factors that have affected different school systems in varying and often unique ways. These factors include such things as community pressure, legal restraints, ideology, and demography, to name but a few. Their influence has been, as we shall see in our examination of the Minneapolis Public Schools, to impinge the ability of those in the schools responsible for curriculum development to implement the ideas of university scholars in anything but a limited and incomplete fashion. Although, then, the ideas proposed by those who teach and write about curriculum in the university do not tell us exactly what was happening in the schools throughout this century, they do provide a picture on a national scope of the general shape and direction that the school curriculum was taking.[6]

The development of the American school curriculum in the twentieth century parallels the nation's transformation from a rural, agrarian society to an urban, industrialized one. Those who write about urban America typically introduce certain themes to provide structure and coherence to their analysis. Historians working in this area have relied on such diverse themes as individualism, equality, organization, collectivism, and cooperation, to name but a few. I, too, have some themes to guide my work. One, social control, I have already mentioned and will have more to say about it later in this introductory chapter. The other is that of community. It is by looking at educational thought during this century through the lenses provided by these two themes that we will, I believe, come to understand the nature and development of the American school curriculum.

III

To understand the importance that the theme of community has played in the development of the American school curriculum, we need to look at the forty-year period of urbanization and industrialization. that followed the Civil War. In the beginning, at least, this was a time of confidence for most Americans. Post-Civil War industrial expansion, the availability of cheap land in the West, and a growing national consciousness embued Americans of the day with a sense of optimism about their future and that of the nation. They saw America as a model of progress and opportunity for the rest of the world, fueled by its ability to take within its midst the disaffected of Europe, to assimilate them to its ways, and to offer them almost limitless economic and political possibilities. Based on this faith, Americans from all walks of life promoted and encouraged unrestricted European immigration.

By the mid-1880s, this sense of confidence began to wane.

Although immigration had provided the labor that had spurred industrial growth and populated new urban centers, it brought with it a sense of fear and doubt to many native-born Americans. Labor unrest, the disappearance of the frontier, and the influx into the population of German Jews and German and Irish Catholics led many to have second thoughts about the assimilative power of the nation. They began to see the immigrant not as a positive element in society but as a danger to the social order. Native-born Americans, depending on their own place in society, came to see the immigrants as competitors for American jobs, as the bearers of anarchist ideas that would radicalize American labor, as the tools of a 'Popish' plot to overthrow American democracy, or as a crude and coarse element that threatened an emerging genteel culture.

During the last years of the nineteenth century, this pattern of immigration changed. The number of entrants from Northern and Western Europe, who had been the main source of immigration up into that time, began to decrease. At the same time a group of so-called 'new immigrants' from Eastern and Southern Europe began to enter the country in increasing numbers. Unlike the German and Irish who preceded them, these immigrants were markedly different in ethnicity, religion, language, and life style from the native-born population. The result was a heightening of the concerns of the previous decades about the ability of the nation to assimilate diverse cultures.[7]

One group affected by this diminished sense of self-confidence was a loose collection of individuals in the emerging professions of social work and education and in the new social science disciplines, a group we can describe as constituting a new middle class. In background, the members of this new class were quite similar. They were native-born and for the most part products of Eastern and Midwestern small, rural towns. They were Anglo-Saxon in heritage, the descendants of those who originally came to this country from Northern and Western Europe, and Protestant in religion.

The rural roots of this new class of intellectuals led them to see American democracy as being embodied in the values and attitudes of the small town. They believed that the growing diversity of the population in the wake of the increasing emigration from Eastern and Southern Europe threatened what they viewed as a homogeneous American culture reflecting the way of life of the native-born, Protestant inhabitants of America's small, rural towns. To these middle-class thinkers, the society that their Anglo-Saxon and Protestant forebearers had carved from a wilderness seemed to be crumbling before an expanding, urban, industrial America.

The small, rural town for the members of this new middle-class assumed an almost mystical character as the guarantor of order, stability, and progress for the nation. What attracted their allegiance to the small town was the intimate and deep face-to-face relationships which their childhood experiences had shown them were possible in a restricted geographic area containing few individuals. Such deep relationships, they argued, allowed the small town to provide almost naturally and spontaneously for all its residents' needs, from birth, through initiation and sickness, to death within its boundaries. Such deep relationships also tended to mitigate the existence of difference and discord and allowed for the emergence of a commonality in values, attitudes, and standards of behavior. If growing up in the small town taught these Americans anything, it taught them that stability, order, and progress were ultimately dependent on the degree to which beliefs and attitudes were shared. It taught them that if American society was to be both orderly and progressive, a homogeneous culture and a spirit of like-mindedness and cooperation had to exist within its population.[8] It was the effort of this emerging group of American intellectuals to construct a homogeneous culture which they came to talk about as their search for community.

This yearning for consensus in the name of community can be linked, I believe, to what the historian J.G.A. Pocock describes as the struggle between virtue and corruption within the Western political tradition from the days of the Florentine Republic in the fifteenth century onward. According to Pocock, that struggle, first seen in the writings of the Florentine political theorist Machiavelli, pitted the self-governing republic of active and equal citizens, characterized as virtue, against diverse forces that threatened the existence of this polity, characterized as corruption.[9]

As this notion was developed in the works of other political theorists, first in seventeenth-century England and later in the American colonies, it took the form of a conflict between a virtuous, rural ideal of self-governing landowners and the corrupting forces of commerce and the centralization of political power. Commerce, then, became within this viewpoint an activity that disrupted the kind of political balance that would ensure the position of rural, agrarian elements within society.[10]

The effort of this new middle class of intellectuals to build a sense of community in twentieth-century American society represents, I think, a continuation of this struggle between virtue and corruption.[11] To these native-born Americans, the presence of Eastern and Southern European immigrants within the population undermined the existing social order. We can see this when we look at one of the most important statements of the day of this middle class, nativist sentiment, the *Reports of the Immigration Commission*. According to the Commission, which issued its findings in 1911, the nation was first settled by highly-skilled individuals from Northern and Western Europe who sought to settle permanently in America. With hard work, most of them were able eventually to secure a foothold in America as landowners. They were capable, both those who did speak English and those who did not, of being assimilated into American society.[12]

The new immigrants from Eastern and Southern Europe were, the Commission suggested, far different. They were for the most part unskilled and came to this country in response to the demand for industrial labor. They settled in the nation's largest cities and showed little interest in owning land. Compared to earlier immigrants, their assimilation into American culture had been slow. The Commission went on to point out that these immigrants are:

> far less intelligent than the old, approximately one-third of all those over 14 years of age when admitted being illiterate. Racially they are for the most part essentially unlike the British, German, and other peoples who came during the period prior to 1880, and generally speaking they are actuated in coming by different ideals, for the old immigration came to be part of the country, while the new, in large measure, comes with the intention of profiting in a pecuniary way by the superior advantages of the new world and then returning to the old country.[13]

The Commission blamed many of the nation's political and economic problems on these new immigrants.[14] They were, according to the *Reports*, 'tractable and uncomplaining' workers who were willing to accept existing conditions and wages in American industry. As a consequence, the members of the Commission believed, the presence of these new immigrants retarded improvements in industrial health and safety standards and precluded any increases in industrial wages. The Commission also presented evidence to suggest that Eastern and Southern European women had a higher birthrate than native-born women and that some of these new immigrants, particularly the South Italians, were responsible for increases in the rate of violent crime.[15]

The immigrants were, however, only a visible and vulnerable target for the new middle-class. At the root of their fears, I think, was what they saw as the larger corruption of the nation's rural virtue from the emergence of an urban, industrialized society. The hostile attitude of these middle-class intellectuals to the new immigrants was no doubt a reaction to the most noticeable sign of this national transformation.

When the members of this new middle-class talked about the primacy of community in American society, they seemed to be talking about the central role of the small town and rural values in the life of the nation. The celebration of the rural town, however, left them with a problem. Despite their roots in rural America, these individuals owed their careers and their futures to urbanization and industrialization. It was in the cities, whose growth depended on industrial expansion, that they were to make their mark on American society.

These professionals, then, faced the dilemma of having to resolve the obvious tension between their rural past and what seemed to be an urban future. Their solution was to try to create within an urban, industrialized society the kind of like-mindedness and cooperation which they believed to have existed in the rural town. What they sought was the sense of unity that the sociologist Robert MacIver has called 'the like willing, or the like thinking, or the like feelings of social groups.'[16]

This effort to build a sense of community in American society has not been, as we shall see in this volume, strikingly successful. Many of those who have sought this goal were not able to accept and to come to terms with the twin factors of urbanization and industrialization. Unable to accept this transformation of American society, they responded as have other intellectuals in Western culture, when faced with social and political changes that seemed to disrupt their way of life, by seeking to enforce like-mindedness through manipulation, imposition, and even outright coercion.[17] They confronted what they perceived as threats to their vision of a virtuous America, as the historian Robert Wiebe has noted, 'by striking out at whatever enemies their view of the world would allow them to see'.[18] This would lead them to propose schemes for building a homogeneous society under the rubric of social control that were inconsistent with our historic, liberal-democratic ethic and its twin commitment to liberty and equality. It would also lead them to advance proposals for regulating human behavior that, if not totalitarian, were certainly authoritarian in outlook.[19]

Fortunately for our country, there have been individuals who have been able to transcend their own backgrounds and come to terms with twentieth-century American life. One such individual was the American philosopher George Herbert Mead.[20] Unlike many members of this new middle-class, he was able to assert the ideal of community in urban, industrial America without doing violence to liberal democratic values.

This search for community has been one of the central preoccupations of those individuals within this larger group of middle class intellectuals who founded curriculum as a professional field of work and study. Like their fellow intellectuals in other walks of life, they were divided about urbanization and industrialization. Some could not accept this transformation in American life and found it impossible to embrace both the ideal of community and that of liberal democracy. They typically choose the former. Others, specifically Franklin Bobbitt, W.W. Charters, and Hollis Caswell, were able more or less to reconcile their search for community with their commitment to a liberal democratic ethic. It is to their work that I will address my attention in this volume.

IV

The search for community in and by itself is probably not a distinctive feature of twentieth-century American society. What does distinguish those who engaged in this search, such as the curriculum workers we are considering in this volume, is that they talked about community using 'scientific' constructs borrowed from the social science disciplines of sociology and psychology. The most important of these concepts was that of social control.

When we introduce the concept of social control into our discussion, we immediately face the problem that there is little agreement about what the term means. As the sociologist Jack Gibbs has pointed out, our 'conceptualization of social control remains in a wretched state.'[21] Some who have offered a definition of the term have taken a broad view and identify social control with all efforts at maintaining social order. From this perspective, all forms of social influence become instances of social control, thus yielding a concept that is effectively synonymous with all of sociological study. Others have taken a narrow view of the concept and identify social control with certain formal and institutional means of social regulation. From this point of view, social control is equated with those formal, artificial mechanisms which society constructs to maintain order. Left out are all those informal influences that seem to exist between individuals in social interaction and that appear to regulate human behavior.[22]

This volume is not concerned with the conceptual adequacy of the concept of social control, a topic that has received extensive attention.[23] Rather, our concern is with how one group of middle-class intellectuals used the concept of social control to build the school curriculum. For this, we need a definition of social control that captures the various meanings that these individuals have attributed to this concept throughout this century. When we look, as we will, at how these educators in fact used the term, we find a common theme. For all these thinkers, social control referred to the diverse efforts of social groups to bring the attitudes and behavior of their members into line with accepted and customary social expectations.[24] It is this definition that I will adopt in this volume.

The term social control is decidedly American in origin, having first appeared in an 1894 introductory sociology text authored by Albion Small and George Vincent.[25] Its evolution as a concept in American thought follows two distinct intellectual paths that parallel the distinction I have already made between a so-called narrow and broad definition of social control. One path begins with the sociologist Edward A. Ross who was the first to examine the concept at any length, initially in a series of articles appearing between 1894 and 1900 in *The American Journal of Sociology* and later in the revision of these articles for his 1901 book, *Social Control*. Ross took a narrow view of the idea of social control and identified it with the formal institutions of society. For Ross, social control was an artificial process reflecting the direct effort of society to use its institutions to maintain social order.

A year after Ross published *Social Control*, the sociologist Charles Horton Cooley published his study of the social self, *Human Nature and the Social Order*. Although Cooley did not use the term social control in his study, his treatment of the social self represented a second, intellectual path for the development of this concept. Cooley took a broad view of the idea of social regulation and argued that social order was a spontaneous outcome of social interaction that occurred as individuals acquired their basic social identity with the emergence of the self. For Cooley, social control was a natural process and an indirect outcome of the workings of those internal, psychological mechanisms associated with the development of the personality.

There is a second difference that distinguishes the intellectual path taken by Ross from that taken by Cooley. That difference has to do with how these two sociologists, in talking about the process of control, described the relationship between the individual and society. American intellectuals throughout this century have, it seems, interpreted this relationship in two radically different ways. Some, including Ross, have argued that the interaction between the individual and society is one-directional with the influence flowing, so to speak, from society to the individual. From this viewpoint, the individual is seen as a passive, responding organism, the recipient of his culture and the social expectations it entails. Others including Cooley have argued that the relationship is reciprocal, that is, moving from society to the individual but also from the individual to society. Here, the individual is seen not only as the recipient of his culture but also as an active agent who plays a role in constructing that very culture.[26]

In advancing what were concepts of social control, Ross and Cooley were in effect suggesting how it might be possible to preserve an American ideal of virtue in the face of the potentially corrupting influence of urbanization and industrialization. They were involved in trying to reconcile the liberal democratic values on which they believed the nation was founded with the realities of a transformed American society. This was what they sought when they spoke of a search for an American community.

This is, I think, a search that has absorbed the attention of American intellectuals throughout this century. In the chapters that follow, we will consider how one group of these intellectuals, those members of what we have talked about as a new middle-class who established the field of curriculum, carried on that search. They were not always successful, as we shall see, in spelling out a vision of community that fit the tenor of the times in which they were living. They did, however, in trying to cure the corruption they saw in twentieth-century American society, give shape and direction to the American school curriculum.

Although the focus of our study is on the school curriculum, we will be able to draw conclusions that apply to our intellectual thought in general. This is the case because ultimately the curriculum is more than just a statement of the course of study within the schools. It is, I think, an important artifact of our culture that informs us about that culture. As the historian Frederick Rudolph has noted, the curriculum 'has been one of the places where we have told ourselves who we are'.[27] We can find within the curriculum, in other words, some of those ideas that define and give meaning to our existence as a nation. By identifying those things we wish to convey to future generations, the curriculum in essence can tell us what we as a nation cherish and wish to perpetuate as well as suggest what we fear and wish to eliminate.[28]

Notes

1 I have discussed the importance of this interest in social control among contemporary educators in my review of one book that advances a social control interpretation of American educational history, *Roots of Crisis*. See BARRY FRANKLIN, 'Education for Social Control', essay review of *Roots of Crisis* by CLARENCE KARIER, JOEL SPRING and PAUL VIOLAS in *History of Education Quarterly* 14, spring, 19/4, pp. 131–6.
2 SOL COHEN, 'The mental health movement, the Commonwealth fund, and public education, 1921–1933', in *Private Philanthropy and Public Elementary and Secon-*

dary Education, Proceedings of the Rockefeller Archive Center Conference, 8 June 1979, edited by GERALD BENJAMIN, New York, Rockefeller Archive Center, 1980, p. 44.

3 The most compelling case for this solution to the dissatisfaction with the concept of social control has been made by the educational historian Carl Kaestle. See CARL KAESTLE, 'Conflict and consensus revisited: Notes toward a reinterpretation of American educational history', *Harvard Educational Review* 46, August, 1976, pp. 390–6.

4 WILLIAM J. REESE, 'Neither victims nor master: Ethnic and minority study', in *Historical Inquiry in Education: A Research Agenda*, edited by JOHN HARDIN BEST, Washington, D.C., American Educational Research Association, 1983, p. 230.

5 ANTONIO GRAMSCI, *Selections from the Prison Notebooks*, edited and translated by QUINTIN HOARE and GEOFFREY N. SMITH, London, Lawrence and Wishart, 1971, pp. 12–13; CARL BOGGS, *Gramsci's Marxism*, London Pluto Press, 1976, p. 39; RAYMOND WILLIAMS, *Marxism and Literature*, Oxford, Oxford University Press, 1977, pp. 108–14.

6 HERBERT M. KLEIBARD and BARRY M. FRANKLIN, 'The course of the course of study: History of curriculum', in *Historical Inquiry in Education, op. cit.*, pp. 146–7.

7 JOHN HIGHAM, *Strangers in the Land: Patterns of American Nativism*, New York, Atheneum, 1963, chapters 1–4; JOHN HIGHAM, 'Origins of immigration restriction, 1882–1879: A social analysis', *Mississippi Valley Historical Review*, 39, June, 1952, pp. 77–88; BARBARA SOLOMON, *Ancestors and Immigrants: A Changing New England Tradition*, Cambridge, Harvard University Press, 1956, chapters 1–4.

8 JEAN B. QUANDT, *From the Small Town to the Great Community: The Social Thought of Progressive Intellectuals*, New Brunswick, Rutgers University Press, 1970, chapter 1; ROBERT WIEBE, *The Search for Order, 1877–1920*, New York, Hill and Wang, 1967, chapters 3 and 5.

9 J.G.A. POCOCK, *The Machiavellian Moment: Florentine Political Thought and the Atlantic Republican Tradition*, Princeton, Princeton University Press, 1975, parts 1 and 2.

10 *Ibid.*, pp. 486–7, 503 and chapter 15.

11 I am basing my extension of Pocock's argument on the suggestions advanced by the historian DOROTHY ROSS in 'The liberal tradition revisited and the republican tradition addressed', in *New Directions in American Intellectual History*, edited by JOHN HIGHAM and PAUL K. CONKIN, Baltimore, The Johns Hopkins University Press, 1979, pp. 116–31.

12 Immigration Commission, Reports of the Commission, *Abstracts of Reports of the Commission*, Vol I, 41 vols., New York, Arno Press, 1970, p. 14.

13 *Ibid.*

14 *Ibid.*, p. 491.

15 *Ibid.*, pp. 494, 500–1 and 540–1; Immigration Commission, Reports of the Commission, *Immigration and Crime*, Vol. 36, 41 vols., New York, Arno Press, 1970, p. 2.

16 ROBERT MACIVER, *Community: A Sociological Study*, London, Macmillan and Company, 1917, p. 81.

17 ROBERT A. NISBET, *The Quest for Community*, London, Oxford University Press, 1953, pp. xiv and 221.

18 WIEBE, *op. cit.*, p. 44.

19 The best discussion of this feature of American life is to be found in Gunnar Myrdal's examination of the predicament of blacks in American society. See Gunnar Myrdal, *An American Dilemma: The Negro Problem and Modern Democracy*, 20th Anniversary Edition, New York, Harper and Row, 1962, pp. 15–17.

20 Mead was of course not the only individual who was able during this period to reconcile our liberal democratic ethic with the realities of urbanization and industrialization. Another individual who took on this task and succeeded at it was the American philosopher John Dewey. Dewey and Mead were, as it turns out, intellectual colleagues and personal friends who exerted a mutual influence on the development of each other's thought. In fact, most of what I will be saying about Mead in this volume could as easily be said about Dewey. There are, however, two reasons that led me to highlight Mead in this volume. First, Mead's treatment of the issue of social control, the principal explanatory concept of this volume, is superior to Dewey's. Mead, for example, provides a much more complete picture than does Dewey of how the individual is brought under social control. Further, Mead pays far more attention than does Dewey to the requirements for social control in a democratic society. In light of the concern of this volume Mead simply represents a better choice than Dewey as an example of an individual who came to terms with urban, industrial America. Second, of the two, Mead has always been given less attention by scholars than Dewey. Believing as I do that on many issues on which they both wrote, Mead's formulations were superior, I have taken this opportunity to place Mead at, so to speak, center stage.

21 JACK P. GIBBS, 'Social control deterrence, and perspectives on social order', *Social Forces*, 56, December, 1977, p. 408.

22 A.B. HOLLINGSHEAD, 'The concept of social control', *American Sociological Review*, 6, April, 1941, pp. 217–20; ALEXANDER CLARK and JACK P. GIBBS, 'Social control: A reformulation', *Social Problems*, 12, spring 1965, pp. 398–9.

23 For some recent efforts to define the concept of social control see JACK P. GIBBS, *Norms, Deviance, and Social Control: Conceptual Matters*, New York, Elsevier, 1981, chapters 3–4; MORRIS JANOWITZ, *The Last Half Century: Societal Change and Politics in America*, Chicago, University of Chicago Press, 1978, chapter 2; DON MARTINDALE, 'The theory of social control', in *Social Control for the 1980's: A Handbook for Order in a Democratic Society*, edited by JOSEPH S. ROUCEK, Westport, Greenwood Press, 1978, pp. 46–58.

24 The definition of social control that I am using in this essay is similar to one suggested by the sociologist JOSEPH S. ROUCEK in 'The concept of social control in American sociology', in *Social Control for the 1980s, op. cit.*, p. 4.

25 ALBION W. SMALL and GEORGE E. VINCENT, *An Introduction to the Study of Society*, New York, American Book Company, 1894, p. 328.

26 A roughly analogous framework is currently being used by some historians of psychology to interpret the development of that discipline. See ALLAN R. BUSS, 'The structure of psychological revolutions', *Journal of the History of the Behavioral Sciences*, 14 January, 1978, pp. 57–64; and OWEN FLANAGAN, Jr., 'Psychology, progress and the problem of reflexivity: A study in the epistomological foundations of psychology', *Journal of the History of the Behavioral Sciences*, 17 July, 1981, pp. 375–86.

27 FREDERICK RUDOLPH, *Curriculum: A History of the American Undergraduate Course of Study since 1636*, San Francisco, Jossey-Bass, 1978, p. 1.

28 KLIEBARD and FRANKLIN, *op. cit.*, p. 152.

2 Social Control I: The Origins of a Sociology of Social Control

I

In laying out the conceptual framework for this volume in the last chapter, we stated that those American educators who established the field of curriculum were, like many of their early twentieth-century counterparts in other areas of endeavor, seeking to reconcile the nation's liberal democratic ethic that was part of its rural, agrarian past with the demands of an emerging urban, industrial society. They sought to achieve this reconciliation by making the school curriculum an instrument of social control for the restoration of a sense of community within modern American life. Our task in this chapter and in the next will be to locate the origins of this idea of social control in our intellectual thought.

Identifying the origins of the idea of social control is, as it turns out, almost as difficult as securing any agreement about the meaning of the term itself. This is the case because, as a process, social control is a constitutive property of social life existing wherever and whenever individuals join together in groups to pursue joint endeavors. It is an idea that can be viewed as being synonymous with the concept of society itself.[1] The nature of this volume does, however, make this task somewhat easier. First, our focus on twentieth-century urban America narrows our search with respect to time and place. Second, our focus on an explicit theory of social control, a construct containing assumptions about social interaction and social influence, narrows our search with respect to content. Taken together, these two constraints direct our search to the emerging social science disciplines of sociology and psychology. It was within these two fledgling social science fields that twentieth-century American intellectuals first specifically posed the problem of urbanization and industrialization as one of social control. It was within these two disciplines that twentieth-century American intellectuals first formulated the idea of social control as an explicit theory with an assumed grounding in certain scientific principles of social and individual behavior. In this chapter, we will seek to identify the roots of this theory within American sociology. In the next chapter, we will seek its origins in American psychology.

The idea of social control was clearly embedded in the content of sociology from the very beginning. Lester Frank Ward (1841–1913), one of American sociology's founding theorists, defined the discipline as the study of the planned and conscious efforts of the members of society to use the power of government to realize the 'best interests of society at large', a process he labelled as 'social telesis'.[2] What Ward in effect was talking about here was the use of the government to regulate social life.[3] For Ward, the ideal state of affairs was what he referred to as 'sociocracy', his term for a society brought under the influence of social control.[4]

Social control played an equally central role in the work of another of sociology's founding theorists, William Graham Sumner (1840– 1910). The subject of sociology for Sumner was what he called 'folkways', his term for the habitual actions of individuals within society that seemed to emerge naturally and spontaneously out of their trial and efforts to satisfy their needs and ensure their survival.[5] Folkways were for Sumner, then, the 'regulative' mechanisms of social life, that is, society's means of social control.[6]

Neither Ward nor Sumner, despite what appeared to be their interest in the question of control, ever articulated a theory of social control. For such a theory, we need, as we suggested in our introductory chapter, to turn to two other founding theorists of American sociology, Edward A. Ross and Charles Horton Cooley.

II

The first individual to specifically define an explicit theory of social control was Edward A. Ross (1866–1951). Ross began his professional career as an economist, having earned his PhD at the Johns Hopkins University under Richard T. Ely in 1891. During the next three years, while teaching successively at Indiana, Cornell and Stanford Universities, Ross shifted both his teaching responsibilities and his research interest from economics to the emerging field of sociology. It was a transition inspired first by his reading of Ward's *Dynamic Sociology* while a graduate student and brought to fruition by his personal relationship with Ward after his marriage to Ward's niece in 1892.[7]

The formulation of a theory of social control was Ross's first, and his principal, contribution to American sociology. Despite his close relationship with Ward and, as we shall see, the similarities between his notion of control and Ward's idea of 'social telesis', there is no indication that Ross derived his concept from Ward. Rather, it seems that social control was for Ross one of those conceptual insights that singular individuals hit upon from time to time to organize and synthesize existing knowledge and emerging trends in intellectual thought.[8] As Ross tells us in his autobiography:

> ... the virus of sociology was in my veins, in the autumn of '94. I kept looking for the linch-pins which hold society together. About Christmas in an alcove of the Stanford Library, I set down as they occurred to me thirty-three distinct means by which society controls its members. This is the germ of my social control.[9]

For Ross, the idea of social control constituted 'a great social secret' which he spent the next seven years unlocking.[10] During these years, he contributed twenty articles to the *American Journal of Sociology* on the topic of social control. He reworked these articles into a book which he published in 1901 under the title, *Social Control: A Survey of the Foundations of Order*.

Society, Ross argued in his first article on social control, exerts a shaping influence on its members. That is, society creates within its members 'certain ideals, standards, certain likes and dislikes, certain admirations and abhorrences'.[11] In fact, it was for Ross only when this shaping occurred that society existed. Ross labelled this aspect of social life 'social ascendancy', his term for the preeminence of society over its members. It included social influence or the unintended shaping of the individual by society and social control or the planned shaping of the individual by society.[12] What brought Ross to make this distinction between social influence and social control was his understanding of the nature of order within society.

Individuals possessed, according to Ross, certain inherent tendencies, sympathy, sociability, an innate sense of justice, and individual responsibility, that would naturally create order in society. In the less complex, more culturally homogeneous society of the past, these tendencies did just that. As an example, he pointed to the first Americans to settle in California. These settlers were typically relatives or at least close friends who had migrated to California in groups in hopes of setting up permanent settlements. Within their ranks, there was little in the way of disharmony, either during their move to California or after they arrived.[13] These settlers, Ross argued, exhibited these natural tendencies for order:

> For a brief period, then, all the conditions tended to maximize the impulses that make for harmony. There was no social imperative, no arbitrary code, no traditional requirement, no conventional standard. There were no social institutions to protect, no vague corporate welfare to safeguard. Nearly every moral problem resolved itself into a question between man and man.[14]

With the announcement that gold had been discovered in California in 1849, those who now came to mine gold were a diverse group of people of many backgrounds and often strangers to each other. Their purpose was not settlement, but to get rich quickly. Ross believed that natural tendencies for order did not fare well in this heterogeneous environment, and the developing mining communities found it necessary to establish explicit codes of law and agencies to enfore them.[15]

Ross argued that in the emerging urban, industrial America of his day, these natural tendencies for order were out of place. Sympathy, for example, as manifest in the individual's concern for the group was not a helpful characteristic for a society which, he believed, was not being built by the meek and peaceful but by the aggressive and warlike. The key to the fixed, impersonal relationships that characterized an industrial society was reliability, not kindness. It was more important in this emerging social order for its members to perform their assigned tasks than for them to worry about their fellow individuals.[16]

In modern American society, with all its complexity, Ross believed that order required the development of a system of artificial restraints.[17] It was these man-made restraints that constituted social control for Ross:

> Like the hypothesis that storks bring babies, the theory that moral instincts beget control has a distressing lack of finality. But how the mystery lights up when we reach the idea of society, — a something distinct from a bunch of persons! For we can regard this society as a living thing, actuated, like all the higher creatures, by the instinct of self-preservation. Social control, then, appears as one of the ways in which this living thing seeks to keep itself alive and well. Or, we can regard this society as a person having its good and its evil and a knowledge of this good and evil. And social control would be the limitation

that the social ego for its own sake imposes upon the freedom of the individual ego.[18]

Ross actually talked about four different types of social control with four different regulative mechanisms, sanctions, suggestions, feelings, and judgment. The most direct and explicit types of social control were those governed by the two sanctions of public opinion and law. Public opinion, relying as it did on the power of what people think of each other, was for Ross a type of social control that would play an increasing role in American society. It offered what he believed was an immediate and relatively inexpensive means of preventing undesirable behavior. Yet, public opinion had a weakness in that it was not reliable. People's opinions often changed from time to time and from place to place.[19] Law represented a more reliable and permanent sanction, particularly suitable to control those acts which society most feared and to which they required the most severe response. It was the most specialized agency of control, operating as it did under the administration of professionals and possessing certain definite and 'violent' sanctions. Law served, Ross argued, as 'the cornerstone of the edifice of order'.[20]

Both public opinion and law had, Ross believed, a serious shortcoming in that neither of them could control such hidden aspects of conduct as thought and motivation. What was needed was a more primary sanction that could regulate these inner dispositions before they manifested themselves in behavior. For this, Ross turned to the sanction of belief, particularly religious belief. It offered both an all-knowing, supernatural power that could penetrate individual consciousness to detect inappropriate motivations and thoughts and suitable mechanisms of conformity through the duty of penitence and the threat of damnation.[21]

Sanctions, however, only accounted for one type of control and not the most significant at that. At the root of social order, Ross argued, were certain 'pervasive' and less 'definite' means of control, specifically suggestions, feelings, and judgment, that operated indirectly.[22]

Social suggestion was one of these powerful but intangible influences. As Ross put it, 'between a man and his associates there comes to be a silent, subtle moral osmosis which we are just beginning to perceive; and until we have comprehended this, we shall never quite account for good behavior'.[23] He did not explain the nature of this moral force, a point I will have more to say about later, but instead provided two illustrations, those of example and expectation. In the first case, he argued, individuals typically model their conduct on the behavior of their associates. In the later, individuals seem to in most instances fulfill the beliefs of their associates that they will act rightly.[24]

Ross paid special attention, as we are in this essay, to one mode of social suggestion, education. Teachers, he believed, through their examples as well as by the standards they set could restrain student behavior:

> In this microcosm the too obstreperous ego gets a wholesome dressing down. There is formed a habit of moderating one's claims, of respecting others' rights, and of hitting upon those moral solutions known as 'justice'. Closely related to this is the training to self-control and the habit of obedience to an external law which are given by a good school discipline.[25]

The existence of a system of public schools that touched the lives of all citizens made education, he argued, a particularly suitable means of social control in American society.

Education for Ross represented an alternative means of social control to that provided by sanctions, particularly those involving coercion:

> There seems to be an inverse relation between force and education, between direct and indirect methods of control. Rome, strong in lictors and legions, ignored education. The Jews, backward in political organization or dispersed among alien races, must needs impose the yoke of their law by school and synagogue rather than by scourge and prison.[27]

By initiating individuals into correct modes of thought and conduct, education, unlike law or public opinion, prevents inappropriate behavior rather than attemping to contain it. It thus offered the power of more direct modes of control at less cost to society, both real and emotional. As Ross noted, 'the avowel that free education is an "economical system of police" sounds rather brutal in this smooth-spoken age. It shocks the public and chills teachers. But now and then the cat is let out of the bag'.[28]

Although Ross indicated that different types of social control were appropriate to different situations, he clearly emphasized the power of indirect control in the emerging urban, industrial society of his day. These controls, such as social suggestion, he noted, were often overlooked because they did not function openly or involve the major regulative institutions of society. Yet, they stood, he believed, at the root of social order. They tended to operate invisibly, leaving the mistaken impression that order was a spontaneous, natural process of social life.[29] They possessed the unique power of getting behind 'the well-trimmed prepossessing lawns in front' and uncovering the 'unpleasant slimy things lurking in the rear fens and undergrowth of the human soul'.[30] Ross directed the major portion of his study of social control to identifying these indirect controls. Some, social religion, ideals, ceremony, art, and personality, controlled through appeals to feelings. The remainder, enlightenment, illusion, valuation, and ethics, controlled through appeals to judgment.

These indirect controls, Ross, argued, exhibited a powerful influence. Ceremony, he noted, could embue an event with meaning and solemnity. Art could invoke passion and sympathy.[31] Ross, however, did not explain how indirect control functioned to regulate human behavior. From his description of these controls, it appears that they operated internally within the individual to provide what we may think of, in distinction to the institutional regulation of direct forms of social control, a kind of psychological regulation. It was precisely this kind of psychological direction that Ross did not explain. To understand why he did not do this, we must now turn to the psychology underlying his theory of social control.

III

Ross was an exponent of what has been called an instinct school of psychology.[32] Accepting the evolutionary ideas of Darwin, psychologists of this persuasion located the source of human behavior in certain hereditarily-given responses which they called instincts. These responses were believed to appear spontaneously at or around birth and were thought by those who adhered to this school of thought to represent the fundamental driving forces of animal and human behavior. They included such simple responses as biting and sucking as well as such complex ones as sympathy, play, sociability, and jealousy.[33]

The most important instinct for Ross in explaining human social behavior was imitation. Humans were for Ross suggestible creatures. Their ideas, feelings, beliefs, and actions were acquired as suggestions from others with whom they were involved in social interaction. In explaining his notion of imitation, Ross turned to the ideas of the French sociologist Gabriel Tarde. In a letter to Ward written seven years before he published his *Social Psychology*, Ross indicated that he was planning to write a book on psychology. 'The chief trouble', he pointed out, 'is my vast indebtedness to Tarde. About half would be founded on him'.[34] Before considering Ross's ideas on imitation, we need to briefly say a word about Tarde's views on this same subject.

Imitation, Tarde argued, was the spark of social development as was heredity the spark of biological development. Just as biological alterations were due to heredity, Tarde believed that social inventions were the result of imitation.[35] Imitation was, then, for Tarde the way by which society developed its laws, religious codes, art forms, and industrial processes, in short its institutions.

Tarde defined imitation as '... every impression of an inter-psychical photography'.[37] That is, imitation implied for him some sort of mental interaction and influence between individuals:

> Everything which we see anchored and rooted in our customs
> and beliefs of today began by being the object of ardent
> discussion. There is no peaceful institution which has not been
> mothered by discord. Grammars, codes, catechisms, written and
> unwritten constitutions, ruling industries, sovereign systems of
> versification, all of these things which are in themselves the
> categorical basis of society, have been the slow and gradual work
> of social dialectic.[38]

Tarde, however, was never able to explain the nature of this 'social dialectic'. Imitation was, he pointed out, the outcome of the functioning of two 'psychic units', belief and desire. It was these units that provided for the so-called 'interpsychical photography' of imitation.[39] He could not, however, explain what these units were and how they functioned. 'One might ask in passing, just what is belief, what is desire? I admit my inability to define them'.[40] Tarde, in other words, was able to offer labels for the psychological influences that individuals exerted on each other in social interaction. But he could not explain how these influences brought about the process of imitation.[41]

By fashioning his psychology around the notion of imitation, Ross incorporated the same weakness that plagued Tarde into his system. It left him unable to explain how individuals engaged in social interaction influenced each other to bring their behavior and attitudes under social control.[42] Without this explanation, however, Ross's theory of social control broke down. Although he talked about both direct controls that operated externally through the application of sanctions and indirect controls that operated internally as a natural outgrowth of social interaction, he was only able to explain the former.

Ross was, it seems, aware of the need within his theory for an internal mechanism of psychological control. At least his comments about the contribution of James Mark Baldwin's notion of self seem to suggest this:

What fits us for association, then is not so much resemblance in this trait or that, as identity in mental constitution. However far apart we may be in creeds or standards, the social relation is possible so long as the same self-thought will interpret both ego and alter. What Baldwin has found the root of is . . . sociality.[43]

Yet, Ross never really incorporated the idea of sociality into his system. Embracing an embryonic form of conflict theory similar to the views of such nineteenth-century European sociologists as Ludwig Gumplowicz and Gustav Ratzenhofen, Ross viewed the relationship of the individual to society as one of discord and tension.[44]

Society, Ross believed, acted to suppress what were natural human tendencies.[45] The typical state of society without this suppression was, he believed, one of disorder:

So much for the optimists, the thinkers who are so impressed with the knitting together of men by their contacts and interactions that for them the problem of socialization is solved. In their eyes, union is easy, order natural, tranquility spontaneous, and the struggle for existence a conflict with nature, and not with our fellowmen . . . Is, then, the primitive struggle so easily put aside, the give-and-take spirit proper to social life so easily come by? Fellowship craving may draw together ten or a hundred; but does it unite ten thousand or ten million? . . . 'Pleasure in companionship', 'pleasure in cooperation', are luxuries; and if men have formed groups under the stress of conflict, it is likely that fear, hunger, or greed rather than sociability have brought them to it.[46]

Ross's point was that social life seems to have begun amidst violence and conflict. There was no automatic and spontaneous social feeling among individuals. The issue for Ross was whether social order was 'a matter of silken cords and rose water' or was it a 'matter of "iron and blood"?'.[47] For Ross, it was the latter. Taken together, his inability to explain how indirect social control took place and his denial of spontaneous sociability affected how he viewed the problem of community and the role of social control in its construction and maintenance.

IV

For Ross, social control was more than an abstraction from the realm of sociological theory. He came to what he called his 'great social secret' in response to his fears about the effect of the nation's transformation into an urban, industrial society. The source of his fear was his belief that inherent in this transformation, specifically in industrialization, was a corrupting influence which he attributed to the actions of those financiers and industrialists who were engineering the development of the nation's corporate economy. These individuals had, he believed, injected an unauthentic spirit of 'rampant commercialism' into our national life. In the name of commercial success and profit, they had, he argued, squandered our natural resources, encouraged 'bossism' in municipal politics, resisted the introduction and enforcement of health and safety regulations in industry, and allowed the existence of prostitution, gambling, and other vices.[48]

What troubled Ross most, however, was the support he believed the backers of this new corporate economy were giving to a national policy of unrestricted immigration in what, he maintained, was their quest for a cheap source of labor to aid industrial expansion.[49] Such a policy, he argued, threatened the existence of the nation's native-born population of Anglo-Saxon heritage and Northern and Western European descent. Echoing the sentiments contained in the *Reports of the Immigration Commission*, Ross pointed out that for most of the nineteenth century, a continuing emigration from Northern and Western Europe in search of permanent settlement in America had served to refurbish this native-born population. Industrialization and the labor demands it created, he maintained, altered this pattern of immigration. By the latter part of the century, this Northern and Western European emigration was being replaced by an increasing migration of Eastern and Southern Europeans in search of the kind of jobs that an emerging industrialized economy could offer.

Ross went on to argue that because of what he believed was the high birth rate of Eastern and Southern European immigrants and their willingness to accept a low standard of living, these newcomers would over time compete with and eventually displace native-born labor from the nation's industrial work force. Some native-born Americans would perhaps benefit, he pointed out, by advancing to higher paying positions in some industries. Most, however, would be uprooted from their present jobs and be forced to accept lower paying positions. In their effort to maintain their standard of living as wages fell and working conditions deteriorated, the native-born population would, he argued, decrease their own birth rate, a practice which Ross feared would ultimately lead to their extinction.[50] This new emigration from Eastern and Southern Europe threatened the native-born population of Anglo-Saxon heritage with what Ross called 'race suicide'.[51]

The danger posed by this so-called 'race suicide' and the ethnic conflict it engendered led Ross to doubt that these new immigrants could ever be successfully assimilated:

> The fusing of American with German and Scandinavian immigrants was only a reblending of kindred stocks, Angles, Jutes, Danes, and Normans were wrought of yore into the fiber of the English breed. But the human varieties being collected in this country by the naked action of economic forces are too dissimilar to blend without producing a good many faces of 'chaotic constitution'.[52]

To understand Ross's fear of an urban, industrialized society and specifically his hostility toward Eastern and Southern European immigrants, we must understand something of his background. Although he received his doctorate at the Johns Hopkins University and studied for a year in Germany, Ross's roots were in the rural Midwest of Illinois and Iowa. In some respects his sociology was less a product of Baltimore or of Germany than it was of his childhood in Verdin, Illinois and Marion, Iowa and his high school and college years at Coe in Cedar Rapids.[53] From his vantage point, the changes that were taking place in American society signaled the demise of the small, rural town and the deep, personal relationships and like-mindedness that existed among its members:

> Now these natural bonds, that were many and firm when the rural neighborhood or the village community was the type of aggregation, no longer bind men as they must be bound in the huge and complex aggregates of to-day. Kinship has lost its old sacred significance. Social erosion has worn down the family until now it consists of only parents and young ... Nearness of dwelling means less in the country and nothing in the town. For the intimacy of the countryside the city offers only a 'multitudinous desolation'. Frequent change of domicile hinders the growth of strong local feelings. The householder has become a tenant, the workingman a bird of passage. Loose touch-and-go acquaintanceships take the place of those close and lasting attachments that form between neighbors that have long lived, labored, and pleasured together.[54]

It was a change that Ross described as the transformation of America from a community to a society.[55]

What worried Ross was that without a like-minded, homogeneous population, one could not count on natural and spontaneous mechanisms for maintaining social order. Artificial means of social control were required:

> We must face the fact, therefore, that the community, under-mined by the stress of change, has caved in carrying with it part of the foundation of order. While not overlooking the growth of intelligence which, by enabling us to comprehend large bodies of people at a distance, invites fellowship to overleap the limits of personal contact. I am bound to say that we are relying on artificial rather than natural supports to bear the increasing weight of our social order, and that a return to a natural basis of social partnership seems about as unlikely as a return to natural food or natural locomotion.[56]

It was these artificial means of order that Ross identified in *Social Control*.

In *Social Control*, then, Ross sought the means to restore the like-minded community he identified with the nation's rural past in an emerging urban, industrial society. It was a quest in which he saw himself as the spokesman for the beleagured American masses in their struggle with a privileged, industrial and financial elite. In attacking the nation's existing policy of unrestricted immigration, Ross believed that he was defending the interests of American workers whose livelihood and very existence were being threatened by the importation of so-called 'cheap labor'.[57]

Ross believed that America was in danger of falling under the rule of what he called 'class control', in which those who were building the nation's corporate economy would rule to promote their own interests at the expense of society at large.[58] Invoking the utilitarian notion of the greatest good for the greatest number, Ross argued that social control, which was for him the opposite of class control, should protect the welfare of all with the least possible interference with individual liberty.[59] For this reason, Ross favored the use of those indirect controls that relied on suggestions, feelings, and judgment in favor of those direct and coercive controls that rested on the application of sanctions.[60]

Yet, despite the democratic and progressive veneer which Ross's advocacy of indirect social control gave to his discussion, there was a more ominous side to his ideas that bears consideration. Ross not only made a distinction between two types of social control, direct and indirect, he made a second and more important distinction between how these two types of social control worked. Some types, both direct and indirect, such as public opinion, suggestion, and religion, worked by appealing to the sentiments of the members of society. They were what

Ross referred to as ethical or moral forms of social control. Other types of social control, again both direct and indirect, including law, belief, and education, depended on the ability of those few in society who held the majority of political power to regulate the affairs of the many. Ross called these forms of social control, political.

These two different forms of control were, Ross thought, appropriate for different social conditions. Where the population was homogeneous and like-minded and where the differences in status and rank among people were minimal, ethical controls could and should be relied on to maintain order. Where the population was heterogeneous and where great differences in status separated a privileged few who ruled from the many who followed, political forms of social control were required to maintain order.[61]

It was only in a society that was democratic, Ross maintained, that social order could rest on ethical controls:

> ... the mild, democratic regime is now recognized as presupposing a homogeneous and enlightened population, free social intercourse, minimum interference with the individual, sanctity of the person, and equality before the law. When any of these conditions fail, the democratic forms soon become farcical.[62]

In the absence of these conditions, it was necessary, Ross believed to embrace political forms of social control.

This distinction between ethical and political controls becomes important when we consider Ross's own efforts to resolve the supposed problems of unrestricted immigration. He joined the nativist Immigration Restriction League, served on its national committee, and advanced its program of restricting the entry into the country of emigrants from Eastern and Southern Europe.[63] During the 1920s, in reaction to the seeming threat from 'race suicide', Ross actively embraced the eugenics movement.[64] For Ross, then, the social control of Eastern and Southern European immigrants involved the use of coercive sanctions.

It was not simply the fact that America was becoming a more heterogeneous society that required the application of coercion to maintain social order. Eastern and Southern Europeans were, Ross noted, not only different from the native-born population, they were inferior:

> You are struck by the fact that from ten to twenty per cent are hirsute, low browed, big faced persons of obviously low mentality. Not that they suggest evil. They simply look out of

place in black clothes and stiff collar, since clearly they belong in skins, in wattled huts at the close of the Great Ice Age.[65]

It was not that these immigrants were for Ross simply culturally backward. He believed that there was something inherently wrong with them. As Ross noted, 'our people, moreover, are singularly free from blood taints. One cannot live in Central Europe without observing that the signs of rachitis, scrofula and syphilis are much more numerous there than they are here'.[66]

Because of these inherent differences, Ross felt that Eastern and Southern European immigrants required different forms of social control than did the native-born population. People of Anglo-Saxon heritage, Ross argued, were motivated primarily by pride and self respect. 'They prize their personal liberty, and will not stand for policing and surveillance'. They thus responded best, according to Ross, to ethical forms of social control. The Eastern and Southern European immigrants, on the other hand, Ross noted, 'bow to authorities and feel the prestige of the past'. These were traits, Ross believed, that 'betrays them to State or Church or some other corporation that hoodwinks and bleeds them'. As a consequence, Ross felt that these immigrants were most responsive to those political controls that would allow them to feel the power of institutional authority.[67]

V

In the end, Ross's theory of social control could not accommodate itself to the transformation of American society into an urban, industrialized nation. For Ross, we should remember, the principal problem that threatened the kind of community he envisioned was cultural diversity, the result of the unrestricted emigration from Eastern and Southern Europe. The only solution that his theory of social control offered was the elimination of diversity by the exclusion of these immigrants or by the application of coercive measures that Ross himself admitted were antithetical to the very liberal-democratic values he claimed to be defending.

At the heart of Ross's problem was his acceptance of the one directional pattern of interaction between the individual and society that I described in our introductory chapter and the view it posits of the individual as the passive recipient of his culture. His acceptance of this viewpoint, as evidenced by his reliance on a psychology of imitation, left him unable to account for the kind of indirect, internal mechanism of social control that might have provided spontaneously for the assimilation of Eastern and Southern European immigrants. Although Ross argued that these indirect controls were the most appropriate in modern, twentieth-century America, he did not, within his theory, employ the kind of psychology that would explain how they would work.

At about the same time that Ross was developing his theory of social control, another formative theorist of American sociology, Charles Horton Cooley, was also defining what was in effect a theory of social control. Unlike Ross, however, Cooley assumed the other principal view of the relationship between the individual and society which we described in chapter 1. This view posits a reciprocal pattern of interaction between these two elements and conceptualizes the individual as an active and creative force in the construction of his culture. Our examination of the sociology of social control now turns to his work.

VI

Charles Horton Cooley (1864–1929) began his academic career, as did Ross, with a doctorate in economics. Unlike Ross, however, Cooley's doctoral work, at the University of Michigan from 1892 to 1894, included course work in sociology, which he used to fulfill his minor requirement. In 1892, Cooley assumed a position as an instructor of sociology in the Department of Political Economy at Michigan and began what was to be a lifetime teaching career at that institution.[68]

Cooley did not really formulate a distinct theory of social control in the sense that Ross did. He only made brief reference to the term in his last book, *Social Process*, written in 1918, to describe the efforts of society to apply intelligence in resolving the problems of population control and international relations.[69] His real contribution to the development of the idea of social control, however, is not to be found there. Rather, we need to look elsewhere, at Cooley's concept of the social self. It was in articulating this concept, although Cooley did not approach the topic in terms of the issue of social control, that he spelled out a second theory of social control within early American sociology, one that we might think of as representing an alternative viewpoint to the theory of social control formulated by Ross.

In introducing the concept of the social self, Cooley sought at least in part to explain how the individual took on the values, attitudes, and standards of behavior of the social group to which he belonged. His immediate concern was the question of socialization, namely how the individual internalizes the norms that guide his public and private conduct. Indirectly, however, he was addressing the larger question of how the ability of the individual to internalize social norms allows society to maintain itself. And as it turns out, this was the very question that Ross was addressing, albeit in somewhat different terms, when he talked about social control.

Cooley used the term social self to refer to those ideas which an individual as a member of society comes to accept and to 'cherish' as his 'own'.[70] The most important of these ideas for our understanding of Cooley's view of social control was the idea the individual held of himself, which Cooley referred to as his self feeling. For it was the self feeling, Cooley argued, that acted to regulate what an individual believed and how he behaved.[71]

Self feeling emerged in three phases. In his interaction with others, an individual typically imagined how he appeared to those others. He then imagined how those others might judge that appearance. Third and finally, he took on that judgment, be it one of approval or disapproval, as his own view on himself.

Cooley described the emergence of this self feeling as roughly analogous to what happened when the individual viewed himself in a mirror. When a person looked into a mirror, Cooley noted, he typically examined his dress and physical stature and then judged what he saw in terms of some ideal notion he held of what he would have liked to see. Cooley argued that something similar took place when the individual in his imagination judged how others perceived him.[72] For this reason, Cooley talked about the social self as the 'reflected or looking glass self':

> In a very large and interesting class of cases the social reference takes the form of a somewhat definite imagination of how one's self — that is any idea he appropriates — appears in a particular mind, and the kind of self-feeling one has is determined by the attitude toward this attributed to that other mind.[73]

What is of particular importance to us in this essay about Cooley's notion of the social self is the role it played in the individual's conduct. How an individual imagined others with whom he interacted viewed him, according to Cooley, determined how in the end he behaved as well as how he felt about his behavior.[74] As an example, Cooley cited the case of the 5-year-old child who, when offered a piece of candy, refused saying, 'mama didn't want me to have candy'. The child's refusal, Cooley noted, was the result of his obedience to his mother's command, which was reinforeced by the child's imaginative image 'of the reproving face and voice of his mother'.[75] The child's behavior was under the control, Cooley argued:

> ... of imagined approval or disapproval of others, appealing to instinctive emotion, and giving the force of that emotion to certain views of conduct. The behavior that connects itself with such social sentiment as we like and feel the impulse to continue, is so much more the likely to be judged as right; but if the sentiment is one from which we are adverse, the behavior is more likely to be judged wrong.[76]

It was a regulative power that could, as Cooley said, 'maintain a standard set by a group', or in other words ensure social conformity.[77] In this way, the social self functioned as an instrument of social control.

The kind of social control that Cooley was describing was essentially the indirect types of control that Ross so favored but which he could not explain. Cooley, however, was able to explain how this type of social control worked to maintain order in American society.

Cooley, unlike Ross, did not posit an individual in conflict with society. Rather, he assumed what has been called an organic view of society, characterizing it as a '... vast tissue of reciprocal activity'.[78] Society and the individual for Cooley were not separate elements but aspects of the same underlying reality. Notions such as individual and society were, he believed, abstractions that were not really part of one's actual experience. The real fact of experience, he argued, was human life, which could be examined in either its individual or social aspects.[79]

Cooley believed that it was the ideas that the individual held of himself and of others in his imagination that constituted his reality. These ideas came together, Cooley noted, in the mind:

> My association with you evidently consists in the relation between my idea of you and the rest of my mind. If there is something in you that is wholly beyond this and makes no impression upon me it has no social reality in this relationship.[80]

Mind was Cooley's term for that whole or reality which emerged out of the interaction of individuals in social life.

What is important about Cooley's concept of mind for our purposes, is its social nature. The ideas which an individual held in his mind were inextricably linked to the ideas of others with whom he interacted and through the sedimented traditions or culture of his social group to the ideas held by his forebearers. Self-consciousness in Cooley's system emerged simultaneously with social consciousness. They could not be conceived of separately.[81]

The social self, as was the case with all the ideas which the mind held, emerged spontaneously out of social interaction. Thus, the social control which the self provided was not something as it was for Ross, that was externally imposed on the individual. Cooley's brand of social control was a natural property of social life that operated automatically within the individual. It was, in a sense, an unintentional kind of control.[82]

The social self, Cooley argued, emerged in the primary group, his term for such fundamental social units as the family, the play group, and the neighborhood. It was in these groups, characterized by their 'intimate face-to-face association and co-operation' that individuals established their identities. They established, in other words, within these groups those common and shared sentiments, particularly the 'feeling of social right and wrong', which held them together as a social unit. These sentiments were the raw material out of which the members of these primary groups naturally and spontaneously formed their feelings of self:

> The ideal that grows up in familiar association may be said to be part of human nature itself. In its most general form it is that part of a moral whole or community wherein individual minds are merged and the higher capacities of the members find total and adequate expression. And it grows up because familiar association fills our minds with imaginations of the thought and feeling of other members of the group, and of the group as a whole, so that, for many purposes, we really make them a part of ourselves and identify our self-feeling with them.[83]

Social control, then, for Cooley was dependent on the existence of the primary group. As American society became urbanized and industrialized, Cooley argued, these intimate associations tended to break down and to be replaced by larger, less enduring forms of association, which he called nucleated groups.[84] These groups, however, lacked the characteristics necessary for the emergence of the self and the social control it provided. The result was a crisis in social order. It was this crisis which represented for Cooley, as it did for Ross, the problem of community. Before we address the issue of community in Cooley's thought, however, we need to see why it was that he was able to talk about social control as a spontaneous fact of social life. To do this, we must turn to the psychological orientation that he brought to his work.

VII

Cooley rejected the notion of imitation that in the end was to pose so much trouble for Ross in his psychological explanation of social control. What troubled Cooley about the idea of imitation was its implication that the individual took on the behavior and attitudes of others with whom he interacted in a mechanical way without reflection.[85] On the contrary, he believed that the act of imitation involved conscious effort. When one observed children imitating each other, he noted:

> It is very natural to assume that to do what someone else does requires no mental effort; but this applied to little children, is, of course, a great mistake. They cannot imitate an act except by learning how to do it, any more than grown-up people can, and for a child to learn a word may be as complicated a process as for an older person to learn a difficult piece on the piano. A novel imitation is not at all mechanical, but a strenuous voluntary activity, accompanied by effort and followed by pleasure in success.[86]

Cooley thus saw the individual as an active agent in his interaction with others. The individual did not simply take on the suggestions of those with whom he interacted. He acted on those suggestions in some way.

It is this view of the individual as an inherently active agent in social life that distinguishes Cooley's psychology from that of Ross. Cooley believed that the individual came into the world with a hereditary need for social feeling.[87] Because of this need the new-born individual began almost immediately to act on his environment. At first, this action took the form of undifferentiated visual, auditory, and tactile activity toward sensory objects in the outer environment. Later on, it expressed itself in the child's almost uncontrollable urge to communicate with others, first through smiling, cooing, and babbling and eventually through language. With the acquisition of language, Cooley argued, this desire to communicate became so strong that the child tended to carry on conversations with imaginary companions.[88] The process continued, Cooley believed, into adulthood when it became interiorized in the mind. From this point on, he stated, '. . . the mind lives in perpetual conversation' with itself.[89]

For Cooley, ideas were the result of this interiorized conversation within the mind. Ideas, then, were not hereditary elements, although the basic material for their formation may have been instinctive. They developed out of a social process:

> It is by intercourse with others that we expand our inner experience. In other words, and this is the point of the matter, the personal idea consists at first and in all later development, of a sensuous element or symbol with which is connected a more or less complex body of thought and sentiment; the whole social in genesis, formed by a series of communications.[90]

As an example, Cooley pointed to the way in which the individual formed an idea about an unknown person who he encountered. He did this by imagining how this unknown person would act in a given situation. That is, his experience provided him with a range of images of people confronting different situations. When he saw a new person, he attempted to match that person with one of these images he held in his mind. He then judged that individual according to his evaluation of the image which the individual matched:

> If I can imagine a man intimidated, I do not respect him; if I can imagine him lying, I do not trust him; if I can see him receiving, comprehending, resisting men and disposing them in accordance with his own plans, I abscribe executive ability to him; if I can think of him in his study patiently working out occult problems, I judge him to be a scholar; and so on.[91]

Social reality, for Cooley, was the idea that the mind constituted. The elements of society were the thoughts which its individual members associated with a variety of symbols. One's association with another, according to Cooley, '... consists in the relation between my idea of you and the rest of my mind. If there is something in you that is wholly beyond this and makes no impression on me it has no social reality in this relation'.[92] The focal point of society for Cooley was, then, the mind. Those things that were not part of the individual's imagination were not part of his society:

> In saying this I hope I do not seem to question the independent reality of persons or to confuse it with personal ideas. The man is one thing and various ideas entertained about him are another; but the latter, the personal idea, is the immediate social reality, the thing in which men exist for one another, and work directly upon another's lives. Thus any study of society that is not supported by a firm grasp of personal ideals is empty and dead — mere doctrine and not knowledge at all.[93]

Social reality in Cooley's sociology was a construct formed out of a mutual and reciprocal sharing of mental states. It involved individuals, according to Cooley, in the act of placing themselves in each others' minds and thus entering with each other into a state which Cooley referred to as 'communion'. Cooley also called this state 'sympathy', but the term empathy might better convey his meaning.[94]

Cooley, unlike Ross, was able to offer a psychological explanation of how the members of society were able spontaneously as part of their ongoing interaction with each other to hold those shared sentiments and ideas that made social order possible. His belief in the automatic tendency of interacting individuals to live, so to speak, in each others' minds enabled him to account for the kind of indirect social control that alluded Ross. It would lead Cooley, as we shall now see, to an understanding of the problem of community in twentieth-century America that was fundamentally different from that of Ross.

VIII

Cooley, like Ross, was a product of the rural, small town. He was born in Ann Arbor, Michigan on 17 August 1864, and, except for short stays during his college years in Colorado, North Carolina and Europe to regain his fragile health and a two-year stay in Washington, DC where he worked for the Interstate Commerce Commission and the Census Bureau, he was to spend his entire life there. In fact, throughout his life he seemed to despair whenever his career required him to travel, even for the briefest periods of time, away from Ann Arbor.[95] Cooley's sociology might be seen, just as was the case with Ross, as the effort of a rural Midwesterner to come to terms with America's transition to an urban, industrial society.[96]

I noted earlier in this chapter that the problem of community for Cooley, as it was for Ross, was the problem of the absence of needed mechanisms of social control within modern, American society. His response to this situation, once again like Ross, was to seek to recreate a community of like-mindedness, reminiscent of the small town, within an urban, industrial society. He hoped that such a community would allow for the existence of primary groups and the social control they provided. The primary group, then, provided Cooley with a model for a modern American community.[97]

At its heart, society for Cooley was the organization of a host of specialized activities into a unified whole and directed toward a commonly shared end. That organization, he believed, required a unifying mechanism, which he called communication. Cooley used the term communication broadly to refer to such activities as the exchange of commodities between various regions of the country, the transmission of ideas between people and places through speech, writing, and telegraph, and the perpetuation of customs between generations over time.[98] The development of self was in effect a process of communication for Cooley between individual imaginations that served to unify the attitudes and patterns of behavior of individuals within society.[99]

Communication could not and should not, Cooley believed, remain a static process. It had to be flexible and provide mechanisms of exchange that were responsive to changing social conditions.[100] What was called for with the demise of primary group relations, he argued, were mechanisms that would connect people whose actual relationships were neither intimate, face-to-face, nor long-lasting. Cooley found these mechanisms in the technological advances in communication that the daily newspaper, the telegraph, and the telephone were bringing to modern America.[101] It was through these forms of communication, Cooley maintained, that the members of twentieth-century American society could live in the imaginations of those others with whom they interacted. This would allow them to be brought under social control just as they had been in an earlier day in the primary group relationships of the small rural town.[102]

Cooley held out great hope for these new mechanisms of communication. Not only could they restore the nation's lost community of like-mindedness, they could, he believed, enlarge the sphere of democracy.[103] Printing, for example, made:

> ... communication general or democratic. So long as handwriting was the only means of record, books were costly, newspapers were not to be thought of and direct access to the stores of thought and feeling was the privilege of a few. Under such conditions opportunity was like the early sun: it lit up a hilltop here and there, but left the plain in shadow. Printing, to put it otherwise, may not make the stream of knowledge deeper or improve the taste of the water, but it does open a path along the margin and give every one a cup from which to drink. With popular education, which is its natural complement, it forms the principal free institution, without which no other sort of freedom could long endure, and by the aid of which we may hope to gain more freedom than we have.[104]

What is important about this type of social control for our purposes is that it is a mechanism of regulation that could, unlike Ross's, operate without the overt and direct action of society's institutions. Communication provided a medium for Cooley through which social control could occur. It was, however, a spontaneous and natural part of social interaction whose origins were to be found '... outside the channels of public guidance and formal institutions'.[105] Social control, Cooley believed, was an immediate outcome of social life whether it took place through the vehicle of the primary group in the small rural town or through the process of communication in an urban industrial society.

Cooley's notion of control, as an automatic feature of social life, seems to have enabled him to take a very sanguine view about the very issues that were so troubling to Ross, namely immigration and the emergence of a corporate economy. For Cooley, the influx of Eastern and Southern European immigrants into the population brought the kind of diversity on which, he argued, democracy thrived. It was this diversity, he went on to note, that spurred needed social changes.[106]

Cooley, unlike Ross, placed primary emphasis in his understanding of racial and ethnic differences on the environment:

> It is certain that different spirits are to be found in different races, that there is a deep and ancient unlikeness in the whole inner life of the Japanese, for example, and of the English. But the same is true of peoples like the English and the Germans, who are not of distinct races. In other words, a group soul, a special ethos or mores, is the sure result of historical causes acting for centuries in a social system; so the different souls will exist whether the race is different or not. And as race differences, when present, are always accompanied by historical differences, it is not possible to make out just how much is due to them alone.[107]

He was, therefore, less willing than Ross to accept the view that the native-born population was innately superior to the newly-arriving immigrants.[108] Cooley believed that any differences between these two segments of the population were primarily cultural in nature and would disappear as both groups entered through processes of communication into relationships similar to those found in primary groups.[109]

Cooley, then, did not attribute the social problems of his day to the seemingly hereditary defects of an increasing immigrant population. Poverty among these immigrant groups, he argued, was primarily due to their unfamiliarity with an urban industrial society and their consequent inability to adjust to its demands. It was a problem, Cooley believed, that could be resolved by guaranteeing these new immigrants opportunities for education, decent housing, and leisure.[110]

Cooley, like Ross, recognized that the rise of a corporate economy was leading to the concentration of the wealth of the nation in the hands of a small 'capitalist class'. Unlike Ross, however, he did not view this concentration as being necessarily bad. It was, he thought, not an aberrant occurrence but rather the natural result of industrialization being undertaken in a society that valued competition. The great wealth these capitalists enjoyed could be seen, Cooley suggested, as the reward for their service to the nation in rationalizing its industrial power'.[111]

The problem for Cooley with industrialization was not the accumulation and concentration of wealth itself. Rather, what worried him was how, in the absence of the kind of social control that the primary group provided, to ensure that industrialization benefited the nation as a whole. There were, he pointed out, indications that this common benefit had not occurred. 'The vast transactions associated with modern industry', Cooley noted, 'have come very little under such control, and offer a field for free-booting such as the world has never seen'.[112] Cooley believed that modern American society required new vehicles through which the spontaneous emergence of social control could occur to fill the void left by the demise of the primary group. He suggested, for example, that labor unions and agencies for the regulation and ownership of industry might fulfill this purpose.[113] For Cooley, then, it seems that the problem of a corporate economy, just as the problem of the immigrant, was transitory and could be remedied naturally through the operation of spontaneous mechanisms of social control.

IX

In spelling out his notion of the social self, Cooley hit upon the indirect, internal mechanism of social control that had alluded Ross. It was a mechanism, we have seen, that allowed him to avoid the use of the coercive sanctions that had so dominated Ross's work in favor of a process of regulation that occurred automatically within social interaction. It was, we have also seen, a mechanism of social control that in distinction to Ross's posited a view of the individual as an active organism who through the emergence of a social or 'looking-glass' self helped to define the social expectations that would ultimately regulate his conduct. In other words, the relationship between the individual and society was not, as it was for Ross, one-directional but reciprocal.

Because of these differences, Cooley was able to take a more positive view of the state of urban, industrial America than did Ross. He was neither troubled by increases in immigration nor by the emergence of a corporate economy. Nevertheless, in the end Cooley was no more successful than Ross had been in defining a view of community for an urban industrial society. Cooley, we should remember, assumed that new advances in communication such as the daily newspaper and the telegraph could connect people whose associations were becoming less face-to-face and less long-lasting. His hope was that communications could reestablish the primary group relationships of the small rural town. In effect, what Cooley did was to substitute communication for face-to-face interaction and promote a reconstituted version of the primary group as his model for a twentieth century American community. In a different but less direct way, Cooley like Ross failed ultimately to accept an urban industrial society. Where Ross tried to resist its inroads, Cooley sought to restructure it on the model of the small rural town.

Neither Ross nor Cooley, then, satisfactorily resolved the problem of community. In attempting to address this problem in terms of the issue of social control, they did establish the parameters in which succeeding generations of middle class intellectuals, including the educators we will examine in this volume, would seek to come to terms with an urban industrial society. Some, fearful of the supposed threat these two forces posed to a homogeneous culture, would embrace the direct, coercive controls emphasized by Ross. Others, who were more hopeful about the promise of both urbanization and industrialization, would turn to the indirect and automatic type of social control favored by Cooley. Most, however, would strike a balance somewhere in between.

Other intellectuals in addition to Ross and Cooley made a contribution early in this century to the development of the idea of social control. Most important for our purposes is the work of two individuals affiliated with the emerging discipline of psychology. One was Edward L. Thorndike, a founding theorist of American behaviorism. The other, George Herbert Mead, although a philosopher by professional identity, made his most enduring contribution to American social thought in the murky realm where psychology and sociology come together, the field of social psychology. They would both, as we shall see, further define and in the process refine the very different psychological explanations of social control first advanced by Ross and Cooley. Their work would, just as would that of Ross and Cooley, have an important effect on how those within the field of curriculum would come to define the concept of social control and the problem of community. It is to their contributions to the development of the concept of social control in American thought we must now look.

Notes

1 PETER L. BERGER and THOMAS LUCKMAN, *The Social Construction of Reality*, Garden City, Anchor Books, 1967, p. 55; DONALD BLACK, *The Behavior of Law*, New York, Academic Press, 1976, p. 105.

2 LESTER FRANK WARD, *Pure Sociology* 2nd edn., New York, Macmillan, 1915, pp. 15–20 and 463–6.

3 SAMUEL CHUGERMAN, *Lester Frank Ward, The American Aristotle*, Durham, Duke University Press, 1939, pp. 162 and 167; CLIFFORD H. SCOTT, *Lester Frank Ward*, Boston, Twayne Publishing Company, 1976, p. 212.

4 WARD, *op. cit.*, pp. 544 and 555; LESTER FRANK WARD, *The Psychic Factors of Civilization*, 2nd edn., Boston, Ginn and Company, 1906, pp. 323–5 and 330.

5 WILLIAM GRAHAM SUMNER, *Folkways*, Boston, Ginn and Company, 1906, pp. 2–5 and 34.

6 *Ibid.*, p. iv.

7 JULIUS WEINBERG, *Edward Alsworth Ross and the Sociology of Progressivism*, Madison, The State Historical Society of Wisconsin, 1972, pp. 27–31 and 34–40.

8 This interpretation of the origins of the idea of social control is supported by their correspondence which was collected during the 1930s and 1940s by Bernard Stern. In 1893, Ross wrote to Ward that 'I shouldn't wonder if this year I may run on to some ideas in sociology susceptible of development' (Ross to Ward, 19 October 1893). Two years later, Ross wrote: 'Besides I have a great new discovery in sociology to talk over with you and get your advice on. Fact is I am planning to bring out a book on a certain phase of sociology' (Ross to Ward, 16 September 1895). 'The Ward-Ross Correspondence I, 1891–1896'. *American Sociological Review*, 3, June, 1938, pp. 381–90. Ross dedicated *Social Control* 'to my Master Lester F. Ward ... ' In regard to this dedication, Ward wrote to Ross: 'The idea had never entered my head, and if it had it would have been instantly banished. In all candor, aren't you afraid it was a mistake?' (Ward to Ross, 4 July 1901). 'The Ward-Ross Correspondence II, 1897–1901' *American Sociological Review*, 7, December, 1946, pp. 746–7.

9 EDWARD A. ROSS, *Seventy Years of It*, New York, D. Appleton-Century Company, 1936, p. 54.

10 Ross to Ward, 2 February, 1896, 'The Ward-Ross Correspondence I', *op. cit.*, p. 892.

11 EDWARD A. ROSS, 'Social Control I', *American Journal of Sociology*, I, March, 1896, p. 518.

12 EDWARD A. ROSS, *Social Control: A Survey of the Foundations of Order*, New York, Macmillan, 1912, pp. vii–viii.

13 *Ibid.*, pp. 44–5.

14 *Ibid.*, p. 47.

15 *Ibid.*, p. 45.

16 *Ibid.*, pp. 11–13.

17 *Ibid.*, p. 59.

18 *Ibid.*, p. 67.

19 *Ibid.*, pp. 95 and 98.

20 *Ibid.*, pp. 98, 106, 111 and 125.

21 *Ibid.*, pp. 126–32.

22 Ross, 'Social Control I', *op cit.*, 534–5.

23 *Social Control*, *op. cit.*, p. 152.

24 *Ibid.*, pp. 151–3.

25 *Ibid.*, p. 164.

26 EDWARD A. ROSS, 'Social Control XIII', *American Journal of Sociology*, 3, May, 1898, p. 811.

27 *Social Control*, *op. cit.*, pp. 167–8.

28 *Ibid.*, pp. 173–4.

29 'Social Control I', *op. cit.*, pp. 534–5.

30 *Social Control*, *op. cit.*, p. 197.

31 *Ibid.*, pp. 254–5, 259–60.

32 EDWARD A. ROSS, *Principles of Sociology*, New York, The Century Company, 1920, pp. 42–3.

33 FAY BERGER KARPF, *American Social Psychology*, New York, McGraw-Hill, 1932, pp. 173–5.

34 STERN, 'The Ward-Ross Correspondence II', *op. cit.*, p. 747. Ross made the same point in the preface to *Social Psychology*. 'At the moment of launching this work, I pause to pay heartfelt homage to the genius of Gabriel Tarde. Solicitous as I have been to give him due credit in the text, no wealth of excerpt and citation can reveal the full measure of my indebtedness to that profound and original thinker. While my system has swung wide of his, I am not sure I should ever have wrought out a social psychology but for the initial stimulus and the two great construction lines — conventionality and custom-yielded by his incomparable *Lois de l'imitation*. See EDWARD A. ROSS, *Social Psychology*, New York, Macmillan, 1912, p. viii.

35 GABRIEL TARDE, *The Laws of Imitation*, translated by Elsie Clews Parsons, New York, Henry Holt and Company, 1903, p. 11.

36 *Ibid.*, p. 145.

37 *Ibid.*, p. xiv.

38 *Ibid.*, p. 168.

39 GABRIEL TARDE, *On Communication and Social Influence*, edited by TERRY N. CLARK, Chicago, University of Chicago Press, 1969, p. 16.

40 *The Laws of Imitation*, *op. cit.* p. 198.

41 *On Communication and Social Influence*, *op. cit.*, p. 38.

42 WILLIAM L. KOLB, 'The Sociological Theories of Edward Alsworth Ross', in *An Introduction to the History of Sociology*, edited by HARRY ELMER BARNES abridged edn, Chicago, University of Chicago Press, 1966, p. 458.

43 EDWARD A. ROSS, *Foundations of Sociology*, 5th edn; New York, Macmillan, 1919, p. 267.

44 *Ibid.*, pp. 53 and 63; ROSCOE HINKLE, *Founding Theory of American Sociology, 1881–1915*, Boston, Routledge and Kegan Paul, 1980, p. 116.

45 *Principles of Sociology*, *op. cit.*, pp. 49–50.

46 *Foundations of Sociology*, *op. cit.*, p. 270.

47 *Ibid.*, p. 271.

48 EDWARD A. ROSS, *Changing America*, New York, The Century Company, 1912, chapter 6.

49 EDWARD A. ROSS, *The Old World in the New*, New York, The Century Company, 1914, pp. 198–201.

50 *Ibid.*, pp. 207–22; EDWARD A. ROSS, *Standing Room Only*, New York, The Century Company, 1927, chapters 26 and 27. Compare Ross's views with those contained in the *Reports of the Immigration Commission*. See Immigration Commission, Reports of the Commission, *Abstracts of Reports of the Commission*, I, 41 vols., New York, Arno Press, 1970, pp. 493–501, 521 and 540–1.

51 *Standing Room Only, op. cit.*, pp. 270–2; EDWARD A. ROSS, 'The causes of race superiority', *Annals of the American Academy of Political and Social Science*, 18, July-December, 1901, pp. 88–9.

52 *The Old World in the New, op. cit.*, pp. 288–9.

53 EDWARD A. ROSS, *Seventy Years of It*, New York, D. Appleton-Century Company, 1936, chapters 1–2; R. JACKSON WILSON, *In Quest of Community: Social Philosophy in the United States, 1860–1920*, New York, Oxford University Press, 1968, pp. 90–102.

54 *Social Control, op. cit.*, p. 433.

55 *Ibid.*, p. 432.

56 'Social Control XIII', *op. cit.*, p. 814.

57 WEINBERG, *op. cit.*, pp. 161–9; *Standing Room Only, op. cit.*, chapters 19–23; *Principles of Sociology, op. cit.*, pp. 36–7; EDWARD A. ROSS, *The Social Trend*, New York, The Century Company, 1922, chapter 1; EDWARD A. ROSS, *World Drift*, New York, The Century Company, 1928, chapters 2–3.

58 WEINBERG, *ibid.*, pp. 39–54; *Seventy Years of It, op. cit.*, chapter 7.

59 *Social Control, op. cit.*, pp. 376, 394 and 419–21.

60 *Ibid.*, p. 429.

61 *Ibid.*, pp. 411–2.

62 *Ibid.*, p. 413.

63 WEINBERG, *op. cit.*, pp. 161–2.

64 *Ibid.*, pp. 167–9. By the 1930s, Ross seemed to have abandoned his nativistic sentiments in favor of an environmental explanation of human differences. He noted in his 1936 autobiography, for example, that he once had 'characterized some of our immigrants from Eastern Europe as "the beaten members of beaten breeds". I rue this sneer. Since coming to know the Slavs in their homeland I realize that their cultural backwardness is due not to any deficiency in themselves, but to their having been overrun again and again by mounted barbarians from the Asiatic grasslands and to their living beyond the reach of such powerful stimuli as our ancestors had from the Crusades, the Renaissance, the Geographic Discoveries and the Rise of sea-borne Commerce'. See *Seventy Years of It, op. cit.*, p. 277.

65 *The Old World in the New, op. cit.*, pp. 285–6.

66 *Foundations of Sociology, op. cit.*, p. 389.

67 *Social Control, op. cit.*, pp. 439–40.

68 CHARLES HORTON COOLEY, 'The development of sociology at Michigan', in *Sociological Theory and Social Research*, New York, Henry Holt and Company, 1930, pp. 3–8; EDWARD C. JANDY, *Charles Horton Cooley: His Life and His Social Theory*, New York, Octagon Books, 1969, pp. 32 and 78.

69 CHARLES HORTON COOLEY, *Social Process*, New York, Charles Scribner's Sons, 1918, chapters 19 and 23.

70 CHARLES HORTON COOLEY, *Human Nature and the Social Order*, New York, Charles Scribner's Sons, 1902, p. 147.

71 Cooley writes that '. . . the ordinary motive to conformity is a sense more or less vivid, of the pains and inconveniences of non-conformity. Most people find it painful to go to an evening company in any other than the customary dress, the source of the pain appearing to be a vague sense of the depreciatory curiosity which one imagines that he will excite. His social self-feeling is hurt by an unfavorable view of himself that he attributes to others. This example is typical of the way the group coerces each of its members in all matters concerning which he has no strong and definite purpose', *ibid.*, pp. 262–3.

72 *Ibid.*, p. 152.

73 *Ibid.*, pp. 151–2.

74 *Ibid.*, pp. 152–3.

75 *Ibid.*, pp. 340–1 and 349.

76 *Ibid.*, p. 350.

77 *Ibid.*, p. 262.

78 *Social Process*, op. cit., p. 28.

79 *Human Nature and the Social Order*, op. cit., pp. 1–2.

80 *Ibid.*, p. 84.

81 CHARLES HORTON COOLEY, *Social Organization*, New York, Charles Scribner's Sons, 1914, pp. 3–5.

82 *Human Nature and the Social order*, op. cit., p. 263.

83 *Social Organization*, op. cit., pp. 23, 28 and 33.

84 *Social Process*, op cit., p. 252; HINKLE, op. cit., p. 162.

85 *Human Nature and the Social Order*, op. cit., pp. 14–16.

86 *Ibid.*, p. 25.

87 *Ibid.*, p. 50.

88 JANDY, op. cit., pp. 102–3.

89 *Human Nature and the Social Order*, op. cit., p. 54.

90 *Ibid.*, p. 69.

91 *Ibid.*, p. 70.

92 *Ibid.*, pp. 81–2, 84.

93 *Ibid.*, p. 89.

94 *Ibid.*, p. 102.

95 JANDY, op. cit., pp. 11, 19–32, 62–3 and 76–7.

96 *Social Organization*, op. cit., pp. 27 and 383–6.

97 JEAN B. QUANDT, *From the Small Town to the Great Community: The Social Thought of Progressive Intellectuals*, New Brunswick, Rutgers University Press, 1970, pp. 14–20.

98 CHARLES HORTON COOLEY, 'The theory of transportation', in *Sociological Theory and Research*, op. cit., p. 40.

99 *Social Organization*, op. cit., p. 61.

100 *Social Process*, op. cit., p. 244.

101 *Ibid.*, p. 255; CHARLES HORTON COOLEY, 'The process of social change', *Political Science Quarterly*, 12, March, 1897, p. 81.

102 QUANDT, op cit., p. 59.

103 *Social Organization*, op. cit., pp. 81, 86 and 88.

104 'The process of social change', op. cit., p. 75.

105 CHARLES HORTON COOLEY, 'A Primary Culture of Democracy', *Sociology and Education*, papers and proceedings of the Thirteenth Annual Meeting of the American Sociological Society, Chicago, University of Chicago Press, 1919, p. 4.

106 *Social Process, op. cit.*, pp. 365 and 370–1.

107 *Ibid.*, p. 274.

108 CHARLES HORTON COOLEY, 'Genius fame, and the comparison of races', *Annals of the American Academy of Political and Social Science* 9, May, 1897, pp. 317–58. Cooley, for example, attacked Francis Galton's belief that some races, because of hereditary differences, were more successful than others in producing highly intelligent 'men' who, in turn, attained fame. Cooley noted that 'every able race probably turns out a number of greatly endowed men many times larger than the number that attains to fame. By greatly endowed I mean with natural abilities equal to those that have made men famous in other times and places. The question which, if any, of these geniuses are to achieve fame is determined by historical and social conditions, and these vary so much that the production of great men cannot justifiably be used as a criterion of the ability of races except under rare and peculiar circumstances hereafter to be specified', (pp. 318–9).

109 Cooley was, however, less optimistic about the ability of Asians and Blacks, whose differences from the native-born population he thought to be racial, to be assimilated. In the case of Asians, he supported some manner of restrictive immigration legislation. He was not, however, like Ross an active advocate for this type of legislation nor a member of the Immigration Restriction League. See *Social Process, op. cit.*, pp. 279–80.

110 Cooley's position on the social problems facing the immigrants was somewhat ambiguous. While for the most part he subscribed to an environmental view of poverty, he did admit that hereditary factors could in some instances play a role, particularly in the ability of different racial groups to adjust to social conditions. He was, in fact, willing where the cause for the difficulty was clearly hereditary to employ what he called 'a scientific eugenics, which shall deliberately select some types for propagation and reject others . . .', *ibid.*, pp. 229 and 236.

111 *Social Organization, op. cit.*, pp. 257 and 260.

112 *Ibid.*, pp. 260–1.

113 *Ibid.*, p. 264.

3   Social Control II: The Origins of a Psychology of Social Control

I

In a handwritten notebook that Edward Ross compiled in 1938 in which he sketched some ideas for a revision of his *Social Control*, a project he never did actually undertake, he noted that he would have to pay more attention to the question of psychology, particularly the role of personality, than he had in his original volume.[1] In an untitled and unpublished manuscript he wrote a few years earlier, he suggested that one of the principal weaknesses in his theory of social control was that when he formulated it, he was limited to nineteenth-century developments in psychology. 'Freud, Adler, and Pavlow', he pointed out, 'didn't make their contribution yet'.[2]

In making this confession, Ross at the end of his career was aware that social control involves more than the operation of certain overt social processes. It involves also the operation of covert psychological processes.[3] In fact, at the heart of any concept of social control, we argued in chapter 2, is a psychological mechanism that seeks to account for the influences on individual conduct and belief that emanates out of social interaction. If we are to understand the development of the idea of social control in our intellectual thought and to see how those associated with the field of curriculum were to use this concept in confronting an urban, industrial society, we need to pursue the efforts of those who, during the first three decades of this century, sought to refine what are in the works of both Ross and Cooley first approximations of a psychological explanation of social control. It is this exploration that brings us first to the work of Edward L. Thorndike and then to that of George Herbert Mead.

II

By any measure, Edward L. Thorndike (1874–1949) is a key figure in American intellectual thought. After graduating from Wesleyan University in Connecticut in 1895, he studied for two years, taking a second bachelors degree and a masters, at Harvard University, under William James. He then moved on to Columbia University where he earned his PhD in psychology in 1898 under James Cattell. His connectionist psychology, which we will discuss in this chapter, was an early formulation of what we today call behaviorism and was one of the principal variants of the functionalist orientation that characterized American psychology during the early years of this century. He was a founder of the mental measurements movement and in this role influenced the development and use of the intelligence test. He authored school textbooks, achievement tests, and teacher training texts that supported the efforts of early twentieth-century American educators to establish what they thought was a science of education. He was one of the first American psychologists to become identified with the field of educational psychology. It was in this capacity that he assumed a position at one of the most important schools of education of the day, Teachers College, Columbia University. And it was in his role at Teachers College, where he taught from 1899 until his retirement in 1940, that he guided the training of many of those graduate students who would occupy the nation's most significant educational posts during the first half of this century.[4] One historian of education, Clarence Karier, maintains that Thorndike was certainly one of the most influential figures, if not the most influential, in determining the form that American education has taken in this century.[5]

Connectionism was Thorndike's contribution to the effort of some of the most important formative theorists of American psychology, including in addition to Thorndike, James Cattell, James Angell, and Harvey Carr, to distinguish the subject matter and methodology of their discipline from the German structuralist psychology of Wilhelm Wundt and his American exponent, the transplanted Englishman, Edward Bradford Titchener. Representing what has come to be called a functionalist school of thought, these critics took issue with the structuralist view of the purpose of psychology as the introspective examination and description of the constitutive elements or structures of the mind. In its stead and despite the differences among them, these functionalists argued for a psychology whose purpose was to go beyond simply describing the elements of the mind to explain why and how they worked as they did and how they served the organism in its adjustment to its environment.[6]

The most important statement of the principles of this new school of thought was James Angell's 1906 Presidential Address to the American Psychological Association, 'The Province of Functional Psychology'. In the published version of the address which appeared in the following year in *The Psychological Review*, Angell, then Chairman of the Psychology Department at the University of Chicago, argued that the most 'fundamental category in functional psychology' was that of control. Although he did not discuss this issue in depth, his point seems to have been that the central concern of functionalism was the role of mental processes in the regulation of the organism in its interaction with the environment.[7] For Thorndike, it was structuralism's predominant interest with the examination of consciousness for its own sake at the expense of any concern about controlling behavior, particularly human conduct, that led him to reject this school and articulate his version of functionalism. As he pointed out early in his career:

> an animal's conscious stream is of no account to the rest of the world except in so far as it prophecies or modifies his action. There can be no moral warrant for studying man's nature unless the study will enable us to control his acts. If a psychologist is to study man's consciousness without relation to movement, he might as well fabricate imaginary consciousness to describe and analyze.[8]

III

A peculiar feature of Thorndike's thought given his behaviorist leanings was his acceptance of an hereditarian view of individual differences. He wrote as did Ross and many other intellectuals of his day as if there was a one-to-one correspondence between one's genes and one's social traits and behavior.[9] That is, although he believed that both environment and heredity, or as he put it 'original nature', played a role in determining human characteristics, heredity was the primary factor. The individual's 'response to any situation will be that which by original nature connected with that situation or some situation like it'.[10]

The connections that Thorndike was referring to took the form of certain unlearned tendencies of differing complexities. The most simple and uniform were reflex actions, such as knee jerks. Somewhat more complex and indefinite were instincts, which included feeding, seeking companionship, and play. The most complex and modifiable of these connections were what he called capacities, such as the capacity to learn. Unlike other unlearned tendencies, capacities were subject, Thorndike believed, to improvement by training.[11]

The action of these unlearned tendencies was neurological and involved what Thorndike described as the conduction of electrical impulses across a series of different types of neurons that connected those parts of the body that were excited by environmental stimuli to those parts of the body that reacted to these stimuli. It was this neurological process of conduction and the resulting connections that accounted for the physical and mental activity of the human organism.[12]

Little was known, according to Thorndike, about why the neurons acted as they did. He advanced the thesis that the ability to make connections depended on the adequate functioning of the various life processes of neurons, which he described, likening neurons to unicellular animals whose special activity was that of conduction, as (i) eating; (ii) excreting waste; (iii) growing; (iv) being sensitive, conducting and discharging waste; and (v) movement. When these life processes were, as he put it, 'going on well', neurons were able to receive and transmit stimuli and were in a state of what he called 'satisfaction'. When the life processes were not 'going on well', neurons were not able to receive and transmit stimuli and were in a state of 'annoyance' or 'discomfort'.[13] It was the abiltiy of the neurons to conduct, that is, to be in a state of 'satisfaction' that, according to Thorndike, enabled learning to take place.[14]

Learning occurred for Thorndike when these neurological connections became automatic, that is, became habits.[15] He reached this conclusion in the experiments he carried out for his doctoral dissertation in 1897. In these experiments, he studied how dogs, cats and chickens in various states of hunger were able to free themselves from cages with release mechanisms of differing complexities when food was placed out of the animals' reach outside their cages. It was his contention that an animal was able to escape from a cage through a trial and error process of associating the situation in which it was placed with the appropriate movement to open the release mechanism. If one of the trial and error movements of the animal in the cage accidently opened the release mechanism and enabled the animal to obtain the reward or 'satisfying' state of affairs provided by the food, that movement became associated with the situation. Each time thereafter when the animal was placed in the same situation, it would increasingly respond with the movement that opened the release mechanism while omitting those other trial and error movements that did not. The response that obtained the animal's escape became stamped into a connection with the situation or stimulus of a particular cage. The automatic or habitual response of the animal when placed in the cage became the movement that opened its release mechanism.[16]

Thorndike went on to systematize the conclusions of his dissertation research in his famous Laws of Effect and Exercise. In the Law of Effect, he sought to explain what made the connections come about. Here, he relied on the notions of neurological 'satisfaction' and 'annoyance' we mentioned earlier:

> Of several responses made to the same situation, those which are accompanied or closely followed by satisfaction to the animal will, other things being equal, be more firmly connected with the situation, so that when it recurs, they will be more likely to recur; those which are accompanied or closely followed by discomfort to the animal will, other things being equal, have their connection with the situation weakened, so that when it recurs, they will be less likely to occur. The greater the satisfaction or discomfort, the greater the strengthening or weakening of the bond.[17]

And in the Law of Exercise, he sought to explain how these connections after repeated occurrences became habits:

> Any response to a situation will, other things being equal, be more strongly connected with the situation in proportion to the number of times it has been connected with the situation and to the average rigor and duration of the connection.[18]

It was from these laws of learning that Thorndike would go on to construct a theory of social control.

IV

It has been argued that those American psychologists who first formulated the principles of behaviorism as well as those who came to embrace this school of thought in ensuing years did so in response to what they perceived to be a breakdown in social order and stability which they attributed to the twin factors of urbanization and industrialization. Their response, so the argument goes, was to change the emphasis of their discipline from that of a pure science devoted to the explanation of mental processes to an applied science of behavior control devoted to curtailing this social disruption. They sought in behaviorism an instrument of social control to restore what they believed was a missing community of like-mindedness that historically had been the root of social order in American society.[19]

Of those associated with this emerging behaviorist tradition within American psychology, it was Thorndike who most clearly spelled out an actual theory of social control.[20] In addition to his two laws of learning, which we have already described, he identified five subsidiary laws of learning. It was in one of these laws, the Law of Associative Shifting, that he identified a psychological principle of social control. Thorndike pointed out that any response that was connected to a given situation as a result of the operation of the Laws of Effect and Exercise could be shifted to make a connection with any other given situation to which the organism was sensitive. As an example, he pointed to the case of one holding up a fish in front of a hungry cat and saying at the same time, 'stand up'. If the cat was hungry enough, Thorndike argued, it would stand up on its hind legs. The reward or satisfying situation of receiving the fish in repeated trials would stamp in the connection between the situation and the response, and the cat's behavior would become a habit that was automatically repeated when placed in that situation. After repeated trials in which the fish and the command, 'stand up', were paired, Thorndike suggested that the fish could be discarded, and the cat would stand up as a response solely to the command.[21] It was this principle embodied in the Law of Associative Shifting, which was in essence Thorndike's version of what we now call classical conditioning, which when applied to human conduct could control that conduct:

> As a possibility, the method is omnipotent in the sense that any response of which a person is capable may thus be connected with the situation which he is sensitive. It is theoretically possible to make a person afraid of the sunshine or flowers, or courageous in the face of a jumping tiger ...[22]

It was an idea that was to play a more important role for Thorndike than in simply regulating how individuals reacted to the weather or to even dangerous animals. It was to represent his instrument for the general control of human conduct in twentieth century urban, industrial America:

> In spite of difficulties in making wants, interests, and attitudes available as controlled responses, in shifting them without losing their essential features, and in overcoming resistances met in

trying to put them in desirable connections, the education of the feelings should be much more effective than it has been. Parents, teachers, social workers, and rulers have no difficulties that they did not have before, and they are better off to the extent that they need not waste time in dubious practices. We now know that the fundamental forces which can change desires and emotions, directing them into desirable channels, are the same as change ideas and actions. A human being learns to react to the situations of life by such and such wants, interests, and attitudes, as he learns to react to them by such and such percepts, ideas, and movements. In both cases, the task of education is to cause the desired connection to occur and to attach the confirming reaction to it.[23]

It was a principle that would suggest to him how a sense of community could be restored to twentieth century American society.

V

Thorndike was born on 31 August 1874 in Williamsburg, Massachusetts, a small village in the Connecticut river valley about twelve miles northwest of Northampton. The denominational demand placed on his father, Reverend Edward Robert Thorndike, a Methodist minister, to frequently change congregations, as well as the common practice among Protestant clergy for a minister to move to larger churches in larger towns as he advanced in his career, necessitated repeated moves for the family. Thorndike spent his youth then not only in rural Massachusetts, first in Williamsburg and then in Conway, but also in the somewhat larger town of Easthampton, the emerging industrial towns of Everett, Lynn and Lowell, and eventually in the major urban centers of Boston and Providence, Rhode Island.[24] Thorndike, unlike either Ross or Cooley, grew up in the midst of the social and economic changes that accompanied both urbanization and industrialization in that region of the country that was probably most affected by these changes. He experienced at firsthand, not from a distance, an America that was becoming less Anglo-Saxon, less Protestant, and less rural.

Except for one year which he spent at Western Reserve University in Cleveland after obtaining his PhD, Thorndike was to spend his professional life in New York City at Teachers College. Although he bought a house in rural Montrose, New York, in 1906, because his wife did not enjoy life in New York City and because he thought it would be a better environment to raise their children, his asthma made it difficult for him to live there even for short periods of time. In 1917 he secured an apartment in New York City near Teachers College, which became the family's permanent home except for brief stays at Montrose during weekends and summer vacations.[25]

We do not know for certain if Thorndike's social views were influenced by his urban experiences, but unlike Ross who rejected the city and Cooley who tried to make it conform to the model of the primary group, he appeared to embrace urbanization. His theory of social control seems to have offered him a way to dissociate the yearning for community, which he shared with other early twentieth century theorists of social control, from its roots in nineteenth-century rural America. Before we actually consider the kind of community that Thorndike envisioned for American society, however, we need first to return to the subject of his hereditarianism, which we examined earlier, and consider its effect on his understanding of the problems of American society.

VI

What seemed to trouble Ross, we should recall, about modern American society was the presence within the population of an increasing number of what he believed to be hereditarily deficient immigrants from Eastern and Southern Europe. Not only did he believe that their hereditary defects rendered them unassimilable to a democratic society, he argued that if they were allowed to remain in America, they would, because of what he thought was an excessive birthrate, eventually displace a genetically superior native population of Anglo-Saxon heritage. Now Thorndike shared Ross's fear about the presence within the population of hereditarily deficient individuals. For Thorndike, however, the hereditary issue that concerned him was that of intelligence.[26] It was deficiencies in intelligence that he believed threatened American society:

> If by some biological catastrophe the next two or three generations had nobody over 85 IQ (which is somewhat below the average present intellect), radios, telegraphs and telephones would go dead, our power houses would be wrecked, trains would be at a standstill, typhus, cholera, and dysentery would sweep over the world ... most of mathematics, science, law,

and government would vanish or remain as mysteries like the
Maya language or the 'canals' on the moon, physical force
would work its will' with little restraint until some modus
vivendi on a low plane was hit upon by the few surviving
humans.[27]

Intelligence, Thorndike believed, not only determined a society's
technological character, it determined its moral character. He argued in
this vein that there was a positive correlation between desirable
hereditary traits. Those who were more intelligent were, he thought,
more moral, more successful in school, earned more money, and
possessed a better character:

> To him that hath a superior intellect is given also on the average
> a superior character; the quick boy is also in the long run the
> more accurate; the able boy is also more industrious. There is no
> principle of compensation whereby a weak intellect is offset by a
> strong will, a poor memory by a good judgment, or a lack of
> ambition by an attractive personality. Every pair of such
> supposed compensating qualities that have been investigated has
> been found really to show correspondence.[28]

Intelligence was for Thorndike the key to maintaining a stable and
like-minded American community. It was not necessary, he believed, to
return to a rural society for this purpose. It could be attained in an
urban society populated by able, and hence virtuous, individuals.[29]

Ethnic heterogeneity did, however, pose a problem for Thorndike.
In a study he conducted in 1922 of the comparative intelligence of black
and white high school students in a Midwestern city, he reported that
less than 4 percent of the blacks scored better than their white
counterparts. He concluded on a dismal note about the potential of
blacks in American society:

> Whatever may be the theoretical possibilities of the negro race
> or of the white-colored hybrid, the actual negroes and hybrids
> now existent in this city showed a failure to include variations at
> the high-school age much above the level of the average white
> high-school pupil. In many practical matters the upper limit of a
> group is as important as its average or typical status.[30]

Generally it was the case, he believed, that black Americans were less
intelligent than white Americans.[31]

This supposed intellectual inferiority of the Black population, according to Thorndike, posed problems for American society. In a 1939 study of American urban life, he argued that the presence of Black families in a city's population diminished what he called its 'goodness of life'.[32]

The poor and the socially deviant also shared Thorndike's disdain. In a study he and one of his graduate students conducted of children institutionalized because of delinquency or because their parents were too poor to care for them, he reported that these children were intellectually inferior to ordinary children, and this inferiority increased with age. It was the result of an intelligence deficit among these institutionalized children which he attributed to heredity.[33]

VII

The American community that Thorndike envisioned was first and foremost a community of the able and the good. Any hope for such a community rested, he believed, on the possibility that the intelligence of the American population could be measured. By the beginning of World War I, American psychologists thought they found the means to do just that with Lewis Terman's revision of the Binet-Simon mental test.[34] During the war, Throndike lent credence to this belief in his work for the National Research Council, a government sponsored group that attempted to mobilize the scientific and technical expertise of industry and the university in the war effort. As a member of its Psychology Committee, Thorndike worked on the development of personnel tests to select men for military training, including the famed Army Beta Intelligence Test.[35] This war effort at mental measurements, Thorndike commented at the end of the war, offered the nation '. . . the greatest increase in scientific control over the management of men in any year in any country'.[36]

Thorndike argued that if during the war it had been possible to measure the intelligence of over 300,000 men a month, it would certainly be possible in peace time to measure the intelligence of every child upon reaching the age of 10. It would be desirable, he argued, to establish a national 'census of intellect' to measure the intelligence of every child at the ages of 10, 14, 18 and 22, the results of which would be turned over to a variety of government officials including school superintendents, mayors, and welfare administrators. He hoped that eventually such a 'census' would be expanded to measure attitudes and values.[37] Throughout the remainder of his career, he would continue to advance the cause of mental measurements and its effort to build a science of education through his authorship of numerous achievement and aptitude tests.

Thorndike saw then in his work in mental testing as well as in the mental measurement movement generally a way to assess the nation's intelligence. With this information available, it would be possible, he believed, to establish specific policies to increase the number of able people in the population while decreasing those of less ability. He advocated the creation of a marriage and child allowance which would be given to the nation's most intelligent men between the ages of 21 and 30. He believed that the money would enable these men, in the prime of their youth to marry women, who he assumed would be of equally high intelligence, and to produce a new generation of able children.[38]

The less able segments of the population should, he argued, be prevented from reproducing. Considering, he pointed out, '. . . the fact that genes which makes able and good people also tend to make competent and helpful homes, and the argument for sterilizing anybody near the low end of the scale in intellect and morals whenever it can be done legally is very strong'.[39] It was a policy, he pointed out, which would result in a reduction of the number of individuals who were institutionalized for mental deficiency as well as a decline in the number of violent crimes and rapes, and it would allow the resources of society to be used for hospitals and schools instead of for the custodial care of the genetically defective.[40]

In addition, Thorndike's sought-after community was one, as it was for Ross and Cooley, of common thought and opinion. He argued that individuals were not generally knowledgeable and skillful, but instead they were narrow specialists or experts in a particular skill or area of knowledge.[41] Outside of their particular areas of expertise, Thorndike believed that individuals knew very little. They were what he called, 'half educated'. It would be dangerous, he went on to say, for people to do all of their own thinking. Their lack of expertise in most areas of life would lead them to accept false or naive solutions to important personal and social problems. As a consequence, he advocated that individuals should limit their thinking to matters that were within their areas of competence. Outside of their areas of competence, they should seek out the appropriate expert for direction and guidance. 'The individual should know when not to think and where to buy the thinking he needs'.[42]

But not all experts and their opinions were of equal value for Thorndike. Of paramount importance were those who he called, 'men of affairs', specifically businessmen, lawyers, and scientists. These were men who, he believed, exhibited not only expertise but exceptional ability. And because they were able, they were also, he argued, more moral, more dedicated to their work, and more willing to apply their talents to the benefit of the larger society than were the majority of the population.[43] These men deserved, he thought, a special and privileged place in American society:

> No egalitarian system of weights can be just or wise. More weight should be given to the wants of superior men than to the wants of inferior men. What able and good men want is more likely to be better for their community or nation or race or the world as a whole than what stupid and bad men want. Providing for their wants will presumably enable them to do more of what they want to do; and this will improve the world and its customs for future residents.[44]

The nation's corporate executives, he noted in this vein, deserved their large salaries because they really earned more in benefits to society than they earned in rewards for themselves. An annual salary of $400,000 for the President of the American Telephone and Telegraph Company would be, he argued, a greater investment in ensuring efficiency in telephone service than using the same amount of money to hire additional operators and linemen.[45]

Not only should these able and expert individuals be accorded a privileged economic position, he argued that political power should also be concentrated in their hands. The majority of the population, he suggested, could not govern themselves, nor should they try.[46] It would be better, he thought, to do away with the existing practice in elections of counting each person's vote equally and replace it with a weighted system of voting that would give more value to the votes of those who were most intelligent. It would also be preferable, he argued, to reduce popular participation in the political process by establishing boards of trustees throughout the nation composed of 'men of affairs' to select candidates for public office.[47]

His intent was to place the direction of American society under the control of these able and good 'men of affairs' he so admired. We can see this most clearly when we consider his view on the education of the American population. Thorndike shared the common assumption of most Americans that education was the nation's great instrument of social progress. He believed, however, that it only made an indirect contribution toward this end by preparing the most able members of society to assume positions of expertise in which they would work for the benefit of all. Early in his career, for example, Thorndike criticized Lester Frank Ward's *Applied Sociology* on the grounds that the book advanced the mistaken view that it was more important for education to ensure 'opportunity for the many mediocre' than for the 'gifted few'. He argued that it was a better investment to support the work of fifteen research professors at the university than to spend an equal amount of money on the annual education of 1500 children.[48]

Thorndike in fact advocated two distinct types of education, education for leadership and education for what he called 'following'. The most able members of society should be educated, he argued, to assume their rightful positions as 'men of affairs' and lead American society. Those of average and below average abilities, however, should be educated for 'following', that is to submit themselves to the rule of the most able in all aspects of life outside of their narrow spheres of competence.[49]

Education for 'following' as Thorndike described it required a degree of external imposition. As he pointed out, 'we must all learn to accept in many lines doctrines which we cannot evaluate or even understand, and persons whose thoughts and ways are alien to us or even distasteful'.[50] It was his concept of social control as embodied in the Law of Associative Shifting that would ensure this needed compulsion. Through this principle, he argued, it was possible to '... shift hatred from truly odious behavior to perfectly smooth and genial words like Progressive, Jew, or Labor Union'.[51] And similarly, the Law of Associative Shifting made it possible to shift the allegiance of the various segments of American society from their longstanding values and beliefs to new and different ones defined for them by the most able and influential members of the population. It was a principle in other words that could at the behest of those of most ability in American society impose a community of like-mindedness built on what they cherished and considered of importance on all of American society.

VIII

During the 1930s Edward Ross in the unpublished manuscript we cited at the beginning of this chapter noted the promise that behaviorism held out as an instrument of social control:

> Watson and others have proven it possible to 'condition' infants so as to produce regularity and consistency in their behavior. This not only promotes their control of their psychological processes ('good habits') but furnished the ground work of later conditioning in matters of moral and social importance. Atti-

tudes of submissiveness or resistance to authority reflect early conditioning.[52]

What Ross seems to be indicating in this statement is that he recognized the compatibility between his explanation of the psychology of social control as a process of imitation and the conditioning process that Thorndike and other behaviorists were using to provide a psychological grounding for their account of social control. Both Ross and Thorndike in describing the psychological process underlying social control posited a view of individuals as passive, responding organisms that were formed and molded by their external environment. Both theorists conceptualized social interaction as a one-way relationship between individuals and their culture in which these individuals were essentially the recipients of their culture in the form of predefined cultural expectations. But where Ross's notion of imitation did not explain how the relationship and any resulting influence occurred, Thorndike's concept of conditioning as detailed in the Law of Associative Shifting did. In a sense then behaviorism offered Ross the kind of psychological explanation of social control that was missing in his theory.

We are not arguing that either theorist was influenced by the other in developing his theory of social control. Rather, we are offering an illustration of the suggestion I advanced in chapter 1 about the relationship between the ideas that intellectuals seem to embrace and the social views to which they subscribe. Our argument was that notions such as social control are important not simply in and for themselves but because they emerge out of and inform us about the views their exponents hold about the nature of society and the individual's role within it. What one believes about social control as well as any of a number of other similar ideas tells us about what he considers important, what he cherishes, and most importantly what he fears. We mentioned in chapter 1 that at least in American society these viewpoints have tended to take two broad forms. One, which we first saw in our examination of Ross and have seen again in Thorndike's work, posits a one-directional pattern of interaction between the individual and society and conceptualizes the individual as the passive recipient of his culture. The other, which we first saw in our consideration of Cooley and will see again when we look at Mead, assumes a reciprocal pattern of interaction between the individual and society and conceptualizes the individual as an active constructor of his culture. These are viewpoints, we argued, that have essentially been competitors throughout our history for the allegiance of American intellectuals.

Although at any given time one can find exponents for each, they seem to alternate as the dominant view of the moment in different periods of our intellectual history. They provide in this way a good barometer of the prevailing tenor of our intellectual thought.

When we look then at Ross and Thorndike, we see a certain commonality in their social views. In his later years, Ross actually came to embrace a view of a community of like-mindedness that was indistinguishable from Throndike's. In the notebook he kept to jot down ideas for his proposed revision of *Social Control*, he argued as did Thorndike, that American society should be governed by a minority of the most able, those with IQs above 130. These able individuals, he argued, should be given financial incentives to encourage them to reproduce. Those with IQs below 70, the 'dull' as he put it, should be sterilized. It was his belief that these eugenic efforts would eventually create an American population in which at least 90 per cent of the members were of high ability.[53] It was Thorndike, not as a conscious intellectual heir, but as one who shared the same view of the relationship of the individual to society and the concept of social control that it entailed, who brought a certain refinement to ideas that Ross first articulated. He provided Ross's theory of social control with a psychological explanation of social influence which Ross could not provide.

Similarly, other American intellectuals who shared the same social viewpoint as Cooley brought refinements to his theory of social control. One such individual, to whose work we will now turn, was George Herbert Mead.

IX

George Herbert Mead (1863–1931) might be thought of as representing the other side of the functionalist coin from Thorndike. After graduating from Oberlin College in 1883 and working for three-and-a-half years, first as a school teacher and then as a member of the survey crew that established the route which the Soo Line Rail Road was to take from Minneapolis to Saskatchewan, Mead enrolled at Harvard University to study philosophy and psychology. He completed his bachelors degree in 1888 and spent the next three years in Germany studying at the universities of Leipzig and Berlin. In 1891, although he had not completed his doctorate, he replaced James Hayden Tufts, who had left to study for his doctorate in Germany, at the University of Michigan, where John Dewey headed the Department of Philosophy and Charles Horton Cooley was completing his doctorate in economics. Three years later, on the recommendation of Dewey who had just assumed the Chairmanship of the Department of Philosophy of the new University of Chicago, President Harper appointed Mead to the faculty as an Assistant Professor of Philosophy. By 1907, he had attained the rank of Professor and remained at Chicago until his death in 1931.[54]

In his Presidential Address to the American Psychological Association, which we mentioned at the beginning of this chapter, James Angell noted that one of the virtues of the functionalist position in psychology was that it provided an account of how consciousness arose within the individual and organized itself as a system for the control of human conduct. He then went on to cite Mead as one who had contributed to the development of this explanation.[55]

Mead's explanation of the relationship of consciousness to conduct represented a critique of Wundt's structuralism. For Mead, the problem with Wundt's psychology was his assumption of the doctrine of parallelism, the view that what occurs in consciousness in the form of psychical processes corresponds with what occurs in the central nervous system in the form of physiological activity.[56] Parallelism, Mead argued, represented a certain advance in psychology because it sought to find a relationship between the mind on the one hand and human conduct on the other. Yet, the relationship it established, he believed, was not complete. What was missing was an interactive element that explained how consciousness acted on the central nervous system to translate psychical processes into physiological action. All parallelism could do, Mead pointed out, was to note the correspondence, not explain it. In the end, he argued, parallelism could not account for the existence of the unique and subjective experiences of individuals in terms of the common, objective experience of the social group.[57] It ultimately led to solipsism, a point we will pursue when we consider Mead's criticism of Cooley later in this chapter.

Mead, then, like Thorndike and others in the functionalist camp argued for a psychology that went beyond the description of mental processes to explain how those processes controlled human interaction within the social environment. Because of the central position that conduct played in his scheme of things, he viewed his psychology as being behaviorist in its orientation.[58] But it was a different kind of behaviorism than that of Thorndike or Watson. At the core of the difference, Mead noted in a letter he wrote to his daughter-in-law, Irene Tufts Mead, was the tendency of Watson to view the 'cortex as at most a mere inhibiting organ'.[59] It was a viewpoint, he noted in a letter to his son, Henry, that had helped psychology attain the status of a natural science. But it was not a psychology that '. . . can answer the questions which have to do with the relation of the self to the body, or state the method of thought and implications of the judgments of science itself'.[60]

Where Watson and Thorndike began with the environmental situation or stimulus and explained its control of the human response, Mead began with the human impulse to adjust to the environment, which he called the 'act', and explained its control of environmental stimuli.[61] Mead criticized both Watson and Thorndike because in focusing on the external environmental situation and ignoring the initial impulse of the human organism to attempt to regulate the environment, they had in effect denied the existence of human consciousness.[62] To distinguish his brand of behaviorism from that of Watson and Thorndike as well as to make clear that his interest was not on the individual as such but on the individual as a social organism, he called his psychology social behaviorism.[63]

X

Mead's theory of social control, as was Cooley's, was rooted in his concept of the self.[64] But self for Mead presupposed the existence of mind. So our route to understanding Mead's theory of social control must of necessity begin with his concept of mind.

Mind was Mead's concept for the social process in which organisms in their interaction with each other established control over meaning.[65] In examining social interaction, for example in the simple case of two organisms in interaction with each other, which for Mead was an instance of the act, he noted a process in which the action of the first organism served as a stimulus for the response of the second organism which, in turn, served as another stimulus for the action of the first organism.

These actions, which Mead called, borrowing an idea from Wundt, gestures, represented the fundamental elements in the social process of the act. As an illustration, he cited the case of two antagonistic dogs approaching each other. As they walked around each other, the two dogs alternatively growled and snapped as if in response to each other until one attacked the other and a fight began. What was happening, Mead suggested, was that the anger of one dog as manifested in a certain vocal gesture, say a growl, evoked a response in the other dog in the form of another vocal gesture, in this case a snap, which evoked another vocal gesture from the first dog, and so on. It was, as Mead put it, a conversation of gestures in which the attitude of one dog evoked an attitudinal response in the other.[66]

Although an apparent conversation was taking place between the two dogs, Mead noted that it, as well as all similar interactions among lower organisms, was a non-significant conversation, that is, a conversation without consciousness and meaning. This was the case, he argued, because there was no shared meaning between the animals involved in the conversation of gestures. In making its gesture, the first dog, for example, did not suggest the same meaning to itself as it did to the second dog. And similarly in making what appeared to be a responding gesture, the second dog did not indicate the same meaning to itself as it did to the first dog.[67] For gestures to be significant, that is for consciousness to be present, they had to, Mead argued, indicate the same meaning to those who made them as to those to whom they were directed.[68]

When gestures became significant, that is had shared meaning for those involved in the act, they became for Mead language.[69] Only humans, Mead argued, however, had language.[70] It was only their gestures:

> . . . by serving as prior indications, to the individuals responding to them, of the subsequent behavior of the individuals making them, . . . make possible the mutual adjustment of the various individual components of the social act to one another, and also by calling forth in the individuals making them the same responses implicitly that they call forth explicitly in individuals to whom they are made, . . . render possible the rise of self consciousness in connection with this mutual adjustment.[71]

Language then allowed human individuals to control what they meant in their gestures and thereby to control the nature of their responses. It was at this point for Mead that mind emerged.[72]

The control over meaning that mind allowed, Mead pointed out, enabled the individual to speak to himself as others speak to him. In these internal conversations, according to Mead, the individual took on the same attitudes toward himself that others assumed toward him in their external conversations with him.[73] More, however, was involved than simply the establishment of shared attitudes. These internal conversations which the individual had with himself led him to change his behavior:

> We are continually following up our own address to other persons by an understanding of what we are saying, and using that understanding in the direction of our continued speech. We are finding out what we are going to say, what we are going to

do, by saying and doing, and in the process we are continually controlling the process itself. In the conversation of gestures what we say calls out a certain response in another and that in turn changes our own action, so that we shift from what we started to do because of the reply the other makes.[74]

As the individual took on the same attitudes toward himself that others held toward him and regulated his behavior accordingly, his self, according to Mead, emerged.

Self emerged, Mead argued, is a two-stage social process. In the first stage of this process, which we have just illustrated with the above quotation by Mead, the individual took on the attitudes of the various other individuals with whom he interacted. This, however, was not sufficient. The individual in the second stage of the development of the self had to take on the collective attitudes of the social group or community of which he was part, which Mead referred to as the generalized other.[75] As Mead pointed out:

If the given human individual is to develop a self in the fullest sense, it is not sufficient for him merely to take the attitudes of other human individuals toward himself and toward one another within the social process, and to bring that social process as a whole into this individual experience merely in these terms: he must also, in the same way that he takes the attitudes of other individuals toward himself and toward one another, take their attitudes toward the various phases or aspects of the common social activity or set of social undertakings in which, as members of an organized society or social group, they are all engaged: and he must then, by generalizing these individual attitudes of that organized society or social group itself, as a whole, act toward different social projects which at any given time it is carrying out, or toward the various larger phases of the general social process which constitutes its life and of which these projects are broad manifestations.[76]

Mead illustrated this two stage process in the emergence of the self by comparing the difference between the child's experience in play and in a game. In play, Mead argued, the child acted out different roles, such as teacher, parent, or Indian, at different times. In doing this, he had to at different times take on these various roles and the responses they entailed. That is, the child had to take on, in Mead's terminology, the attitudes of these various others. In the game, on the other hand, the child faced an activity organized according to certain rules and procedures expressed in terms of the role requirements of the participants. To act according to these rules the child had to take on the roles and accompanying attitudes of not just one participant at a time but of all the participants simultaneously. He had to in other words govern his conduct in terms of what the other participants of the game in terms of the rules expected. That is, in Mead's terminology the child had to take on the attitudes of the generalized other.[77]

The emergence of self for Mead was a process with two phases, the 'me' and the 'I'. The 'me' represented the attitudes of the generalized other as they were assumed by the individual, and the 'I' represented the response of the individual to the attitudes of the generalized other.[78] Self came forth, according to Mead, because these two phases allowed for what he called 'reflexiveness', the turning back of the experience of the individual upon himself. This meant that the individual could through the interaction of the 'me' and the 'I' be both a subject as well as an object of which he could gain a total view or perspective. He could in other words become self conscious of himself. Only the self, Mead maintained, had this quality of reflexiveness. Other parts of the body were not reflexive. The eye, for example, could see the feet, but it could not see the back. It could not see itself whole.[79]

We can see the reflexiveness between the 'me' and the 'I' when we examine the actual emergence of the self. The individual when he confronted the attitudes called for by the generalized other had to in some way act on these attitudes. He had to make a response. That response was his 'I'. The nature of that response was, however, always uncertain. It remained hidden outside of the individual's consciouness as an 'I' until it occurred. Once it was made, however, it became an historical event in the individual's self conscious memory that could be known. It became the 'me' of which the individual was aware.[80] In the emergence of the self then we have a process in which the individual as an 'I' examined himself as an object in terms of the attitudes of the generalized other and then responded. As Mead put it, 'the "I" is the response of the organism to the attitudes of the others; the "me" is the organized set of attitudes of others which one himself assumes. The attitudes of the others constitutes the organized "me", and then one reacts toward that as an "I" '.[81]

The reflexiveness that the 'me' and the 'I' allowed for should be seen as representing an adjustment between two different forces. The 'me' in embodying the attitudes of the generalized other, suggested conventionality and regularity. The 'I' as an individual's unique response, represented initiative and novelty. The 'me' attempted to summon forth a particular kind of response. But the response, the 'I', was usually different than the 'me' intended, and when it occurred, it created a new 'me'.[82] It was a relationship that Mead most precisely caught in the following terms:

> Whatever we are doing determines the sort of stimulus which will set free certain responses which are there ready for expression, and it is the attitude of action which determines for us what the stimulus will be. Then in the process of acting we are constantly selecting just what elements in the field of stimulation will set the response successfully free. We have to carry out our act so that the response as it goes on is continually acting back upon the organism, selecting for us just those stimuli which will enable us to do what we started to do.[83]

XI

Mead defined social control as a process in which the individual brought the act, his impulse to adjust to his environment, into relation with what he called the object, those situations, agencies, institutions, and other things that the individual encountered in social life.[84] The relationship he seemed to have in mind was one in which the individual took on the attitude of his social group toward the object and in so doing assumed a role as a member of society in defining that object:

> The human individual is a self only in so far as he takes on the attitude of another toward himself. In so far as this attitude is that of a number of others, and in so far as he can assume the organized attitudes of a number that are cooperating in a common activity, he takes the attitudes of the group toward himself, and in taking this or these attitudes he is defining the object of the group, that which defines and controls the response. Social control, then, will depend upon the degree to which the individual does assume the attitudes of those in the group who are involved with him in his social activities.[85]

Social control for Mead, then, was a process that took place with the emergence of self. In so far as the individual took on the attitudes of the generalized other, that is, acquired a self, he was brought under social control.[86] Mead thus shared Cooley's view of social control as an internal psychological process that occurred spontaneously as the individual entered into social life.

The actual mechanism of social control for Mead was the reflexivity provided by the two phases of the self, the 'me' and the 'I'. In the emergence of the self, we should recall, the response that the individual made to the attitudes of the generalized other appeared as a 'me', the attitudes called for by the generalized other which the individual took on as his own. The 'me', then, had the effect of placing a restriction on the response of the individual. Its appearance as a 'me' set parameters as to its nature.[87] The process for Mead was one of self criticism. In taking on the attitudes of the generalized other, the individual not only became self conscious of his conduct, he also became critical of it. 'Self criticism is essentially social criticism, and behavior controlled by self criticism is essentially behavior controlled socially.'[88]

Thus far in our discussion, the idea of social control has implied a degree of restriction on the individual's conduct. Ross and Thorndike turned to the idea of social control to curtail the role that certain individuals, Eastern and Southern European immigrants and the less able respectively, would play in American society. Cooley embraced the idea, although his view did not have the malevolent implications of either Ross's or Thorndike's, to restore the commonality and like-mindedness of the small town and its primary group relationships. Mead, on the other hand, denied that social control actually restricted the individual. The individual was, he maintained, only an individual in so far as he was a member of society, that is, acquired a self. And acquiring a self brought the individual's conduct under social control. 'Hence social control', Mead argued, 'so far from tending to crush out the human individual or to obliterate his self-conscious individuality, is, on the contrary, actually constitutive of and inextricably associated with that individuality ...'.[89]

This was the case because social control as Mead interpreted it required that the individual have a part to play in defining the situations, agencies and institutions of his social experience or in Mead's terminology, the object. In taking on the attitudes of the generalized other, the individual in effect defined the object in terms of a 'me' which itself reflected a unique individual contribution in the form of a response, an 'I'. It was this response as it expressed itself in the 'me' that offered the individual this definitional role:

> Social control depends, then, upon the degree to which the individuals in society are able to assume the attitudes of the others who are involved with them in common endeavor. For the social object will always answer to the act of developing itself in self-consciousness. Besides property, all of the institutions are such objects, and serve to control individuals who find in them the organization of their own social responses.[90]

Social control broke down for Mead when individuals within society were excluded from defining the various objects they encountered. He argued, for example, that the Marxian system of exclusive state ownership of the means of production as well as the political machines that controlled many American cities during the early twentieth century represented examples of the breakdown of social control because they both restricted, each in their own way, participation in their functioning to a small segment of the population.[91]

The distinguishing feature of Mead's theory of social control was the reciprocal relationship he posited between the individual and society. The individual for Mead did not simply take on the attitudes of the generalized other as they were given. The reflexiveness that the 'me' and the 'I' brought to the emergence of self required that before the individual took on these attitudes, he had to make a response to them. And in this response he could examine, judge, and even reconstruct them. What emerged in the form of his 'me' were attitudes that reflected his own unique contribution. They were in effect shared attitudes, whose nature he played a role in defining.[92] Although Mead's self, according to the philosopher Maurice Natanson, 'is an emergent from the social process ... there is an individual contribution that each self makes to this process. It is not a one-way relationship. The emergent self is at the same time a unique quality that impinges tellingly upon the social process'.[93]

This view of self and the notion of social control it entails is, I think, important. It made the individual as we just have seen an active participant in the process of social control. And as we shall now see, it led Mead to a view of the problem of community that was fundamentally different from the views of Ross, Thorndike, and even Cooley.

XII

Born in South Hadley, Massachusetts on 21 February 1863 and raised from the age of 7 until he graduated from college in Oberlin, Ohio, where his father, Reverend Hiram Mead, taught at the local theological seminary, Mead was a product of the rural small town.[94] Yet unlike the other theorists of social control we have previously considered, the sense of community that Mead envisioned for American society required neither a return to the small town nor the homogeneous culture it implied. As Mead pointed out in his critique of the Russian novelist Leo Tolstoy:

Retreat from the complex to the concrete was represented by Tolstoy. He was seeking the simplest type of social organization, built up on the basis of the very simple agricultural community. In a certain sense many social problems are solved in that way, e.g. by the Mennonites. But this has never been worked out in communities engaged in large production.[95]

American society, he believed, would have to find its sense of community, not in its past but in its 'complex' future.

Ross and Cooley modeled their notion of community on the intimate, face-to-face relationships they identified with the small rural town, Thorndike, although he accepted urbanization, yearned for the kind of like-mindedness those relationships implied. For Mead, on the other hand, geographical size and personal intimacy were not important features of community.[96] What was important was that the individual took on the attitudes of the generalized other:

> It is the ability of the person to put himself in other people's places that gives him his cues as to what he is to do under a specific situation. It is this that gives to the man what we term his character as a member of the community; his citizenship, from a political standpoint; his membership from any one of the different standpoints in which he belongs to the community. It makes him a part of the community, and he recognizes himself as a member of it just because he does take the attitude of those concerned, and does control his own conduct in terms of common attitudes.[97]

All that was really required for Mead in the way of uniformity would be provided for as the individual took on the attitudes of the generalized other and acquired his self. And human society was only possible, Mead believed, in so far as its members had acquired selves.[98] In Mead's scheme no special provisions were really necessary to retain a sense of community as America became an urban industrialized nation.

Industrialization did not, for example, pose the kind of threat to Mead that it did to Ross and Cooley. On the contrary, industrialization seemed to him to represent a promising social advance. A central feature of the nation's emerging industrial economy for Mead was the standardization of work and the resulting division of labor that had replaced the artisan who was responsible for the entire process of production with a corps of specialized workers who each took responsibility for a part of the production process. It was a transformation that had replaced those who he called 'handworkers' in favor of machine production.

Machine production, he argued, required new types of specialized workers who possessed the intelligence, skill and efficiency to keep up with the 'regularity, precision, and timelessness' of the machine. These workers could demand and obtain the higher wages, shorter working days, and increased leisure time that would offer them 'adequate social and economic status'. They would not become as some have feared 'an inferior part of the machine' but rather would become 'a class of machine tool makers and high grade mechanics who control the machine'.[99] Consequently, he argued:

> ... we must approve of every mechanical advance which replaces human labor in the manufactory. Every such invention brings society nearer the position in which man will control instead of being part of the machine.[100]

Neither did Mead perceive a threat from the nation's growing immigrant population. He, in fact, challenged the hereditarian viewpoint of intellectuals such as Thorndike that identified the nation's social problems with the inherent defects of its immigrant population. He believed that in the case of Chicago, for example, Eastern and Southern European immigrant labor and had played a critical role in adding to the city's industrial growth.[101]

He recognized, however, that this influx of immigrants into the population brought with it problems. In a survey Mead conducted of one Chicago neighborhood populated primarily by Slavic immigrants who worked in the meat packing industry, he noted the substandard conditions in which they lived. The conversion of single family houses into tenement apartments had made the neighborhood overcrowded. There were, he pointed out, many violations of city ordinances relating to sanitary facilities and living space requirements. Landlords seemed unwilling to make needed repairs to their tenement buildings. Mead, however, did not blame the immigrants for the conditions of their neighborhoods. Rather, he placed the blame on American industrialists. It was, Mead claimed, their single-minded desire for profit that led them to advocate the admission of immigrants into the country to take advantage of their labor while at the same time maintaining that it was the immigrants' 'own affair if they were wretched, helpless and shamelessly exploited after they arrived'.[102]

We can account for Mead's optimism about the twentieth century transformation of American society by the fact that his theory of social control unlike the others we have examined could accommodate the kind of social changes that urbanization and industrialization had brought. The emergence of self resulted in what he called a 'fusion' of the 'me' and the 'I' into the kind of shared understanding that made cooperative social life a possibility. Yet, it was not a 'fusion' that quashed diversity in the name of like-mindedness.[103] Because the process of social control that took place with the emergence of self involved both a social attitude, a 'me', and an individual response, an 'I', there was in Mead's theory allowance for diversity. In fact, social control for Mead was not simply a process of molding the individual to the requirements of the social group as it was for Ross and Thorndike, and even to some degree for Cooley. It was rather a process of reconstructing society in terms of the shared needs of the diverse members of society:

> Human society, we have insisted, does not merely stamp the pattern of its organized social behavior upon any one of its individual members, so that this pattern becomes likewise the pattern of the individual's self; it also at the same time, gives him a mind, as the means or ability of consciously conversing with himself in terms of the social attitudes which constitute the structure of his self and which embody the pattern of human society's organized behavior as reflected in that structure. And his mind enables him in turn to stamp the pattern of his further developing self (further developing through his mental activity) upon the structure or organization of human society, and thus in a degree to reconstruct and modify in terms of his self the general pattern of social or group behavior of which his self was originally constituted.[104]

The members of society were for Mead shaped by their social environment, a viewpoint shared to varying degrees by the other theorists of social control we have examined. But these same members of society could in turn, and this distinguished Mead's theory of social control from the others we have considered, shape that environment to respond to emerging conditions. He therefore believed that:

> ... the laws governing the social and economic order, can actually be worked out by the people experiencing them. They are no longer thought of as arbitrarily imposed by an external being. The individual is no longer a traveller through a foreign country where he must suffer without understanding why. He is an integral part of the world in which he finds himself.[105]

It was a belief that led Mead in distinction to Ross and Thorndike to view the problems of the immigrants as environmental problems that could be remedied by environmental change.

Mead himself took an active role in trying to improve the social conditions faced by Chicago's immigrant population. In 1908, he joined with Jane Addams and Grace Abbott to establish the Immigrants' Protective League as a means of helping immigrants after their arrival in Chicago. He served as the League's First Vice President and a member of its Board of Trustees until 1919 and contributed substantial financial support to the League's work.[106] During the years of his involvement, the League lobbied for the establishment of a Federal Protective Bureau for immigrants in Chicago, established a corps of visitors who met immigrants upon their arrival in Chicago and located lost immigrants, provided legal assistance for immigrants, and supported state legislation to regulate employment agencies that contracted for immigrant labor.[107] In addition, Mead came to the assistance in 1910 of garment workers, who were predominately immigrants, who had struck Hart, Schaffner and Marx. He was a member of a subcommittee, organized by a Citizens Committee interested in bringing an end to the strike, that investigated the causes of the strike and the complaints of the workers. He and the other members of the subcommittee issued a report substantiating many of the workers grievances, and they then worked successfully to get both labor and management to agree to the establishment of an arbitration board to resolve them.[108]

His most extensive effort on the behalf of not only immigrants but labor in general was his advocacy of vocational education. It was here that we can see most clearly the view of community he envisioned for twentieth-century American society. In 1912, Mead chaired a committee organized by the City Club of Chicago to investigate vocational education in Chicago and other cities. The Committee was troubled by an increasing elimination rate in the Chicago Public Schools in which 43 percent of the students entering the first grade left before they reached the eighth grade, which they attributed to the fact that students were finding little of value and importance to their later lives in the existing curriculum. To counteract this elimination rate and the underlying student dissatisfaction with the curriculum, the Committee recommended the introduction of vocational training into the curriculum of the seventh and eighth grades as well as the establishment of vocational and commercial programs in the high schools.[109]

The kind of vocational training that Mead advocated was quite different from the system of vocational education that was taking root in the nation's schools during this period. He criticized that form of vocational education on the grounds that it separated out one class of students, those of working class backgrounds, and provided them with a narrow sort of trade training that prepared them to operate one type of machine or for one occupation while ignoring their need for an academic education. He favored a broader, more 'liberally' oriented form of vocational education. It should, he believed, prepare students to operate a wide range of different machinery. And it should provide them with the mathematical and language skills and historical knowledge they needed to 'comprehend' the entire process of production and 'to criticize the tool and its use'.[110]

This type of vocational training, Mead argued, would improve the conditions of the nation's industrial working class. We have already mentioned that Mead believed that industrialization had created the demand for a class of highly skilled and well paid 'machine tool makers' and 'mechanics' who would in effect control the machine. At the same time, however, he noted that industrialization had displaced a class of less skilled and less efficient 'handworkers', as he called them, who found themselves out of work or in less developed industries where the pay was low and the hours long. Only a system of vocational training, Mead argued, would enable these displaced individuals to obtain the higher level of skill and understanding they needed to upgrade their position in an industrial economy.[111]

This was, he believed, especially true of the children of the immigrants. It was only an appropriate education, that is, an education that included the kind of vocational training he advocated, that would provide these children with the skills they needed to realize the promise of life in a democratic society:

> We need such an application of our Democratic principles to force us to recognize the worth in humanity in the hundreds of thousands to whom we yearly open our door, who come at our invitation, often to be despoiled of what they bring and what they are.[112]

The issue for Mead was not whether there would be vocational training. The nation's industrial economy required it. The question was who would provide and control that education? Industrialists themselves, he believed, would be willing to establish their own systems of vocational training. Their concern, he argued, would be profit, and consequently they would favor the kind of narrow training that would enhance worker productivity and efficiency. Fearing this, Mead argued that vocational training had to be the responsibility of the public schools. Under public control vocational training would serve all the members of the community, providing them a voice in defining the

nature of the training which, in turn, would define the nature of work and ultimately the industrial process itself.[113]
As Mead put it:

> ... the community is putting itself into the position where it will have to introduce standards for industry. It is of enormous importance that these industries should be introduced at a point where the community is obliged to say they must be hygienic ... It is of great importance that the community should take over into its hands the standardizing of industries in the school, and just so far as we introduce trade industries into our schools we are putting the community into the place where it will sooner or later have to pass upon the standards of life of those working in the industries.[114]

Mead's belief that the inclusion of vocational training within the public schools would allow the members of society to define the nature of the industrial process illustrates the active role his theory of social control allowed the individual as the constructor of the community in which he lived. 'We control our conduct', he noted, 'by determining the objects to which we will respond — by constructing the objects, by determination of the stimuli.'[115] The life of the community for Mead was one of constant reconstruction mediated by the reciprocal interaction and mutual adjustment between its members.[116]

Mead's view of community as distinct from Ross and Thorndike's did not require the kind of artificial like-mindedness that was achieved by allowing one segment of society to impose its will on the rest. There was for Mead no necessity for the conflict and hostility among various social groups and classes which Ross and Thorndike took for granted. Nor was there for Mead the necessity to resist the kind of social changes that industrialization and urbanization brought. The reflexivity that Mead posited between the 'me' and the 'I', between the society and the individual, always held out the possibility that society could be reconstructed to meet the needs of its members as they confronted new situations.[117] Notwithstanding the differences that existed within society, it was possible to obtain the kind of coordination and cooperation implied by the idea of community without the damping effect on individuality we saw in the views of Ross and Thorndike:

> One may say that the attainment of that functional differentiation and social participation in the full degree is a sort of ideal which lies before the human community. The present stage of it is presented in the ideal of democracy. It is often assumed that

democracy is an order of society in which those personalities which are sharply differentiated will be eliminated, that everything will be ironed down to a situation where everyone will be, as far as possible, like everyone else. But of course that is not the implication of democracy: the implication of democracy is rather that the individual can be as highly developed as lies within the possibilities of his own inheritance, and still can enter into the attitudes of the others whom he affects. There can still be leaders, and the community can rejoice in their attitudes just in so far as these superior individuals can themselves enter into the attitudes of the community which they undertake to lead.[118]

XIII

Earlier in this chapter I argued that Thorndike's behaviorism offered a certain refinement to the concept of social control originally suggested by Ross by providing a better explanation than Ross had of the psychological mechanism by which control actually was brought about. Similarly, I believe that Mead's ideas represent a refinement of the theory of social control articulated by Cooley. Self for Cooley, we should remember, emerged as the individual in his interaction with others came to view himself in his mind as these others viewed him. It was this imaginative reconstruction of how others viewed him that gave the individual his self and brought him under social control. It was a notion of social control, as we have mentioned, that saw the individual as an active participant in defining the nature of the attitudes and standards of behavior that would ultimately control his conduct.

Mead recognized the advance that Cooley had made over such earlier attempts as Tarde's theory of imitation to account psychologically for the social individual.[119] Yet, he found fault with Cooley's understanding of the self as a 'psychical' element located in the mind. Mead on the other hand, argued that there was a psychical phase involved in the emergence of the self, as we in effect interpreted our social world by making a response to the attitudes of the generalized other in the form of an 'I'. But the raw material of the self was in our objective experience of the social world in the attitudes of the community which we take on as our own in the form of the 'me'. Mead did not believe that conceptualizing the self as a totally 'psychical' element as Cooley did would enable us to account for the objective or as he called them the 'solid facts' of society.[120] It was a position, Mead believed, that left Cooley with a psychology of parallelism and led him ultimately to the solipistic view that society only existed within the individual's mind.[121]

Mead's theory of social control made the connection between the individual and society that Cooley could not. His conceptualization of the self in two phases, one social and objective and the other individual and psychical, represented a conceptual advance over Cooley's theory of the self. It brought out the full potential inherent in the idea of the individual as an active participant in the formation of society by identifying the psychological mechanism by which the individual was able to both construct and reconstruct his social world.

Mead was able also to carry the notion of community a step further than Cooley. The community that Cooley envisioned for twentieth-century American society was in effect the community of the primary group. What he yearned for was the intimate, face-to-face primary relationships he knew in the rural small town of his youth. It was not really a vision of a community for an urban industrial society. It was rather as Mead suggested 'an account of the American community' to which Cooley himself belonged.[122] Mead's view of community, on the other hand, was one that embraced the very social transformations that Cooley in the end seemed to reject. Of all the notions of community we have considered in our examination of the historical roots of the idea of social control in American thought, it was only Mead's view that came to terms with modern, twentieth-century America in all its aspects.

XIV

In the last two chapters we have sought to locate the origins of the idea of social control in our intellectual thought. Toward that end, we have examined the work of those early twentieth-century American intellectuals who, we argued, first articulated what we might think of as theories of social control, Edward A. Ross, Charles Horton Cooley, Edward A. Thorndike, and George Herbert Mead. In doing this, we suggested that these theories, at least as they were initially formulated, took two different forms, each reflecting what we believe is a basic concept of the relationship between the individual and society. One conception of social control, articulated by Ross and Thorndike, posited a one directional pattern of interaction between the individual and society and depicted the individual as the passive recipient of his culture. Within this perspective, social control was defined as a process of direct and planned imposition in which the individual was molded to fit certain predefined social expectations. The other conception of social control, spelled out by Cooley and Mead, posited a reciprocal pattern of interaction between the individual and society and depicted the individual as an active constructor of his culture. Within this perspective, social control was defined as an indirect and spontaneous process occurring simultaneously with the emergence of self in which the individual and society cooperatively formed a set of shared and mutually agreed upon social expectations.

In the introductory chapter of this volume, I argued that one of the central driving forces in twentieth-century American intellectual thought has been the search for social unity and stability in an urban, industrial society, a pursuit I have described as the search for community. Throughout this century, middle class, American intellectuals have sought to define the nature of this hoped for community by invoking the idea of social control. In examining the work of those thinkers who first spelled out theories of social control, only one of them, George Herbert Mead, was able to reconcile liberal-democratic values with the forces of urbanization and industrialization. The other theorists we have considered, Ross, Cooley, and Thorndike, each in their own way, failed to achieve this adjustment. They sought instead a return in one form or another to the like-mindness and unity they identified with the nineteenth century small, rural town and the democracy they thought to have thrived there.

In the remainder of this volume, I will follow the idea of social control as it has found its way into one aspect of our twentieth-century intellectual thought, those ideas and practices that make up the field of curriculum. I will first examine the work of those American educators who identified themselves professionally with the field of curriculum during the first half of this century. I will look at how these educators, using ideas that first appeared in the writings of Ross and the other theorists of social control we have considered, addressed the seeming gap between our liberal democratic ideals and the realities of urbanization and industrialization as well as how they resolved or failed to resolve the problem of community. Second, I will examine the effort of educators in one urban school system, the Minneapolis Public Schools, who were responsible for the selection and organization of the curriculum to actually use the school program as an instrument of social control for addressing the issue of community in twentieth-century America.

Notes

1 EDWARD A. ROSS, 'Notes for a revision of social control, 1938', *The Edward A. Ross Papers,* State Historical Society of Wisconsin, Madison, Box 31.

2 EDWARD A. ROSS, 'Untitled, undated manuscript', *ibid.,* Box 26.

3 According to Roucek and his associates, any explanation of social control must involve the interaction of both social and psychological processes. See JOSEPH S. ROUCEK and Associates, *Social Control,* New York: P. Van Nostrand Company, 1947, chapter 2. For an examination of how different psychological processes can account for social control see RAJ S. GANDHI, 'Socialization and personality', in *Social Control for the 1980's: A Handbook for Order in a Democratic Society,* edited by JOSEPH S. ROUCEK, Westport, Greenwood Press, 1981, pp. 63–76.

4 The most extensive treatment of Thorndike's life and his contribution to American intellectual thought is to be found in GERALDINE JONCICH, *The Sane Positivist: A Biography of Edward L. Thorndike,* Middletown, Wesleyan University Press, 1968. The range of Thorndike's work can be seen in his extensive bibliography which appeared in three issues of the *Teachers College Record* covering three periods of his life: 1898–1925, 27, February, 1926, pp. 466–516; 1926–1939, 41, May, 1940, pp. 717–25; 1940–1949, 60, October, 1949, pp. 42–5.

5 CLARENCE J. KARIER, 'Elite views on American education', in *Education and Social Structure in the Twentieth Century,* edited by WALTER LACQUER and GEORGE L. MOSSE, New York, Harper Torchbooks, 1967, pp. 149–54.

6 For a good summary of this school of thought see EDWIN G. BORING's classic, *A History of Experimental Psychology,* 2nd. ed, New York, Appleton-Century-Crofts, 1950, chapters 16 and 22, pp. 410–20. For a more recent treatment see ROBERT L. WATSON. *The Great Psychologists* 3rd. ed, Philadelphia, J.B. Lippincott Company, 1971, chapters 12 and 17. The best view of the conflict between structuralism and functionalism is to be found in two papers by major participants in the struggle, Edward Titchener and James Angell. See EDWARD BRADFORD TITCHENER, 'The postulates of a structural psychology', *The Philosophical Review,* 7, September, 1898, pp. 449–65; and JAMES ROWLAND ANGELL, 'The province of functional psychology', *The Psychological Review,* 14, March, 1907, pp. 61–91.

7 ANGELL, *ibid.,* p. 88–9.

8 EDWARD L. THORNDIKE, *Animal Intelligence,* New York, MacMillan, 1911, pp. 15–6.

9 For a good discussion of the rise of hereditarianism in American psychology see HAMILTON CRAVENS, *The Triumph of Evolution: American Scientists and the Heredity-Environment Controversy,* 1900–1941, Philadelphia: University of Pennsylvania Press, 1978, chapters 1–2; and MERLE CURTI, *Human Nature in American Thought: A History,* Madison: University of Wisconsin Press, 1980, chapter 9. The best treatment of the social implications of hereditarianism remains RICHARD HOFSTADTER's classic, *Social Darwinism in American Thought,* rev. edn; Boston, Beacon Press, 1955.

10 EDWARD L. THORNDIKE, *The Original Nature of Man,* Vol. I of *Educational Psychology* 3 Vols., New York, Arno Press, 1969, pp. 2–3.

11 *Ibid.,* p. 5.

12 *Ibid.,* pp. 209–17 and 221–2.

13 *Ibid.,* pp. 224–7.

14 *Ibid.,* pp. 227–8.

15 EDWARD L. THORNDIKE, *The Elements of Psychology*, New York, A.G. Seiler, 1905, pp. 14 and 16.

16 *Animal Intelligence, op. cit.*, pp. 26 and 35–6; EDWARD L. THORNDIKE, *The Psychology of Learning*, Vol. 2 of *Educational Psychology, op. cit.*, p. 10; JOHN C. BURNHAM, 'Thorndike's puzzle boxes', *Journal of the History of the Behavioral Sciences*, 8, April, 1972, pp. 159–67.

17 *Animal Intelligence, ibid.*, p. 244.

18 *Ibid.*

19 DAVID BAKAN, 'Behaviorism and American urbanization', *Journal of the History of the Behavioral Sciences*, 2, June, 1966, pp. 5–29; JOHN C. BURNHAM, 'On the origins of behaviorism', *Journal of the History of the Behavioral Sciences*, 4, April, 1968, pp. 143–51; FRANZ SAMELSON, 'Struggle for scientific authority: The reception of Watson's behaviorism, 1913–1920', *Journal of the History of the Behavioral Sciences*, 17, July, 1981, pp. 399–425.

20 Those who write on the history of American behaviorism usually credit John B. Watson as the founder of this school of thought. If Thorndike is given any mention, it is typically in passing as one of many who followed in the path first laid out by Watson. Actually, a good case can be made that it was Thorndike and not Watson who was the founding theorist of behaviorism. In 1898, fourteen years before Watson described the nature of behaviorism in his paper, 'Psychology as the behaviorist views it', Thorndike in his Law of Effect had spelled out the principal explanatory concept of behaviorism, the idea of conditioning. Pavlov who also had defined the concept of conditioning gave Thorndike credit for having done so two to three years before him. See JONCICH, *op. cit.*, pp. 415–6. The important question for us, however, is not who was the first to define the nature of behaviorism but rather who articulated the implications of this perspective for social control. Clearly Watson was interested in the problem of social control and talked about the role that a behaviorial psychology could play in the control of behavior. But he did not formulate as did Thorndike a clear concept of social control. For Watson's thoughts on the role that behaviorism could play in the control of behavior see his *Psychology from the Standpoint of a Behaviorist*, Philadelphia, J.B. Lippincott, 1919, pp. 1–8. For a discussion on the implication of Watson's behaviorism for the issue of social control, see LUCILLE C. BIRNBAUM, 'Behaviorism in the 1920s', *American Quarterly*, 7, spring, 1955, pp. 15–30; and DAVID COHEN, *J.B. Watson, the Founder of Behaviorism: A Biography*, London, Routledge and Kegan Paul, 1979, chapter 5.

21 *The Psychology of Learning, op. cit.*, p. 215.

22 EDWARD L. THORNDIKE, *The Psychology of Wants, Interests, and Attitudes*, New York, D. Appleton-Century Crofts, 1935, p. 192.

23 *Ibid.*, p. 217.

24 JONCICH, *op. cit.*, chapters 1–2.

25 *Ibid.*, pp. 220–4.

26 EDWARD L. THORNDIKE, *Mental Work and Fatigue and Individual Differences and their Causes*, Vol. 3 of *Educational Psychology, op. cit.*, p. 250.

27 EDWARD L. THORNDIKE, *Human Nature and the Social Order*, New York, Macmillan, 1940, p. 440.

28 *Ibid.*, pp. 264–9; EDWARD L. THORNDIKE, 'Intelligence and its uses', *Harpers*, 140, January, 1920, pp. 233–4.

29 *Human Nature and the Social Order, op. cit.*, p. 431.

30 EDWARD L. THORNDIKE, 'Intelligence scores of colored pupils in high schools', *School and Society*, 18, 10 November, 1923, pp. 569–70. In this study it is interesting to note that Thorndike did not seem troubled by the fact that the black and white students he compared attended different schools within the city and that the majority of these white students were enrolled in private schools.

31 Thorndike made this point clearly in his *Human Nature and the Social Order* by presenting a picture of two overlapping curves which supposedly illustrated the comparative distribution of intelligence between black and whites. In the picture the upper tail of the curve for the black distribution intersects the lower tail of the curve of the white distribution thus indicating that over half of the black population fall below the mean intelligence score of the white population. See *Human Nature and the Social Order, op. cit.*, p. 431.

32 EDWARD L. THORNDIKE, *Your City*, New York, Harcourt, Brace and Company, 1939, pp. 77–80.

33 J.L. STENQUIST, E.L. THORNDIKE, and M.R. TRABUE, 'The intellectual status of children who are public charges', in *Archives of Psychology*, Vol. 5, edited by R.S. WOODWORTH, New York, The Science Press 1915, pp. 48 and 52.

34 CRAVENS, *op. cit.*, pp. 80–2.

35 JONCICH, *op. cit.*, pp. 360–7.

36 EDWARD L. THORNDIKE, 'Scientific personnel work in the army', *Science*, 49, 17 January, 1917, p. 54.

37 *Ibid.*, pp. 55–6. In 1921, the *Journal of Educational Psychology* published a panel discussion on the measurement of intelligence which included several of the nation's leading psychologists including Thorndike. One question posed to each panel member was for their views on what new work needed to be done in the future in the area of intelligence and its measurement. A majority of them stated that tests should be developed that could measure character and values in the same way that existing tests measured intelligence. EDWARD L. THORNDIKE, 'Intelligence and its measurement', *Journal of Educational Psychology*, 12, March/April, 1921, pp. 123–4 and 195–216.

38 *Human Nature and the Social Order, op. cit.*, p. 458–9.

39 *Ibid.*, p. 456.

40 *Ibid.*, p. 437.

41 In arguing that individuals were narrow specialists and not generally knowledgeable, Thorndike was only reaffirming what he had said about the theory of formal disciplines that dominated nineteenth-century American educational thought and practice. According to the idea of formal disciplines, which was a variant of the older theory of mental disciplines, education was seen as a process of developing the capacities of the mind, which were thought to exist in the form of a number of mental faculties or abilities, by exercising them through the study of certain school subjects, specifically subjects that were thought to be difficult such as the classical languages and mathematics. Thorndike, first in a series of experiments with Robert Woodworth on the effects of improving one mental function on the ability of certain school subjects to improve general intelligence, took issue with the idea of formal disciplines. He argued that general training, such as the training or exercise which certain school subjects supposedly offered according to the advocates of formal disciplines, did not in fact improve mental performance. Mental performance, he went on to argue, could only be improved by specific training in the particular skills required by the performance. This was the case, he believed,

because what were called mental functions actually existed in the form of particular capabilities that were highly independent of each other. There were, he said, no faculties of memory and attention as those who subscribed to formal disciplines claimed but only a number of specific memories and specific things to which one was attentive. Learning, according to Thorndike, was not a broad and general process but a narrow and specific one consisting of the acquisition of a multitude of particular and specific elements of knowledge and skill in the form of connections or bonds that were stamped in as habits according to the Laws of Effect and Exercise. See EDWARD L. THORNDIKE and ROBERT S. WOODWORTH, 'The influence of improvement in one mental function upon the efficiency of other functions, I, II, III', *Psychological Review*, 8, May, July, November, 1901, pp. 247–61, 384–95, and 553–64; EDWARD L. THORNDIKE, 'Mental discipline in high school studies', *Journal of Educational Psychology*, 15, January/February, 1924, pp. 1–22 and 83–98. For an examination of Thorndike's work in relation to the idea of formal disciplines see, WALTER B. KOLESNIK, *Mental Discipline in Modern Education*, Madison, University of Wisconsin Press, 1962, chapter 3.

42 EDWARD L. THORNDIKE, 'The psychology of the half-educated-man', *Harpers*, 140, April, 1920, pp. 666–70.

43 *Human Nature and the Social Order, op. cit.*, pp. 72–4; EDWARD L. THORNDIKE, 'A sociologist's theory of education', *The Bookman*, 24, November, 1906, pp. 290–1.

44 EDWARD L. THORNDIKE, *Selected Writings from a Connectionist's Psychology*, New York, Appleton-Century-Crofts, 1949, pp. 338–9.

45 *Human Nature and the Social Order, op. cit.*, pp. 94–5.

46 *Ibid.*, p. 808.

47 *Ibid.*, pp. 792–4 and 800–2.

48 'A sociologist's theory of education', *op. cit.*, pp. 290–4.

49 EDWARD L. THORNDIKE, 'How may we improve the selection, training, and life work of leaders', in *How Should a Democratic People Provide for the Selection and Training of Leaders in the Various Walks of Life*, New York, Teachers College Press, 1938, pp. 29–41.

50 *Ibid.*, p. 41.

51 *The Psychology of Learning, op cit.*, p. 31.

52 'Untitled undated, manuscript', *op. cit.*

53 'Notes for a revision of social control, 1938', *op cit.*

54 GEORGE DYKHUIZEN, *The Life and Mind of John Dewey*, Carbondale, Southern Illinois University Press, 1973, pp. 64–8 and 77; DAVID L. MILLER, *George Herbert Mead: Self, Language and the World*, Austin, University of Texas Press 1973, pp. x–xxxviii; DAVID WALLACE, 'Reflections on the education of George Herbert Mead', *American Journal of Sociology*, 72, June, 1967, pp. 396–408.

55 ANGELL, *op. cit.*, p. 89.

56 GEORGE HERBERT MEAD, *Mind, Self and Society from the Standpoint of a Social Behaviorist*, edited by CHARLES W. MORRIS, Chicago, University of Chicago Press, 1934, pp. 18–21.

57 *Ibid.*, pp. 21–37 and 42–51.

58 *Ibid.*, p. 2.

59 Mead to Irene Tufts Mead, 21 February, 1917, *The George Herbert Mead Papers*, University of Chicago Library, Box 1, Folder 14.

60 Mead to Henry Mead, 3 March, 1916, *ibid.*, Box 1, Folder 9.

61 *Mind, Self and Society, op. cit.*, p. 6; GEORGE HERBERT MEAD, 'Suggestions toward a theory of the philosophical disciplines', *Philosophical Review*, 9, January, 1900, pp. 2–3, 9 and 16; GEORGE HERBERT MEAD, 'The definition of the psychical', in *Selected Writings of George Herbert Mead*, edited by ANDREW J. RECK, Indianapolis, Bobbs-Merrill, 1964, pp. 36–43 and 50; GEORGE HERBERT MEAD, *The Philosophy of the Act*, edited by CHARLES W. MORRIS, Chicago, University of Chicago Press, 1938, p. 364.

62 *Mind, Self and Society, op. cit.*, pp. 10–11; GEORGE HERBERT MEAD, 'Concerning animal perception', in RECK, *op. cit.*, pp. 73–81.

63 *Ibid.*, p. 6

64 GEORGE HERBERT MEAD, 'The genesis of self and social control', in RECK, *op. cit.*, p. 290.

65 *Mind, Self and Society, op. cit.*, p. 133.

66 *Ibid.*, pp. 13–14, 42–3 and 48–9.

67 *Ibid.*, p. 81; Miller, *op. cit.*, pp. 70–1.

68 *Mind, Self and Society, ibid*; GEORGE HERBERT MEAD, 'A behavioristic account of the significant symbol', in RECK, *op. cit.*, pp. 244 and 246.

69 *Mind, Self and Society, ibid.*, pp. 45–6; GEORGE HERBERT MEAD, 'The mechanism of social consciousness', *Journal of Philosophy, Psychology, and Scientific Methods*, 9, 18 July, 1912, p. 403.

70 *Mind, Self and Society, ibid.*, pp. 118–20.

71 *Ibid.*, p. 69.

72 *Ibid.*, pp. 132–3.

73 'A behavioristic account of the significant symbol', RECK, *op. cit.*, p. 243.

74 *Mind, Self and Society, op. cit.*, pp. 140–1.

75 *Ibid.*, p. 158.

76 *Ibid.*, pp. 154–5.

77 *Ibid.*, pp. 153–4; 'The genesis of the self and social control', RECK, *op. cit.*, pp. 284–5.

78 *Mind, Self and Society, ibid.*, p. 175.

79 *Ibid.*, pp. 134–7, 163 and 165–73.

80 J. DAVID LEWIS, 'A social behaviorist interpretation of the meadian "I"', *American Journal of Sociology*, 85, September, 1979, pp. 269–70.

81 *Mind, Self and Society, op. cit.*, p. 175.

82 *Ibid.*, pp. 177–8. According to Mead's student David Miller, 'the generalized other is included in the "me", and the "me" consists of those attitudes and habits of the community (of which the self is a member) that have been accepted by the individual and applied under customary circumstances in performing his social role in the community. The "I" component of the self is the impulsive, creative component. The "I" is the initiator, the actor, but the "me" furnishes the "tools" for acting.' And further, '. . . by help of the generalized other (institutions) the "I" is able to reconstruct; it is able to formulate new attitudes with correspondingly new habits, even as men have made new tools and our finest instruments by starting with the clumsy hand and sticks and stones.' See DAVID MILLER, 'Mead's theory of universals', in *The Philosophy of George Herbert Mead*, edited by WALTER ROBERT CORTI, Winterthur, Switzerland, Archiv fur genetische Phisolophie, 1973, pp. 96 and 97.

83 GEORGE HERBERT MEAD, *Movements of Thought in the Nineteenth Century*, edited by MERRITT A. MOORE, Chicago, University of Chicago Press, 1936, pp.

389–90.

84 'The genesis of the self and social control', RECK, *op. cit.*, p. 289; *The Philosophy of the Act, op. cit.*, pp. 6–7; J. DAVID LEWIS and RICHARD L. SMITH, *American Sociology and Pragmatism: Mead, Chicago Sociology and Symbolic Interaction*, Chicago, University of Chicago Press, 1980, pp. 124–5.

85 'The genesis of the self and social control', *ibid.*, p. 290.

86 *Mind, Self and Society, op. cit.*, p. 254.

87 *Ibid.*, p. 210.

88 *Ibid.*, p. 255.

89 *Ibid.*

90 'The genesis of the self and social control', RECK, *op. cit.*, p. 291.

91 *Ibid.*

92 HERBERT BLUMER, 'Sociological implications of the thought of George Herbert Mead', *American Journal of Sociology*, 71, March, 1966, p. 536.

93 MAURICE NATANSON, *The Social Dynamics of George Herbert Mead*, Washington, D.C. Public Affairs Press, 1956, pp. 14–15.

94 HENRY MEAD, 'Biographical notes', in *The Philosophy of the Act, op. cit.*, pp. 1xxv–1xxvii.

95 'Student notes for Mead's social psychology, 1912', *The Mead Papers op. cit.*, Box 3, Folder 5, p. 103.

96 *Mind, Self* and Society, *op. cit.*, pp. 266–7.

97 *Ibid.*, p. 270.

98 Mead's assumption that the existence of self, which emerged out of a social process, was a precondition for the emergence of society is not as it may seem at first glance a circular argument. Mead argued that there existed prior to the emergence of self certain cooperative activities of a primitive type among interacting individuals in which these individuals through the conversation of gestures were able to take the same attitude toward themselves as others took toward them. Given his account of the emergence of mind and self, this primitive kind of social process was a necessary precondition. The more highly developed form of organization that we would call society, however, required that the interacting individuals had previously acquired selves, See *Mind, Self and Society, op. cit.*, pp. 227 and 240.

99 GEORGE HERBERT MEAD, 'On the effects of industrialization', unpublished , undated manuscript, *The Mead Papers, op. cit.*, Box 3 Addendum, Folder 14, pp. 1–15.

100 *Ibid.*, p. 15.

101 'On the effects of industrialization', *op. cit.*, pp. 35–7; GEORGE HERBERT MEAD, 'On the role of social settlements', unpublished, undated manuscript, *The Mead Papers, op. cit.*, Box 3 Addendum, Folder 24, p. 3.

102 'On the effects of industrialization', *ibid.*; GEORGE HERBERT MEAD, 'Untitlted, unpublished, undated manuscript on the living conditions of slavic immigrants in Chicago', *The Mead Papers, op. cit.*, Box 9, Folder 25.

103 *Mind, Self and Society, op. cit.*, pp. 273–7.

104 *Ibid.*, p. 263.

105 GEORGE HERBERT MEAD, 'On humanity, happiness, and the moral order', unpublished, undated manuscript, *The Mead Papers, op. cit.*, Box 2 Addendum, Folder 26.

106 'Annual reports of the Immigrants' Protective League, 1913–1919', *The Papers of the Immigrants' Protective League*, University of Illinois-Chicago Library, Supple-

ment II, Folder 59; Immigrants' Protective League, 'Aims and purposes', *The Papers of the Immigrants' Protective League*, University of Illinois-Chicago Library, Box 66, Folder 66.

107 'Statement of the Immigrants' Protective League', in *Statements and Recommendations Submitted by Societies and Organizations Interested in the Subject of Immigration*, Reports of the Immigration Commission, Vol. 41, 41 vols New York, Arno Press, 1970, pp. 55–78.

108 MARY JO DEEGAN and JOHN S. BURGER, 'George Herbert Mead and social reform: His work and writings', *Journal of the History of the Behavioral Sciences*, 14, October, 1978, pp. 365–9; 'Report of the Subcommittee of the Citizens Committee on the Strike', *The Mead Papers, op. cit.*, Box 9, Folder 22.

109 GEORGE HERBERT MEAD, WILLIAM J. BOGAN, and ERNEST A. WREIDT, *A Report on Vocational Training in Chicago and in Other Cities*, Chicago, City Club of Chicago, 1912, pp. 2, 4 and 7.

110 *Ibid.*, p. 9; GEORGE HERBERT MEAD, 'Industrial education, the working man and the schools', in *George Herbert Mead: Essays on His Social Philosophy*, edited by JOHN W. PETRAS, New York, Teachers College Press, 1968, pp. 57–60.

111 'On the effects of industrialization', *op. cit.*, pp. 10–12, 16 and 25–7.

112 *Ibid.*, pp. 38–9.

113 GEORGE HERBERT MEAD, 'Educational aspects of trade schools', in PETRAS, *op. cit.*, pp. 46–7.

114 *Ibid.*, p. 48.

115 JULIET HAMMOND, 'Notes for Mead's lectures on the philosophy of education, 1910–1911', *The Mead Papers, op. cit.*, Box 8, Folder 9, p. 8.

116 *Mind, Self and Society, op. cit.*, pp. 303–10 and 335. The reflexivity that Mead posited between the 'me' and the 'I' in his description of the emergence of self became his model for describing the relationship he saw between the individual and society. The idea which Mead advances that the individual is an active constructor of his society is essentially the notion of reflexivity writ large.

117 *Ibid.*, pp. 303–8 and 314–6; JAMES CAMPBELL, 'George Herbert Mead on Intelligent Social Reconstruction', *Symbolic Interaction*, 4, Fall, 1981, pp. 191–205.

118 *Mind, Self and Society, ibid.*, p. 326.

119 GEORGE HERBERT MEAD, 'Cooley's contribution to American social thought', *American Journal of Sociology*, 35, March, 1930, pp. 699–700.

120 *Ibid.*, pp. 701–4.

121 *Mind, Self and Society, op. cit.*, p. 224.

122 'Cooley's contribution to American social thought', *op. cit.*, p. 705; 'Student notes for Mead's social psychology, 1912', *op. cit.*, p. 102.

4 Building an Efficient Community: The Origins of the Idea of Social Control in Curriculum Thought

I

Americans, Edward Ross noted, writing in 1920 in *The Principles of Sociology*, had numerous instruments of social control available to them to contain the seeming threat posed by the growing diversity of the population. Newspapers, popular magazines, religious revivals, and the settlement house could all serve, he pointed out, to instill the population with common ideas.[1] No instrument, however, he suggested, was more appropriate for this effort than the school:

> Thoroughly to nationalize a multitudinous people calls for institutions to disseminate certain ideas and ideals. The Tsars relied on the blue-domed Orthodox church in every peasant village to Russify their heterogeneous subjects, while we Americans rely for unity on the 'little red school house.'[2]

It was increasingly to the schools that American intellectuals would turn in this century as they sought to socially control the twin forces of urbanization and industrialization. Ultimately, then, educators would take the leading role in this twentieth century effort to regulate society in the name of community. No educators, as it turned out, were more committed to this task than were those individuals who identified themselves professionally with the field of curriculum.

As a field of research and practice, curriculum first appeared on the American intellectual scene at just about the time that Ross was defining his concept of social control in the pages of *The American Journal of Sociology*. In fact, what we might think of as the first explicit American curriculum theory, Herbartianism, emerged at least in part out of the effort of individuals to respond educationally to the demands they believed urbanization and industrialization posed for the nation's population.

For Charles De Garmo, one of the founding theorists of American Herbartianism, Herbart's injunction that education should 'furnish a moral revelation of the world to the child' required more than the mental training that dominated the schools of his day. The preeminent function of education, he argued, was to provide the child with the 'ideals, dispositions, and habits' that were required for social life.[3] Urbanization and industrialization, he noted, had created a host of new problems for Americans to solve. The streams that had in an earlier day provided the nation with a source of pure water have become polluted. The increased population density of the city required new forms of mass transportation. The absence of free land in the West has transformed those who might have in an earlier day settled the nation's frontier into a new class of urban slum dwellers.

Resolving these problems, De Garmo argued, required the development within the population of a new viewpoint, one that was decidedly more social in outlook than the prevailing individualism of the moment. A new type of American was required, one who placed his social responsibilities ahead of his individual interests. Instilling this view in the population, De Garmo went on to say, required 'a readjustment of our theory and practice in education to our new social and economic conditions'.[4]

The kind of reorientation that De Garmo and other Herbartians had in mind was one, it seems, that would make education an instrument of social control. Ira Howerth, a sociology instructor at the University of Chicago, writing in *The Fifth Yearbook of the Herbart Society*, noted the need, as did the theorists of social control we considered earlier, for unity in American society. Education, he went on to say, 'because of its power to develop personalities in the direction of a perceived good' could serve to realize this needed solidarity.[5] In fact, when Howerth talked about how the schools might accomplish this goal, he sounded reminiscent of Ross and Thorndike:

> So long as certain classes or certain individuals refuse to recognize their natural relations to society, that is, are unsocialized, so long will they retard the advance of society toward its ultimate goal. The great problem of the age is how to get rid of our unsocial classes. Obviously, the only way to get rid of them is to socialize them. And this may be done by education, and this should be, we contend, its main object.[6]

Despite this apparent interest in using education as a means of social regulation, Herbartianism represents a conceptual dead end for our understanding of the role that the idea of social control has played in the development of the school curriculum. No one in the Herbartian camp, excluding of course John Dewey whose affiliation with the movement was anyway at best marginal, talked about social control or, for that matter, explained how the curriculum could serve this function. Further, Herbartianism had a rather short life span as an educational movement. By the time Ross published his book on social control in 1900 and before the other founding theorists of social control had begun to write on this subject, Herbartianism's influence on American educational thinking had begun to subside.[7]

Our study, then, must turn elsewhere if we are to learn anything about the role played by the idea of social control in the development of the American school curriculum. As it turned out, the impact of Herbartianism extended beyond the life of the movement itself. At the heart of American Herbartianism was the belief, which was variously referred to as correlation or concentration, that the subjects of the curriculum should be organized around a unifying theme.[8] Herbartianists, however, were never very successful in getting school people to embrace this principle of curriculum organization. Far more fortunate in this vein was a group of educators who in the years following World War I sought to organize the school curriculum around certain social issues or problems. These educators, who identified themselves with the idea of social efficiency, brought to their work of curriculum organization an explicit concept of social control.[9] It is to this social efficiency movement which we now must turn to see how the idea of social control found its way into the American curriculum field.

II

The problem with Herbartianism, pointed out William Chandler Bagley, an early advocate of the idea of social efficiency, writing in 1905 in *The Educative Process* was the vagueness of the movement about its ultimate social objectives.[10] What no doubt troubled Bagley was that despite the interest of Herbartianists in using education to socialize youth for life in an urban, industrial society, they never explicitly stated the direction that effort should take. Bagley, who had taken courses with De Garmo while pursuing his doctorate at Cornell University, was, on the other hand, quite clear as to the social function of education. The fundamental aim of education, he stated, was 'the development of the socially efficient individual'.[11]

Such an individual, according to Bagley, was one whose willingness to engage in productive work and to place the interests of society as a whole above his own, would advance the cause of social progress. The task of education, he went on to say, was to prepare individuals who would as citizens and workers carry on their day-to-day lives so that 'society will maximally profit'.[12]

There was nothing terribly remarkable about an educator such as Bagley in 1905 invoking the idea of efficiency. We have already noted the fears that plagued many middle class American intellectuals during this period about urbanization and industrialization and their desire to cope with what they saw as the disruptions accompanying this social and economic transformation of the nation. America, they believed, had to find some means of reconciling its historic liberal democratic ethic with the growth of the corporation, particularly the financial speculation and waste of natural resources it appeared to bring, and with the threat to social order they identified with the growing diversity of the population. What these intellectuals sought were new forms of social organization which would, they hoped, preserve existing democratic values within this new social and economic context.[13] No notion better conveyed the aspirations which these intellectuals held for modern American society than did this idea of efficiency.

Efficiency meant several things for these individuals. It referred to certain personal characteristics, particularly hard work and discipline, which they admired. It also described the increased productivity and enhanced profits that industrialization had made possible. Most important, however, the term typified the harmony in human relationships these intellectuals thought necessary in an urban, industrial society.[14] As two of the most influential thinkers of the day, Herbert Croly and Walter Weyl, noted, an efficient social order, that is one that was unified, would curb the destructive, selfish and wasteful aspects of industrialism and allow the progressive promise of this new economic system to be realized.[15]

Nowhere during the early years of this century was the connection between efficiency and social harmony made more visible than in the pronouncements of those professionals in engineering and business who sought to reorganize industrial production in the name of what they called scientific management. At the center of this effort was the most widely known of the founding theorists of the scientific management movement, Frederick Winslow Taylor.

For Taylor, the problem of American industry was the apparently intractable antagonism between management and workers. Employers, he noted, were primarily motivated by the need to reduce their labor costs and therefore sought to pay their workers as little as possible, certainly less than the wages offered by their competitors. Workers were, on the other hand, impelled by the desire to obtain the highest wages they could for the least amount of work. Neither group, then, believed that they had any shared interests. As a consequence, the relationship between management and labor was marked by discord and mutual suspicion, a situation that ultimately led to both low productivity and low wages.[16]

Taylor identified two interrelated factors that were responsible for this inefficiency in the functioning of American industry. Employers were ignorant of the principles of sound management, particularly the time required for the completion of the different types of jobs within the plant. As a result, they established a uniform rate of daily pay for all their workers. In response, workers, recognizing that there was no incentive for hard work, did only what was minimally necessary to earn their day's pay. Often, he noted, they adopted the practice of 'soldiering' or slowing down the pace of their work which led to a reduction in output.[17]

There was, Taylor went on to argue, a science of management that could make our industrial process more efficient. Its most important principle was what he called the 'task idea', the notion that each worker should be given a narrowly defined task which he was to perform at a specific rate using certain predefined procedures.[18] The key to scientific management was to determine the appropriate rate and the procedures for completing the task.

For Taylor workers fell into two broad groups. There were the masses of American workmen, whom he referred to as 'average' men, whose devotion to the practice of 'soldiering' was responsible for the existing state of inefficiency in American industry. There were also, however, a few so-called 'first-class' men, individuals who could on a regular basis without undue stress produce twice or even four times as much as their fellow workers. Taylor argued that an analysis of the work performance of these 'first-class' men offered a way to determine the optimum rate and procedures for carrying out the various jobs within a plant.[19] He advocated the use of a number of observational procedures, which he referred to as 'scientific time studies' or what we today would call task analysis, to time these efficient workers as they carried out their tasks and to identify the particular steps they followed. The results of this kind of analysis, Taylor believed, would reveal the most productive standards by which to conduct the work of American industry.[20]

The goal of efficient or scientific management was to ensure that all workers adhered to these standards. Taylor advanced two policies to achieve this end. First, he sought to curb the long-standing and what he believed was inefficient practice of allowing workers to follow their own inclinations as to the speed at which they would work and the procedures they would follow. He recommended instead a system of what he called 'functional management'. Each plant was to have a centralized planning department staffed by specialists in scientific management who would use 'scientific time studies' of the various jobs of the plant to determine the standards workers should follow.[21]

Second, he sought the elimination of the prevailing system of uniform rates of daily pay in favor of differential wages based on output. In carrying out his own time studies, Taylor had noted that 'first-class' men could be motivated to work at their peak rate if they were paid anywhere from 30 to 100 per cent more than 'average' workers. He therefore advocated what we might think of as a piece-rate system in which workers would be paid according to output on a scale that was from 30 to 100 per cent higher, depending on the job, of the prevailing daily wages of most American workers.[22] Taken together, these two policies would, Taylor believed, fulfilled the overall promise of scientific management for increasing the efficiency of American industry.[23]

The drive for efficiency implied more for Taylor than simply a change in the material conditions of industrial work. At a hearing in 1912 before a special House Congressional Committee investigating the scientific management movement, Taylor suggested that his system would lead to a 'mental revolution' in the attitudes of both management and labor. They would 'become friends instead of practical enemies'.[24] Governed by the principles of scientific management, Taylor argued, employers and employees would overcome the historical antagonism that has divided them and '. . . arrange their mutual relations that their interests become identical'.[25] It was for Taylor the possibility that scientific management offered for harmony and unity in the work place that would allow employers and employees to join together to reduce labor costs and increase wages.[26]

In extolling the idea of social efficiency, then, Taylor, Bagley, and other like-minded early twentieth-century American thinkers were expressing sentiments similar to those of individuals in the previous century who longed for the cultural homogeneity they identified with the rural, small town. The notion of efficiency allowed these twentieth-century intellectuals to carry into modern urban industrial life what was essentially an older rural ideal of social unity or, as we called it, community. It signaled in fact that these thinkers had been able to separate the notion of community from a particular place in time and to generalize it as a principle of human relations in a set of social arrangements that were far different.[27] As we shall see, it was under the rubric of social efficiency that the first educators identified with the field of curriculum would assert their commitment to the value of community. And it was in the name of efficiency along lines first laid out by Frederick Taylor that they and many of their intellectual heirs would seek to make the school curriculum an instrument of social control.

III

The Herbartians were only one of several groups of educators whose concern with the problems posed by urbanization and industrialization led them to question the doctrine of mental disciplines. There were individuals such as the psychologist G. Stanley Hall who advocated the cause of child study, an early variant of development psychology, as a means of developing a more adequate curriculum for twentieth-century youth. There was a loose collection of individuals including Mead and John Dewey who shared the view most insistently expressed by the sociologist Lester Frank Ward that education should serve to redress the inequities of urban industrial society. And there were educators such as Bagley who extolled the virtues of social efficiency.[28] It was this last group who were, as we shall see, most significant in the development of American curriculum thought and practice.

What troubled efficiency-minded educators about the doctrine of mental disciplines was its devotion to the goal of mental training. Under the sway of this doctrine, they argued, the school curriculum had come to be overcrowded with subjects, such as the classical languages and higher mathematics, that possessed little in the way of social utility. That is, they were areas of study whose only function was to prepare a small segment of the school population for admission to college. These subjects offered nothing to the mass of American youth as they prepared to assume adult citizenship and work roles in twentieth-century American society.[29] It was this functional view of the course of study that would provide the intellectual foundation for the emergence during the decade following World War I of a professional field of curriculum. And similarly, it was this viewpoint that would govern the work of school people from the 1920s onward in shaping and directing the curriculum within American schools.

Initially, at least, the efforts of efficiency-oriented curriculum workers to reform the school program took two distinct directions. At the center of the movement and ultimately most influential was the attempt of educators such as Franklin Bobbitt and Werrett Wallace Charters to apply the principles of scientific management to the design of the curriculum. At the fringe of social efficiency thinking, however, was the less successful effort of one Ross L. Finney to use the curriculum to resist the changes that industrialization and urbanization had brought. In the remainder of this chapter, we will consider these two strands of efficiency thinking, looking first at Finney and then at Bobbitt and Charters.

IV

Born in Postville, Iowa, a small town in the Northeast part of the state, Finney (1875–1934) began his career as a Methodist minister serving several churches in Minnesota. Just before completing his doctorate in theology at Boston University in 1911, Finney abandoned the active ministry for a teaching position in philosophy of education and economics at Illinois Wesleyan University. In 1914, he was appointed Professor of Education at the State Normal School in Valley City, North Dakota, and in 1919 he came to the University of Minnesota where he taught sociology of education until his death in 1934.[30]

Writing in 1922 in the *Causes and Cures for the Social Unrest*, Finney argued that the emergence of industrial capitalism, or as he put it 'machinofacture', was threatening the position of the nation's middle class population. Equating the middle class with the native-born population of Northern and Western European heritage, he was echoing the same concerns that his fellow Iowan, Edward Ross, had raised over twenty years earlier.

From above, the small monied class who had financed the development of the corporations that had come to dominate the scene, had so concentrated money in its own hands as to virtually squeeze the middle class out of the economic life of the nation. From below, a largely immigrant working class whose labor had made industrialization possible, had brought to this country a 'Bolshevik' ideology which would in time bring about a revolution similar to the Russian Revolution of 1917. Once destroyed by the upper class, the middle class would have no choice but to join the workers and under the influence of their radical philosophy to become part of a new American proletariat. Parroting Ross, he saw America's twentieth-century economic transformation as endangering the middle class with 'race suicide'.[31]

The middle class was to Finney's way of thinking the mainstay of democratic values and stability in American society. As a consequence, he bemoaned the passing of the nation's rural agrarian past where this class had, he believed, exerted a significant influence in the affairs of the nation:

> In the olden days almost any apprentice might hope, by industry and thrift, to get together the tools, materials and shop to set up on his own account. Under those circumstances owner and worker were the same; capital and labor were united in one person. But under modern machinofacture conditions that is out of the question. Ownership and labor are quite naturally and inevitably separated. And that, reader, is the crux of the whole modern situation; that is the fundamental cause of the modern social unrest.[32]

It was his hope, he noted in 1928, that in some way this past could be restored to twentieth-century life:

> In the really good society of the future the lower classes will have escaped en masse from a status of poverty, ignorance, and cultural deprivation, into a really humanizing condition of living. Such is a society from which will have disappeared both the squalid misery of the present lower classes and the sordid luxury of the so-called upper classes; and in which all will be middle class together, sharing equitably in the cultural resources of civilization.[33]

What Finney sought was a homogeneous social order in which all its members were middle class in both 'mental contents' and 'overt behavior'. Such a society, Finney believed, would embody the sense of community which seemed to him to have been lost in twentieth-century America.[34]

It was to education that Finney looked to secure this needed social homogeneity. The schools were to be his vehicles for ensuring that everybody thought and acted alike. This was to his way of thinking the fundamental aim of education for social efficiency.[35] Compulsory school attendance, he noted in this vein, could curb the radicalism of the immigrant working class and bring their interests into line with those of the middle class:

> A far wiser propoganda for the workers is one that will ally and amalgamate them with the middle class. And such an alliance and amalgamation should be forced upon the lower classes, whether their agitators like it or not, by compulsory attendance

laws that will make high school graduation practically universal.[36]

In securing social homogeneity, the schools, Finney argued, would become democracy's instrument of social control, the term he used for the action of a person or group to constrain the conduct and behavior of others.[37]

To explain how the schools would provide for social control, Finney turned to the ideas of Cooley and Ross. Claiming to embrace Cooley's social psychology, he argued that there was no independent ego that could be conceived of apart from society. The mind was in truth a social mind that emerged as individuals in social interaction came to share the same mental states. At the mental level, Finney pointed out, '... we are participants in a common substance'.[38]

Both Cooley and Finney argued that it was the existence of a shared mental state that allowed the members of society to be brought under social control. The social self, Cooley's mechanism of social control, emerged, as the individual came to see himself as the others with whom he interacted saw him. For Cooley, we should remember, the individual was an active participant in this process. That is, the individual actually acquired his self feeling when he evaluated the view that others held toward him. Finney, on the other hand, saw the individual as acquiring his social mind by passively imitating the suggestions of others with whom he interacted:

> The sources of almost all our learning are social also. It is from other people, through sheer social suggestion, that we absorb almost our entire stock of knowledge. One is said to get ideas by social suggestion when he takes them from other people without critical resistence. Much of the content of the mind has been derived in that way. The percentage of one's information which he acquires by original inferences from his own observatioins, is very small indeed; the percentage from which the element of social suggestion is wholly absent is almost negligible ... The power of the individual mind to draw new inferences independently is very much less than our conceit would like to suppose; thinking is very much more a collective enterprise than it pleases us to admit.[39]

For Finney, then, the individual was essentially passive as he acquired the ideas that would ultimately regulate his conduct:

> The term social suggestion has been familiar for some time. It indicates the source of ideas. But when the mind accepts ideas

uncritically from social sources the learning process is relatively passive, as compared with original perception and conceptual thinking. And the fact that has been too little observed and reckoned with in theory, especially in pedagogical theory, that the contents of our minds is derived very largely from process of relatively passive mentation. If the learning process is a social process, it follows that the learning process is just to that degree a passive process.[40]

Mental and hence social life for Finney was more of a process of 'blind followership' than original thought. Because the individual learned by imitating the suggestions of others, he saw social control as a matter of habituation. The individual, Finney argued, was brought under social control in so far as he took on those habits that would ensure proper conduct and belief. It was the fact that learning at the core was habituation that allowed education, according to Finney, to function as an instrument of social control.[41]

Finney obtained his understanding of how social control was to be brought about from Ross. If educators were to understand the problem of social order, he noted, that should 'read and ponder well Professor Ross's monumental work on *Social Control*'. Ross's great contribution, Finney believed, was to identify the overt acts undertaken by society's institutions to bring about individual conformity. These institutions offered the social stimuli which the individual took on 'without conscious resistance' or thought, for that matter, in the form of habits.[42]

Ross's work was critical, Finney pointed out, because he was willing, unlike Cooley, to admit that social control sometimes did not occur automatically and required coercion:

> And only practical disaster can result from over-looking in educational theory and practice the fact that society often crosses the purposes of its members and breaks their wills. Indeed, compulsion has everywhere and always been an outstanding phenomenon in social organization and evolution. Society has never displayed the pale squeamishness about killing an individual wish that some contemporary theorists profess themselves to feel. The routine element in social life has always been too important to tolerate such trifling.[43]

Finney was particularly critical of John Dewey on this score. Dewey, he noted, viewed social control as arising out of the give and take of individuals in social interaction. Such a viewpoint, with its assumption of individuals as active and thinking participants in bringing about control, ignored, according to Finney, the role of habit and drill in controlling human conduct. Dewey, Finney argued, placed too much emphasis on the role of individuals as original thinkers. Dewey forgot, he went on to say, that it was '. . . even more important, especially in the present crisis, that they be trained to revere and to obey'.[44]

Finney believed that the best hope for the restoration of community lay with American educators, especially those whose work involved the curriculum. 'Salvation, if there be any', he once remarked, 'would seem to be with the curriculum makers'.[45] What created the kind of like-mindedness which Finney thought so essential for addressing the existing social crisis was the existence of a common social heritage, the stock of knowledge in the humanities, sciences, and technology which society had accumulated over the ages. The task of curriculum workers, he believed, was to design a course of study for the schools that would assure that all members of society acquired this heritage.[46]

The curriculum that Finney recommended was organized around certain disciplines of knowledge. They were not, however, the classical subjects favored by the mental disciplinarians. Rather, they included (i) language; (ii) vocational subjects; (iii) sports, games and amusements; (iv) sciences; (v) the fine arts; and (vi) the 'new humanities', Finney's term for the social sciences. Where advocates of the doctrine of mental disciplines saw the subjects of the curriculum as instruments for training the mind, Finney viewed them, as we might expect of one with an efficiency orientation, as vehicles for socializing youth for adult citizenship and work roles. Higher mathematics, he argued, should not be a required subject in high school. It should be available for those small number of students who would need this study as preparation for certain technical careers. All that should be required, Finney argued, was that students should possess the skills necessary to do simple computations. Similarly, he recommended that the study of formal English grammer be replaced in the public schools by instruction in functional literacy.

At the heart of Finney's curricular recommendations were the so-called 'new humanities'. They included ten subjects: geography, biology, psychology, anthropology, sociology, economics, politics, ethics, metaphysics, and history. The study of these subjects was important, Finney argued, because they would reveal to students the conclusions of our social heritage as to the proper form our social institutions should take. They would, in fact, make the institution of society the objectives of education. By instilling students with correct information about how American social institutions should function, they would enhance their efficiency as citizens and workers.

Finney, like Mead, favored a system of vocational education as part of a comprehensive high school. A program of vocational training required of all students would, he believed, reduce the number of unskilled individuals in society. For the working class, particularly, it would ensure that they received both training for work as well as a liberal education. Such a curriculum, Finney argued, would provide them not only with the skills they needed to earn a living but with the knowledge they required to demand a decent standard of living while resisting the appeal for violent revolution.[47] A curriculum composed of functionally oriented courses in mathematics and English, the 'new humanities', and vocational education would create the like-minded citizenry, firmly rooted in the values of the middle class, that was necessary, Finney argued, for restoring a sense a community to twentieth-century American society.

In advancing this curriculum proposal, Finney had to resolve the dilemma of how students of differing intellectual capacities could partake of a single, common course of study. Finney was writing, we should remember, during the height of the mental measurements movement when many educators were advocating that the curriculum should be differentiated into tracks in which students would be placed according to their abilities. Finney, it seems, shared the hereditarian viewpoint of Ross and many of these proponents of mental measurements. He pointed out, for example, '... that half the people have brains of just average quality or less, of whom a very considerable percentage have very poor brains indeed'. This lower half of the population, he went on to say, had little to contribute to society because 'IQs below .99+ are not likely to secrete cogitations of any great social fruitfulness'.[48] Actually, it was for Finney this fact of human existence that would allow his recommended common curriculum to make everybody middle class.

Despite individual differences in mental capacity, Finney believed that the imitative and passive nature of the human mind rendered the overt behavior of all members of society the same. Except under very special conditions, it was not possible, he argued, simply from observing their behavior to distinguish the bright from the dull. Because learning was, as he put it, a process of 'passive mentation', all members of society no matter what their station in life or their ability could be conditioned to perform the same routinized habits. Thus if the curriculum were to embody middle class values and standards of behavior expressed in the form of certain desirable habitual responses, everyone could learn in the same way at the same time:

> Ours are the schools of a democracy, which all the children attend. At least half of them never had an original idea of any general nature, and never will. But they must behave as if they had sound ideas. Whether these ideas are original or not matters not in the least. It is better to be right than to be original. What the duller half of the population needs, therefore, is to have their reflexes conditioned into behavior that is socially suitable. And the wholesale memorizing of catchwords-provided they are sound ones-is the only practical means of establishing bonds in the duller intellects between the findings of social scientists and the corresponding behavior of the masses. Instead of trying to teach dullards to think for themselves, the intellectual leaders must think for them, and drill the results, memoriter, into their synapses. For the dullards it is that or nothing.[49]

Many of Finney's recommendations for the curriculum were in tune with the prevailing opinion of his day. His view of learning as a process of 'passive mentation' was not appreciably different from the behavioral viewpoint that came to dominate psychological and educational thinking during the 1920s. His advocacy of a functionally oriented course of study was consistent with existing efforts at curriculum reform. The comprehensive high school that took shape during the period he was writing did, as he suggested, provide for both liberal and vocational education. And many of the subjects he called the 'new humanities' did find their way into the school curriculum in the decade following World War I. Yet, despite the seeming currency of Finney's proposals, his influence on the development of efficiency oriented curriculum thought and practice was minimal, if not non-existent.

There are at least two good reasons for Finney's lack of influence. First, his hostility to industrialism coupled with his advocacy of the values of an agrarian, middle class made him at best an anachronism. Two decades earlier, when Ross was writing on social control, one might have been able reasonably to entertain the possibility of preserving certain features of America's nineteenth-century rural past. By the end of World War I that hope was naive at best. The nation had in fact become both urbanized and industralized. If a sense of community was to be created in twentieth-century America, it had to be done by coming to terms with both the city and the factory.

Second, there was a certain harshness to Finney's thought that no doubt made it difficult for many to embrace his views. Like Thorndike he advocated a dual system of education, one for leadership and one for followership. Beyond the public schools, Finney argued, stood the colleges and graduate schools. Here, those of high intelligence who would ultimately lead American society would be prepared to understand the social heritage as well as to use their own creative powers to infuse that heritage with new ideas.[50] Such a dual system of education led him to a vision of a rigidly stratified society that seemed out of keeping with the nation's historic commitment to equality:

> At the apex of such a system must be the experts, who are pushing forward research in highly specialized sectors of the front. Behind them are such men and women as the colleges should produce, who are familiar with the findings of the experts and are able to relate part with part. By these relatively independent leaders of thought, progressive change and constant readjustment will be provided for. Back of these are the high school graduates, who are somewhat familiar with the vocabulary of those above them, have some feeling of acquaintance with the various fields, and a respect for expert knowledge. Finally, there are the duller masses, who mouth the catchwords of those in front of them, imagine that they understand, and follow by imitation. The homogeneity of society, involving its capacity for unified purposive mobilization, lies in the fact that the findings of science and our best philosophy permeate the whole mass, much as Catholic theology permeated the whole mass of west European society during the Middle Ages. Such solidarity can be secured only by practically universal instruction on the lower secondary level of the sort that drills slogans into the dullards, but at the same time selects the brightest for creative thinking on the higher levels, while doing some of both for the great average mass. By no other means can public opinion be organized around the leadership of the better intellects. The problem of leadership is at bottom, therefore, a problem of followership; and the followership of the masses can be secured only by memoritor drill on the epitomized philosophies of the leaders.[51]

Finney claimed to have derived his notion of social control at least in part from Edward Ross. Yet Ross, throughout his writings, was able to convey a basic sympathy for the plight of the American masses that was clearly absent in Finney's work. Finney's ideas also bear a striking resemblance to the positions espoused by Thorndike, whose influence was clearly much greater. In Thorndike's case, however, it was quite easy for educators to embrace his behaviorism while rejecting his less than egalitarian social vision. Finney was a different matter. To reject his social vision was to reject all for which Finney stood. There was little of any uniqueness that was left.

If Finney represented social efficiency's conceptual dead-end, Franklin Bobbitt and W.W. Charters were its influential core. It was these two individuals whose willingness to accept the reality and permanence of an urban industrialized society led them to discover an educational use for the ideas of scientific management. And by applying these ideas to the task of curriculum work, they were able to suggest how the school program could be used to build a sense of community in American society.

V

At about the same the time that Finney was describing the separation of labor and ownership under industrialization, Franklin Bobbitt (1875– 1956), Professor of Educational Administration at the University of Chicago, was describing a related characteristic of this economic system, the division of labor:

> In the old days a shoemaker was master of his entire craft. He took the original order, prepared the leather, designed the shoe and each of its parts, cut each piece, did the sewing, the finishing, and finally the selling. ... At the present time, however, one man cuts out the sole; a second cuts the parts for the upper; a third, the lining; a fourth man sews the top to the vamp; a fifth sews on the toe-cap; a sixth gashes the insole preparatory to sewing it to the vamp; and so the process continues, the shoe passing down the line of several dozen workmen before it reaches the last one who places the finished shoe in the box ready for shipment.[52]

Born in English, Indiana, a community of less than one thousand in the Southeast part of the state, Bobbitt earned his undergraduate degree at Indiana University and then went on to teach, first in several rural schools in Indiana and later at the Phillipine Normal School in Manila. After receiving his doctorate at Clark University in 1909, he joined the faculty of the University of Chicago where he remained until his retirement in 1941.[53]

For Bobbitt, it seems, industrialization was less a break with past economic practices than a reorganization of these practices. The critical difference, he thought, between the artisan shoemaker and the manager of the twentieth-century shoe factory was that the latter simply possessed more intricate means to perform essentially the same task. 'Like the old-time shoemaker he has command of the technical information, makes all the necessary judgments, and operates his man-and-steel machine in such a way as to perform all the processes.'[54]

Similarly, Werrett W. Charters (1875–1952) also emphasized the continuities that linked twentieth-century America with its past. Writing in 1927 in an editorial that would be published in the *Journal of Educational Research*, Charters suggested that Americans should not be alarmed at the prospect of change. 'Though much is discarded', he noted, 'much remains, and as in times past, so now in these disquieting times, the fundamentals of our civilization stand solidly as a base from which to push out with confidence toward new adventures.' Those changes that have occurred, he went on to say, have affected less the 'fundamentals' of our civilization than its 'marginal totals'.[55]

Charters, like Bobbitt, was a product of the small town. Born in rural Hartford in the Province of Ontario, Canada, Charters began his career as a teacher in a rural school in Rockford, Ontario. After completing undergraduate work at McMaster University, the Ontario Normal College and the University of Toronto, Charters migrated to the United States where he earned his PhD in 1904 at the University of Chicago. During the next forty-three years, until his retirement in 1947, he served on the faculties of the State Normal School at Winona, Minnesota, the universities of Missouri, Illinois, Pittsburg and Chicago, the Carnegie Institute of Technology and the Ohio State University.[56]

Unlike Finney, both Bobbitt and Charters held a favorable view of industrialization. In May 1945, toward the end of his career, Charters delivered the commencement address to the graduates of Fisk University in Nashville. Pointing to the various changes that industralization had made possible, he noted that 'much will remain but much will be changed and probably for the better'. America was entering a period, he went on to say in which the promise of democracy would be realizable by all.[57] In a similar vein, Bobbitt pointed out twenty-seven years earlier that with industrialization had come the expansion of democracy throughout the nation.[58]

Nevertheless, both Bobbitt and Charters recognized the potential for discord that existed in industrial America. The specialization of labor, Bobbitt argued, had made the American population interdependent. Efficiency, under those conditions, required cooperation. Such a collaboration would require, he pointed out mirroring the views of Taylor, that labor and capital would need to overcome their long-standing antagonism. They needed, Bobbitt stated, 'to be partners, to cooperate intelligently, and effectively, to be able mutually to recognize and respect the interdependent interests of the other ...'.[59]

Similarly, Charters noted the conflict between labor and capital. Both groups, he noted, were currently struggling for the control of American education, particularly vocational education, in hopes of using the schools to advance their own narrow interests. At the least, he argued, such a conflict would damage American education by robbing it of the political and economic support of society's major interest groups. It could, however, destroy our educational system as interest groups of various persuasions abandoned the public schools to develop private schools that reflected their own points of view. Even more ominous for Charters was the possibility that the conflict between labor and capital over the schools could spread to other issues and 'break the nation into two great camps'.[60]

Charters, like Bobbitt, emphasized the value of a cooperative ideal for resolving the social strife of his day. During the 1930s, Charters was particularly interested in identifying the essential characteristics of American democracy, which he referred to as 'Democraciana'. In a set of handwritten notes on the essential features of education for a democractic society, which he apparently made around 1935, he suggested the inclusion of certain values in the curriculum, including industry, ambition, intelligence, and cooperation.[61]

Unlike Finney, however, neither Bobbitt nor Charters identified the seeming conflict that industrialization had brought with either ethnicity or class. Bobbitt, in fact, warned against the dangers of 'exaggerated nationalism'. Although he favored, as we shall see, an element of like-mindedness in society, it should not be achieved, he believed, at the expense of turning one social group against another. The great lesson to the American population of World War I, he argued, was their 'recognition of the fundamental interdependence of all people'.[62]

Charters shared Thorndike's view that human behavior was a reflection of certain original inborn tendencies. Unlike Thorndike, however, he went on to argue that environmental factors played a key role in developing, refining, and modifying that behavior. For Charters, then, human behavior was rooted in both heredity and environment.[63] Consequently, Charters seemed to reject the hereditarian thinking of his day that saw the problems of twentieth-century America as the result of an increase within the population of those of less intelligence. He argued that intelligence was far less a determinent of individual success than was character, personality, or effort, qualities that were not inborn but could be acquired. His view of the educational value of the intelligence test was fundamentally at odds with that of Thorndike:

What right has any person to predict failure because an intelligence quotion is somewhat low? To be sure, three percent of the pupils in the school may be so defective as to be hopeless, but the other ninety-seven percent may possibly be able to develop compensating traits of personality which far outweigh mediocrity in mental ability. We of the classroom are inclined to feel sorry for the industrious child with a comparatively low mental score, who by dint of hard work keeps abreast of his class. 'Isn't it unfortunate', we say, 'that he isn't bright?' We should rather say, 'Isn't it fortunate that he is so industrious, ambitious, and friendly? What a fine chance he has for success in the game of life where there is no particular correlations between success and brightness ...' In making an inventory of the assets of a man industry, forcefulness, leadership, sympathy, and ambition are major headings, which combined yield nothing in importance to brains and mental brightness.[64]

If America was to revive its seeming lost sense of community, both Bobbitt and Charters believed, cooperation and interdependence would have to become widely shared values among the population. Bobbitt, however, did not believe that building a sense of community required a return to the past. Like Mead, he embraced an urban, industrialized society. An industrial economy, it seems, provided Bobbitt with his model for such a community spirit, the modern corporation.[65] It was the harmonious relationships that he believed could exist between the specialized workers of the modern corporation that needed to be expanded to society at large.[66] For this to occur, the principles of scientific management, which he thought could govern all group interaction, had to be applied throughout society.[67]

Bobbitt referred to this desired pattern of relationships as 'large-group consciousness'. It was this awareness among its members that would create the like-minded population needed to transform modern American society into a community:

How does one develop a genuine feeling of membership in a social group, whether large or small? There seems to be but one method and that is, *To think and feel and ACT with the group as a part of it as it performs its activities and strives to attain its ends*. Individuals are fused into coherent small groups, discordant small groups are fused into the large internally-cooperating group, when they act *together* for common ends, with common vision, and with united judgment.[68]

A critical task of the school curriculum, Bobbitt argued, was to create this 'large-group consciousness' or sense of community. The existing school curriculum with its devotion to mental training was inadequate for this task. Such a curriculum did nothing to inform youth of their responsibilites as citizens and specialized workers, let alone involve them in the day to day life of society. What was needed was a new, functionally oriented school program built out of the 'living experience' of the members of society.[69] It was to attain this kind of curriculum that Bobbitt, and Charters too, turned to the principles of scientific management.[70]

For both Bobbitt and Charters, Taylor's idea of the 'scientific time study' provided the means for reforming the curriculum along more functional lines. By observing so-called 'first class men' on the job, the 'time study' allowed employers to identify the precise steps needed to complete an industrial task efficiently. Under Taylor's system, these steps would constitute the standardized procedures for carrying out the task. In a roughly analogous manner, Bobbitt and Charters suggested that educators should identify the standards for efficient citizenship and work by observing the specific activities of adults in their day-to-day lives. They recommended that these standards become the objectives of the curriculum.[71] As Bobbitt pointed out:

> Human life, however varied, consists in the performance of specific activities. Education that prepares for life is one that prepares definitely and adequately for these specific activities. However numerous and diverse they may be for any social class, they can be discovered. This requires only that one go out into the world of affairs and discover the particulars of which these affairs consist. These will show the abilities, attitudes, habits, appreciations, and forms of knowledge that men need. These will be the objectives of the curriculum. They will be numerous, definite, and particularized.[72]

The heart of curriculum making for Bobbitt and Charters was this identification of the very specific, almost minute, day-to-day activities of the members of society, a process they referred to as job or activity analysis. In his 1922 curriculum study in Los Angeles, Bobbitt presented teachers with a list of around 600 very narrow and particular life activities from which to select objectives for their course of study. Similarly, Charters's recommendations for the training of secretaries was based on his identification of the 871 day-to-day duties of secretaries in a variety of different types of offices.[73] Once these activities were stated as educational objectives, the curriculum became simply the procedures to be followed to teach these various activities to students.[74]

There was, we should note, a difference in the approach that Bobbitt and Charters took to using job analysis. For Bobbitt, the first step in curriculum development was the description of the day-to-day activities of adult men and women. Charters, on the other hand, argued that it was necessary prior to describing these activities or immediately thereafter to identify those ideals or desired standards which the curriculum should attain. For Charters, then, the process of curriculum construction involved the identification of not only the activities of adult life but the ideals as well.

This difference in their approach to curriculum making does not, however, seem to be of great significance. In a February 1923 article in *The School Review*, Charters criticized Bobbitt's Los Angeles curriculum study on the grounds that he had failed to classify his curriculum objectives in terms of any ideals toward which they were to be directed.[75] In the letter acknowledging receipt of the article the preceding year, the journal's editorial board reported that Bobbitt had examined Charters's article and had indicated 'that there is nothing in it to which he would object.'[76] Where Charters's concern with ideals becomes important, we shall see, is in his discussion of the issue of social control.

One of the special virtues of job analysis, Charters argued in a speech he delivered at the University of Kentucky in October 1928, was that its use could mute existing discord among American educators. According to Charters, curriculum workers of the day were divided on the issue of curriculum selection. Educators who were, as he put it, 'located on the right wing' favored the selection of content from the traditional academic disciplines. 'Left wing' educators, on the other hand, advocated the selection of content that would help children solve the current problems of the day whether or not that content came from 'the great fields of knowledge'. There was, however, a middle way, Charters argued, whereby educators could use the traditional disciplines for utilitarian purposes and avoid the conflict that had divided them into two extreme camps. This middle way, Charters stated, was the approach of job analysis. Using job analysis, educators could select educational objectives that had the most functional value for youth and still 'appreciate the necessity for systematic organization of the fields of knowledge at times which are pedagogically and psychologically appropriate'.[77]

We can in fact see in Charters's advocacy of job analysis the same devotion to gradualism and evolutionary change that led him to distrust radicalism in the larger society. Job analysis was for Charters more than a practice borrowed from industry for the reorganization of the curriculum along functional lines. Its origin was actually to be located. he pointed out, in the penchant of the ancient Greeks for breaking things into their component parts. It was in this sense related to a host of other analytical procedures including logical analysis, chemical analysis, grammatical analysis, and psychoanalysis.[78] In a handwritten manuscript on the history of curriculum making which he probably prepared during the 1930s, Charters described job analysis as the culminating stage in the historic effort of humans to transmit useful knowledge from one generation to the next.[79] It represented for him, then, the evolutionary refinement of our past practices of curriculum making.

VI

Not only did Bobbitt and Charters borrow their methodology for curriculum making from the scientific management movement, they also, it seems, took their cues for the organization of the curriculum from the same source. Bobbitt, for example, embraced job analysis because it enabled the teacher to identify specific standards for the education of different individuals much as it enabled those in industry to determine the manufacturing standards for different products. He went on to argue that just as there were distinct standards for different products, there should be separate educational standards for individuals of different abilities and social classes.[80]

The first task of the curriculum worker, Bobbitt argued, was to use job analysis to identify the broad areas of human activity to be found within society. After identifying these activities, the curriculum worker needed to subdivide them into the narrower activities of which they were composed, which in turn would become the objectives of the curriculum.[81] Bobbitt identified ten such broad activities including social intercommunication, citizenship, health and the raising of children. Of these activities, nine represented what Bobbitt believed all children should acquire by way of general education.

While the major areas of activity encompassed by general education should be the same for all students, Bobbitt suggested that the particular objectives as well as the actual curriculum content should be differentiated according to the child's ability and social class.[82] In planning the curriculum, Bobbitt pointed out:

> . . . our first responsibility is to work out the pupil activities and
> experiences that will carry the gifted pupils most effectively to

the highest practicable heights. This done, we shall have the average pupil travel the same road so far as it is in their power to normally do so; but modify it so far as their limitatioins make it necessary. The sub-average will travel the road laid out for the average so far as they can; but they will depart from it when their limitations make departure necessary.[83]

The tenth broad activity of education for Bobbitt was that of occupation. Here, the objectives of education were to be those abilities that were necessary for youth to prepare for any of the many specialized work roles available to them as adults. This segment of the curriculum would be highly differentiated in that both the objectives and the actual content to be taught would be distinct for each occupation.

Bobbitt offered the case of trigonometry as an example. Through the use of job analysis, the curriculum worker would discover that trigonometry was required in the work of the engineer, but not in the work of the typist or medical doctor. 'As a consequence, trigonometry will be prescribed as occupational training in the courses for engineers, but not in courses for the other occupations named; nor for general education.'[84]

Charters also accepted the practice of differentiating the curriculum according to the child's interest, ability, and vocational goals.[85] Perhaps because he believed that intelligence was a poor predictor of one's success, he was less willing than Bobbitt to rely solely on ability for making this differentiation. This was particularly the case if it resulted in permanently assigning children to particular classes or courses of study:

> ... classes should be only tentatively sectioned upon the basis of intelligence tests. The sections should not be permanent in their composition. This does not mean that the lazy but superior child should be placed in a lower section, when he fails to maintain his ranking; he needs to be kept where he is and the pressure increased. Yet the highly nervous child or the sickly pupil of superior mentality may be benefited by a change to what we call a lower section. And particularly may the child of great industry and ambition, who according to the intelligence ratings belongs in the next lower section, be advanced to a higher section when the teacher feels that he can successfully carry the work because of his industry. The door should not be shut in the face of ambitious youths, just because there is a slight question as to their mental level. As I have said, success is far too complexly conditioned to be measured by a formula which involves mentality only.[86]

Bobbitt and Charters's fundamental message to educators, then, was that the curriculum had to directed to more utilitarian or functional ends and that these ends had to be related to the occupational and social destiny as well as the ability of American youth. Despite, however, their obvious dissatisfaction with the idea of mental training, neither Bobbitt nor Charters completely rejected the view held by mental disciplinarians that the curriculum should be organized around the widely accepted disciplines of knowledge. Bobbitt, for the most part, in his writings talked about a curriculum composed of such subjects as English, history, mathematics and the foreign languages. His concern was not so much with what was taught but with ensuring that whatever content was part of the curriculum was derived from the life activities of the members of society. The curriculum could be composed of traditional disciplines so long as the content within these subjects reflected the work and citizenship demands placed on the adult members of American society.[87]

Bobbitt's 1914 survey of the schools of San Antonio, Texas is illustrative of this view. Although he accepted the existing organization of the curriculum around such traditional disciplines as English, geography, and mathematics, he criticized San Antonio school officials for their failure to analyze the day-to-day activities of the city's population in selecting curriculum content. He chided the school administration, for example, for including words on the sixth grade spelling list, such as antithesis, javelin, and myriad, that were 'just as unintelligible to the sixth grade pupils as ... to adults in general'. He was particularly critical of the fact that in selecting these words, no one in the schools bothered to survey the business leaders of the city about the actual frequency of their use in their correspondence.[88] Similarly, he criticized the mathematics curriculum in San Antonio for its emphasis on algebra and geometry instead of on the application of arithmetic to 'the practical civic, social, industrial, recreational and other matters which are greatly needed by this rising generation of young people ...'.[89]

Bobbitt did not, however, oppose efforts to integrate the curriculum around the social problems of youth, a practice that would become the hallmark of curriculum reform in the 1930s and thereafter. He favored, for example, the introduction of a civics course, a curriculum reform first advocated by the Social Studies Committee of the Commission on the Reorganization of Secondary Education in 1916 as a way of integrating social science disciplines around the problems of citizenship.[90]

Charters, too, believed that the curriculum be derived from objectives which, in turn, were to be drawn from the life activities of the adult members of society. Once these objectives were stated, he argued, 'the material which ordinarily is classified under the great divisions of subjects begins to emerge and can be gathered together without serious difficulty'.[91]

It was also possible, Charters pointed out, to alter the existing arrangement of the school program and organize the curriculum around the situations that youth might face in the larger society outside the school or, as he put it, around 'life projects'.[92] The use of projects, he pointed out, would fundamentally alter the school curriculum. 'Arithmetic, geography and spelling would disappear and in their place we would have such projects as personal cleanliness, the decoration of the home, the writing of letters, the growing of flowers, city sanitation . . .'[93]

Charters, it seems, did not necessarily want such a complete transformation of the school curriculum. Instead, it appears that the kind of projects he had in mind would continue to provide instruction in those traditional disciplines that had made up the course of study, albeit it would be instruction that was indirect and incidental:

> To discover what shall be included in the subject of grammar we begin, let us say, with the life project of correct speech, and derive the broken rules and the necessary grammar . . . To determine what tool processes to teach in manual arts we analyze home repairs, or some other activities, and derive the processes. Keeping fit leads to hygiene. From hygiene we go to physiology, and from that we derive biology to understand the physiological facts.[94]

If curriculum workers were to organize the school program around projects, it was important, Charters argued, that they be certain to include not only the treatment of adult life activities but instruction in significant elements of the traditional school subjects.[95] Charters's advocacy of the use of projects was an attempt similar to Bobbitt's to integrate subject matter content and certain life problems and activities.

VII

For Bobbitt and Charters, America's urban industrial future seemed one of promise, the gradual and evolutionary advance to what we might think of as the nation's next stage in the quest for progress. The key to that progress lay for both in the willingness of the various factions that industrial capitalism had spawned to put aside their antagonism and work together harmoniously. They saw in the principles of scientific management the path to attaining this cooperation and coordination among all Americans. As Bobbitt pointed out in advocating the applicability of these principles throughout society:

> Management, direction, and supervision are functions of all cooperative labor. While men act singly, direction can find no place; but when men cooperate for common ends, one must direct the diverse labors of the group in order to secure unity and effectiveness. The tasks of direction arose with the rise of human organization. Directive labors differ naturally from group to group in their specific details; but whether the organization be for commerce or for manufacture, philanthropy or education, transportation or government, it is coming to appear that the fundamental tasks of management, direction, and supervision are always about the same.[96]

The task of social control, Bobbitt argued, was to bring about this cooperation by instilling a sense of 'large-group consciousness' in the members of society. It was necessary, he thought, that all Americans, despite their narrow, specialized roles show a certain common understanding about their various functions in the life of the nation and about the mutual obligations these functions entailed. As he put it, 'each has rights; and each has duties'.[97]

Bobbitt believed that the schools, particularly the curriculum, would play a large role in the realization of social control. For Frederick Taylor, we should remember, 'scientific time studies' provided workers with the particular knowledge and skill they needed to coordinate production. Similarly, Bobbitt believed that job analysis would yield a school curriculum that would provide all youth with the specialized knowledge appropriate for both their abilities and their social position.

His emphasis on specialized knowledge as the basis of social control seems at least at first glance quite similar to the kind of social regulation that Thorndike advocated when he described individuals as being 'half educated'. Yet, Bobbitt never carried the idea of specialization as far as Thorndike or even Finney to embrace a hierarchical society of leaders and followers. Rather, he took a position not dissimilar to that of Cooley and Mead in which individuals had a role to play in defining the nature of the control to which they would be subject.

We can see Bobbitt's concern for the participation of individuals in the affairs of society when we examine his criticism of Taylor's brand of scientific management. Taylor, we have already noted, believed that efficient management could not exist if workers were allowed to make their own decisions about either the procedures they followed or the rate of speed at which they worked. These decisions had to be standardized throughout the plant, which required that they be made for all workers involved in a particular task by certain experts in a centralized planning department.[98] Workers, it seems for Taylor, did not need to know anything beyond the requirements of performing their narrow industrial task. They did not need to know anything about the nature of the product they were producing or about the work of others and their relationship to it.

Bobbitt faulted this approach to organization on the grounds that it offered workers no opportunity to use their own insights and skills in enhancing production. If workers did not understand the instructions they received from the planning department or if the planning department erred in the instructions they gave, the entire production process would come to a halt. 'It is hard to see', he warned, 'how this could do otherwise than mechanize the worker, destroy all powers of thought and initiative, and in the end undermine in large degree his working efficiency'.[99]

Taylor's ideas on the role of workers, Bobbitt asserted, was based on a 'feudal theory' of social organization that was out of place in a democratic society. If individuals were to be truly efficient as both workers and citizens, they needed both specialized knowledge about their particular social duties as well as broad knowledge of the overall effort of the total group to which they belonged. It was this latter knowledge that would enable them to arrive at that common understanding which Bobbitt and other efficiency oriented thinkers thought necessary for harmonious social living and united effort:

> And as workers are changed from industrial serfs to freemen with minds and rights to think and with responsibility resting upon them for thought and suggestions, they are filled with a new spirit. Recognized as men, they become men; act like men; and the curve of their operative efficiency mounts rapidly upward.[100]

In talking about social control, Charters sought the middle ground, much in the same way as his advocacy of job analysis placed him, at least as he saw it, mid-way between the so-called educators of the 'right wing' and 'left wing'. The aim of education, he wrote in 1923 in his most famous book, *Curriculum Construction*, was to prepare youth to accept the 'ideals that society thinks are valuable'. Only five pages later, however, he noted that in a democratic society there was room for a diversity of opinion.[101] Writing five years later in *The Teaching of*

Ideals, which provided the most explicit statement of his social views, he expressed a position on the role of individuals in society that was quite similar to that of Mead:

> Everyone is both player and judge. In part we follow the decisions of leaders ≏ the church, the Bible, the words of elder statesman ≏ and in part we make our own decisions, as should always be the cae in a democracy.[102]

Charters did not write extensively on the social and political issues of his day, and it is thus difficult to determine how he would resolve the problems facing urban industrial America. Late in his career, however, he commented briefly on the educational problems facing American Indian children, thus giving us a glimpse of his views on the problem of cultural diversity. In 1945 Ralph Tyler, Charters's former colleague at Ohio State, then at the Univeristy of Chicago, wrote Charters concerning the soon to be released report of a Congressional committee investigating the schooling of American Indian children. The Committee, he reported to Charters, was about to recommend a number of proposals to make the Indian child, as he put it, a 'better American' rather than a 'better Indian', including support for the continued expansion of boarding schools outside the reservation and provision for teaching Indian children English in order to make their native languages 'secondary' in importance to them. Tyler thought that these recommendations were 'contrary to the findings of educational research' and urged Charters to voice his own concerns to the Committee.[103] A month later Charters wrote to Tyler to tell him that he would be happy to write to the Committee to tell them that their recommendations were 'all wet'.[104] For Charters, unlike Finney, social control did not require the obliteration of diverse cultures within American society.

The key to social control for Charters was to develop within individuals a 'unified' personality or a 'single integrating principle of conduct'.[105] To achieve this goal, he argued for a school curriculum directed to the teaching of ideals, his term I noted earlier for such desired human traits as honesty, loyalty, and courage, to name but a few.[106] Individuals would be brought under social control, he pointed out, in so far as they acquired the ideals necessary for guiding their conduct. Job analysis, Charters believed, would allow educators to identify appropriate ideals and to connect them to the-day-to-day life activities through which they expressed themselves in conduct.

Although social control for Charters rested on the acquisition of certain ideals, he was in most of his writings and speeches remarkably silent about the particular ideals he had in mind. In one instant, however, he did suggest the ideals he thought appropriate for American youth. In his 1945 graduation address at Fisk University which we mentioned earlier in this chapter, Charters offered his formula of the four ingredients for successful living: '1) establish aims, 2) learn, 3) work, and 4) cherish integrity'.[107] What Charters seemed to be telling these young Black Americans, and by implication all American youth, was that success in twentieth-century America was at bottom a simple matter of thoughtful planning. If they would only approach their lives as he approached the task of curriculum making with a systematic and deliberate plan, there was little that could stand in their way. Most important, it seems, was the second element in his prescription, learning:

> Education is the safeguard of democracy. As education in-
> creases, intelligence grows and men are prepared for new
> problems as they arise. The surest way for a people to prepare for
> the future is to passionately nurture the ideal of an educated
> people. Opportunities are sometimes closed because those who
> control the opportunities maintain that the people are not ready.
> If the people are trained, opportunity more freely opens its
> doors. A trained people are a secure people.[108]

Despite whatever faults existed in modern American society, Charters believed that education would cure them. Addressing the particular conditions of Black Americans in his speech, he pointed to the fact that unlike the past, the educational opportunities that were created as part of the nation's war effort were open to 'all races and creeds'. He maintained that the facilities for training minority groups established by the Federal government during the war and even earlier during the Depression were 'as good as those for whites'. The only difficulty, he believed, that remained for minorities was that of securing employment. 'But', he noted, 'it is improving'.[109] Charters's message, then, to these Fisk graduates, and no doubt to all American youth, was that the growth of industrialization had brought with it the expansion of both democracy and opportunity.

Charters's vision of industrial America was clearly an untroubled one. Although it was a vision that was overly optimistic and uncritical, it was one that seemed to match the man. As Ralph Tyler commented in a 1940 letter to Charters congratulating him on his 65th birthday:

> You have a most remarkable mixture of kindness, clear vision,
> common sense, and tranquillity. The result is that we can all turn
> to you for advice and help with certainty that it will be taken

into consideration. When problems arise, I find myself always trying to analyze them as I have seen you analyze such problems and to apply the kind of common sense generalizations which you make.[110]

It was certainly fitting for a figure who himself was viewed as being unruffled in the face of problems to take the measured view of urbanization and industrialization that he did. It was equally fitting that an individual lauded for his own kindness would take the generous view that he did of the nation's future.

For neither Bobbitt nor Charters did the changes that accompanied the nation's transformation to an urban, industrial society amount to all that much. What occurred in the way of change was, they thought, modest in nature and benign in effect. At bottom, the building of a sense of community in American society was, they believed, simply a matter of instilling the population with the appropriate knowledge and skills required for their specialized work and common understanding. Adopting the ideas of the scientific management movement, they set out to build a functionally oriented school curriculum dedicated to this task.

VIII

In this chapter, we set out to show how the idea of social control found its way into the writings of those American educators who during the decade following World War I established curriculum as a professional field of work and study. The investigation led us to certain key figures in curriculum work who identified themselves with the doctrine of social efficiency, namely Ross L. Finney, Franklin Bobbitt and Werrett Wallace Charters.

Although Finney shared Bobbitt and Charters's commitment to efficiency ideals, he took a fundamentally different view than either of them about the task of building a sense of community in twentieth-century American society. Like Edward Ross, Finney was unable to reconcile the need for liberal-democratic values with the reality of modern society and sought to use the curriculum to resist the inroads that both urbanization and industrialization were making in the life of the nation. As it turned out, Finney's views represented a departure from the mainstream of efficiency minded curriculum thinking. More representative of the movement were Bobbitt and Charters who held a far more sanguine view of urban, industrial America.

For Bobbitt and Charters, neither the rise of cities nor the emergence of the corporation represented fundamental breaks with America's past. The social disruptions that both might bring were, they believed, minimal and could with little difficulty be accommodated to the need for social harmony and solidarity. Adopting the ideas of scientific management to the work of selecting and organizing the curriculum, they sought to construct a functionally oriented school program derived from the day-to-day work and citizenship activities of the adult members of society. Such a curriculum, they argued, could instill the nation's youth with the needed cooperative impulse that would avoid the disruptions which the antagonism between labor and capital seemed to forebode. The advent of both urbanization and industrialization offered, they believed, the promise of increased economic opportunity and the expansion of political democracy. Taking a position similar to Mead's, Bobbitt and Charter argued that the schools could socialize American youth for their roles in the nation's industrial work force while at the same time providing them with the knowledge they needed to actively participate in and influence the economic and political destiny of the nation. Although the idea of social control was at the heart of their thinking about the curriculum, it was a view of control that in contrast to the ideas of Ross, Thorndike, and Finney was remarkably benign.

From the outset, then, those educators, such as Bobbitt and Charters whose views, we argued, dominated the field of curriculum during its formative period, were preoccupied with the question of how the school and its course of study could socially control the twin forces of urbanization and industrialization. Looking to the corporation as their model of how American society should be organized, they found their solution to the problem of social control in the principles of scientific management. The central task of the curriculum for both Bobbitt and Charters was to prepare future generations of selfless and cooperative individuals who possessed the knowledge and skills necessary for the specialized work roles of a corporate economy. In effect, they linked the fate of American schools to the advance of industrial capitalism. The measure of a good education for them was to be found ultimately in the service it provided to the growth of the nation's industrial economy, an expansion they saw as being synonymous with the extension of democracy itself.

In characterizing Taylor's vision of industrial organization as 'feudalistic', Bobbitt did levy some criticism at industrial capitalism. Yet, neither he nor Charters recognized as did Mead the role that the school could play in social betterment. As Bobbitt noted in his supplementary statement in the 1926 *Yearbook of the National Society for the Study of Education*, 'the school is not an agency of social reform'. Its ability to improve society was at best indirect and was to be found in its efficiency in adjusting youth to the prevailing social and economic practices of the moment.[111] Where Mead saw the task of the school as that of mitigating the worst effects of industrial capitalism, thereby fitting the economic system to the needs of individuals in a democratic society, Bobbitt and Charters saw the task of the school as simply fitting the members of society to the demands of the economic system. Although they agreed with Mead that citizens in a democratic society needed to be actively involved in the affairs of the nation, neither of them, unlike Mead, seemed to believe that such participation required any significant changes in the organization of an industrial economy.

Bobbitt and Charters's resolution of the problem of community was, in the end, incomplete. Using the principles of scientific management, they recommended practices for curriculum selection and organization that addressed one of the central problems posed by urbanization and industrialization, discord. Their brand of social harmony, modeled after the work relations of the modern corporation, did little, however, to promote liberal democratic values. Although both of these formative theorists of the curriculum field recognized the need for an active citizenry, they did little to ensure the ability of that citizenry to change existing political and economic arrangements. Bobbitt and Charters were too quick, it seems, to equate democracy with industrial capitalism.

Bobbitt and Charters were not the only early curriculum workers who sought to use the school program to resolve the problem of community. Another individual, Hollis Caswell, undertook this same task in the period after 1930. Abandoning the concept of efficiency, Caswell was able to put forth recommendations for the selection and organization of the curriculum that took into account both the need for social harmony and for real citizen participation in the management of American political and economic life. It is Caswell's effort to use the school curriculum to resolve the problem of community that will constitute the subject of our next chapter.

Notes

1 EDWARD A. ROSS, *The Principles of Sociology*, New York, The Century Company, 1920, pp. 409–10.
2 Ibid., p. 409.
3 CHARLES DE GARMO, 'Some aspects of moral education', *The Third Yearbook of*

the *National Herbart Society for the Scientific Study of Teaching-1897*, edited by CHARLES A. MCMURRAY, The National Herbart Society Yearbooks 1–5, 1895–1899, New York, Arno Press, 1969, pp. 47–8.

4 *Ibid.* , pp. 39–40 and 46.

5 I.W. HOWERTH, 'The social aim of education', *The Fifth Yearbook of the National Herbart Society for the Scientific Study of Teaching-1899*, edited by CHARLES A. MCMURRAY, The National Herbart Society Yearbooks 1–5, 1895–1899, *op. cit.*, pp. 72 and 94.

6 *Ibid.*, p. 76.

7 HAROLD B. DUNKEL, *Herbart and Herbartianism: An Educational Ghost Story*, Chicago, University of Chicago Press, 1970, pp. 277–80.

8 EDWARD A. KRUG, *The Shaping of the American High School, 1880–1920*, Madison University of Wisconsin Press, 1969, pp. 99–108; MARY LOUISE SEGUEL, *The Curriculum Field: Its Formative Years*, New York, Teachers College Press, 1966, pp. 31–6.

9 WALTER H. DROST, 'That immortal day in Cleveland ≏ the report of the committee of fifteen', *Educational Theory*, 17, April, 1967, p. 178.

10 WILLIAM CHANDLER BAGLEY, *The Educative Process*, New York, Macmillan, 1905, p. 59.

11 *Ibid.*, pp. 58–61; ERWIN V. JOHANNINGMEIER, 'William Chandler Bagley's views on the relationship between psychology and education', *History of Education Quarterly*, 9, Spring, 1969, 7.

12 *The Educative Process, ibid.*, pp. 61–4.

13 SAMUEL P. HAYS, *The Response to Industrialism, 1885–1914*, Chicago, University of Chicago Press, 1957, chapter 1; SAMUEL P. HAYS, 'The new organizational society', in *Building the Organizational Society*, edited by JERRY ISRAEL, New York, The Free Press, 1972, pp. 1–15.

14 SAMUEL HABER, *Efficiency and Uplift: Scientific Management In the Progressive Era. 1890–1920*, Chicago, University of Chicago Press, 1964, pp. ix–x.

15 HERBERT CROLY, *The Promise of American Life*, New York, Macmillan, 1909, pp. 358–9; WALTER E. WEYL, *The New Democracy*, rev. edn., New York, Macmillan, 1914, Chapter 10.

16 FREDERICK W. TAYLOR, 'Shop management' in *Scientific Management*, New York, Harper and Brothers, 1947, pp. 22, 23 and 30; FREDERICK W. TAYLOR, 'The principles of scientific management' in *ibid*, p. 10.

17 'Shop management', *ibid.*, pp. 30–1.

18 'Principles of scientific management', *op. cit.*, p. 120.

19 'Shop management', *op. cit.*, pp. 24–5.

20 *Ibid.*, pp. 28–9, 46–8 and 148–75.

21 *Ibid.*, pp. 65–6 and 98–102.

22 *Ibid.*, pp. 25–6.

23 *Ibid.*, p. 22.

24 'Taylor's testimony before the House Special Committee' in *Scientific Management, op. cit.*, p. 280.

25 'Principles of scientific management', *op. cit.*, p. 10.

26 'Shop management', *op. cit.*, pp. 131–2.

27 ROBERT H. WIEBE, *The Search for Order, 1877–1920*, New York, Hill and Wang, 1967, pp. 146–7; THOMAS BENDER, *Community and Social Change in America*, Baltimore, The Johns Hopkins University Press, 1978, pp. 4–6.

28 HERBERT M. KLIEBARD, 'Education at the turn of the century: Crucible for curriculum change', *Educational Researcher*, 11, January, 1982, pp. 16–24.

29 KRUG, *op. cit.*, pp. 278–83; BAGLEY, *op. cit.*, pp. 60–5, chapter 13; FRANKLIN BOBBITT, *The Curriculum*, Boston, Houghton Mifflin, 1918, chapter 1; W.W. CHARTERS, *Curriculum Construction*, New York. 1923, chapter 1; Ross L. FINNEY, *A Sociological Philosophy of Education*, New York, Macmillan, 1928, chapter 9.

30 The University of Minnesota, *The Senate Minutes, 1934–1935*, Vol. 1, Minneapolis, University of Minnesota, 1934, p. 19; ROBERT BECK, *Beyond Pedagogy: A History of the University of Minnesota College of Education*, St. Paul, North Central Publishing Company, 1980, pp. 65–6.

31 Ross L. FINNEY, *Causes and Cures for the Social Unrest: An Appeal to the Middle Class*, New York, Macmillan, 1922, chapter 4–5 and 7–8.

32 *Ibid.*, p. 43.

33 Ross L. FINNEY, *A Sociological Philosophy of Education*, New York, Macmillan, 1928, p. 375.

34 *Ibid.*, p. 417.

35 *Ibid.*, pp. 54–5; Ross L. FINNEY, 'The ultimate aim of education', *Educational Review*, 6, November, 1918, pp. 314–6.

36 *Causes and Cures for the Social Unrest op. cit.*, p. 180.

37 *A Sociological Philosophy of Education, op. cit.*, pp. 428–9; Ross L. FINNEY and LESLIE D. ZELENY, *An Introduction to Educational Sociology*, Boston, D.C. Heath, 1934, p. 34.

38 Ross L. FINNEY, 'The unconscious social mind', *Journal of Applied Sociology*, 10, March/April, 1926, pp. 357–67.

39 *A Sociological Philosophy of Education, op. cit.*, p. 58.

40 *Ibid.*, p. 60.

41 *Ibid.*, pp. 70–1 and 442–52; Ross L. FINNEY, 'Prerequisite to progress', *Teachers College Record*, 20, May, 1919, p. 235.

42 *A Sociological Philosophy of Education, op. cit.*, p. 471.

43 *Ibid.*

44 Ross L. FINNEY, 'Sociological principles fundamental to pedagogical method', *Educational Review*, 55, February, 1918, pp. 100 and 109.

45 *A Sociological Philosophy of Education, op. cit.*, p. 285.

46 Ross L. FINNEY, 'The sociological principle determining the elementary curriculum', *School and Society*, 7, 23 March, 1918, pp. 338 and 344; Ross L. FINNEY, 'Education and the reconstruction', *School and Society*, 8, 6 July, 1918, p. 15; Ross L. FINNEY, 'The educator as statesman', *Journal of the National Education Associatioin*, 18, November, 1929, p. 243.

47 *A Sociological Philosophy of Education, op. cit.*, chapters 9, 12 and 15.

48 *Ibid.*, pp. 386 and 388.

49 *Ibid.*, p. 395.

50 *Ibid.*, pp. 340–5 and 351–5.

51 *Ibid.*, pp. 397–8.

52 *The Curriculum, op. cit.*, p. 76.

53 JOHN FOHLES, *Biographical Dictionary of American Educators*, I, 3 vols., Westport, Greenwod Press, 1978, pp. 143–4.

54 *The Curriculum, op. cit.*, p. 77.

55 W.W. CHARTERS, 'Our education for a changing civilizatioin', *The W.W. Charters*

Papers, Ohio State University Library, Folder L1.

56 FOHLES, *op. cit.*, pp. 259–60.

57 W.W. CHARTERS, 'Fisk commencement speech, 17 May, 1945', *The Charters Papers, op. cit.*, Folder L1, p. 2.

58 *The Curriculum, op. cit.*, p. iii.

59 *Ibid.*, pp. 76, 86 and 88.

60 W.W. CHARTERS, 'The reorganization of women's education', *Educational Review*, 62, October, 1921, pp. 224–5.

61 Charters to Boyd H. Bode, 8 May, 1939, *The Charters Papers*, Folder YB102, *op. cit.*; 'Untitled, undated notes', *The Charters Papers*, Folder L1, *op. cit.*

62 *The Curriculum, op. cit.*, pp. 158–9.

63 W.W. CHARTERS, *The Teaching of Ideals*, New York, Macmillan, pp. 16–19.

64 W.W. CHARTERS, 'Success, personality, and intelligence', *Journal of Education Research*, 11, March, 1925, p. 173.

65 *The Curriculum, op. cit.*, pp. 92–5; FRANKLIN BOBBITT, *How to Make a Curriculum*, Boston, Houghton Mifflin, 1924, p. 105.

66 For a discussion of the corporation as a community, see MICHAEL NOVAK, *The Spirit of Democratic Capitalism*, New York, Simon and Schuster, 1982, chapter VI.

67 *The Curriculum, op. cit.*, pp. 123–9; FRANKLIN BOBBITT, 'Some general principles of management applied to the problems of city school systems', *The Supervision of City Schools, The Twelfth Yearbook of the National Society for the Study of Education*, Part I, Chicago, University of Chicago Press, 1913, p. 7.

68 *The Curriculum, ibid.*, p. 131.

69 *Ibid.*, chapters 11–12.

70 *Ibid.*, chapter 6; CHARTERS, *Curriculum Construction, op. cit.*, chapters 1–2.

71 *How to Make a Curriculum, op. cit.*, pp. 8–11 and 32–5; *Curriculum Construction, ibid.*, chapter 4.

72 *The Curriculum, op. cit.* p. 42.

73 FRANKLIN BOBBITT, *Curriculum Making in Los Angeles*, Chicago, University of Chicago Press, 1922; W.W. CHARTERS and ISADORE B. WHITLEY, *Analysis of Secretarial Duties and Traits*, Baltimore, William and Wilkins Company, 1924.

74 *The Curriculum, op. cit.*, p. 42; *Curriculum Construction, op. cit.*, p. 106.

75 *Curriculum Construction, ibid.*, p. 30; W.W. CHARTERS, 'The Los Angeles high school curriculum', *School Review*, 31, February, 1923, pp. 95–103.

76 Department of Education, University of Chicago to Charters, 9 November 1922, *The Charters Papers, op. cit.*, Folder MD2.

77 W.W. CHARTERS, 'The use of activity analysis in curriculum construction', *The Charters Papers, op. cit.*, Folder L5, pp. 2–4.

78 *Ibid.*, p. 1.

79 W.W. CHARTERS, 'New models for the 40s,' *The Charters Papers, ibid.*, Folder L1.

80 'Some general principles of management applied to the problems of city-school systems,' *op. cit.*, pp. 26–7, 35–6, 39 and 41–42.

81 *How to Make Curriculum, op. cit.*, pp. 8–9; *Curriculum Making in Los Angeles, op. cit.*, p. 7.

82 *How to Make a Curriculum, ibid.*, pp. 41–2 and 71–2.

83 *Ibid.*, pp. 61–2.

84 *Ibid.*, p. 67.

85 *Curriculum Construction, op. cit.*, pp. 111–2 and 152–4.

86 'Success, personality, and intelligence,' *op. cit.*, pp. 174–5.

87 *How to Make a Curriculum, op. cit.*, pp. 69–70, chapters 6–17.

88 FRANKLIN BOBBITT, *The San Antonio Public School System: A Survey*, San Antonio, School Board, 1915, p. 108.

89 *Ibid.*, p. 152.

90 *How to Make a Curriculum, op. cit.*, pp. 120–1; Commission on the Reorganization of Secondary Education, *The Social Studies in Secondary Education*, Bulletin No. 28, Washington, D.C., U.S. Government Printing Office, 1916, pp. 52–6.

91 *Curriculum Construction , op. cit.*, pp. 103–4 and 151.

92 *Ibid.*, pp. 137–9.

93 *Ibid.*, p. 142.

94 *Ibid.*

95 *Ibid.*, p. 140.

96 'Some general principles of management applied to the problems of city-school systems', *op. cit.*, p. 7.

97 *The Curriculum, op. cit.*, pp. 91 and 96.

98 'Shop Management', *op. cit.*, pp. 65–6.

99 'Some general principles of management applied to the problems of city-school systems', *op. cit.*, pp. 91–2.

100 *The Curriculum, op. cit.*, p. 79.

101 *Curriculum Construction, op. cit.*, pp. 27 and 32.

102 W.W. CHARTERS, *The Teaching of Ideals, op. cit.* pp. 29–30.

103 Tyler to Charters, 29 March, 1945, *The Charters Papers*, Folder YD53, *op. cit.,*

104 Charters to Tyler, 4 May, 1945, *ibid.*

105 *The Teaching of Ideals, op. cit.*, pp. 13, 25–6 and 39.

106 *Ibid.*, p. 33; CHARTERS, *Curriculum Construction, op. cit.*, p. 74.

107 'Fisk commencement speech', *The Charters Papers, op. cit.*, p. 3.

108 *Ibid.*, p. 9.

109 *Ibid.*, p. 10.

110 Tyler to Charters 23 October, 1940, *The Charters Papers, op. cit.*, Folder YD53.

111 FRANKLIN BOBBITT, 'The Orientation of the curriculum-maker', *The Foundations of Curriculum-Making, The Twenty-Sixth Yearbook of the National Society for the Study of Education*, Part II, edited by GUY MONTROSE WHIPPLE, Bloomington, Public School Publishing Company, 1926, p. 54.

5   Building a Cooperative Community: Social Control and Curriculum Thought, 1930–1955

I

At the core of both Bobbitt and Charters's interest in the idea of social control, we saw in our last chapter, was the place of the individual in an emerging industrial economy. Bobbitt was particularly worried, I noted, lest the division of labor and the standardization of work that seemed to be required under corporate capitalism would limit the role that individual intellect and initiative could play in industrial production. Writing in 1941, the year he retired from the University of Chicago, he addressed this issue one last time. Commenting on the difference between work that ennobled individuals and that which degraded them, he stated:

> If the work forces him to be an automaton, as mindless as a machine, the lack of mental functioning lets his mental powers wither away and he is in some degree dehumanized. If the work calls for an excessive proportion of his time or energy, then he is shut out from the social, aesthetic, and intellectual activities necessary for maintaining flexibility and virility of powers. If he is hardened and consumed on the physical level, then his more human powers must atrophy. If his work is so specialized as to exercise but a narrow range of mental powers, the rest of them are left to die away ... If the work is such as to deprive one of genuine responsibility for understanding, thought, planning, self direction, and effort, then, like a child, the worker remains a dependent in spirit and is thwarted from becoming or remaining an independent, resourceful, and responsible adult.[1]

In the years around World War I when Bobbitt first raised this concern, he found his solution in the principles of scientific management. Under the direction of these principles, with perhaps some slight modification, Bobbitt argued, production would be carried out not only more efficiently and harmoniously, but under conditions that would enhance both the profits of management and the status of labor. Bobbitt believed that when these same principles were used to design the curriculum, the result would be a school program that would infuse throughout the population a cooperative spirit and the elevated status it brought.

At the end of his career, Bobbitt maintained his commitment to the twin goals of efficiency and cooperation. He described American society as a 'great cooperative enterprise.'[2] Yet, his faith in scientific management seemed to wane. Where Bobbitt once spoke of using the schools to fit individuals to the occupational demands of an industrial economy, he now spoke, as did Mead, of the need for the schools to help to mitigate the worst apsects of industrialization.[3] Where he once described the task of curriculum work as that of 'making' a standardized course of study for all American youth, he now described the task as that of 'discovering' the individual curriculum that would enable each person to live the life he or she desired.[4]

Bobbitt was not the only erstwhile proponent of the so-called scientific movement in curriculum making who seemed during the 1930s and early 1940s to abandon its principles. In 1924 Charles Peters, of Ohio Wesleyan University, authored an educational sociology text in which he claimed that 'the same viewpoint dominates this book as that which controls in the books of Charters and Bobbitt',[5] In 1942 in his *Curriculum of Democratic Education,* Peters, too, seemed to abandon his earlier viewpoint. Curriculum making could not, he argued, simply rely on uniform objectives derived from an analysis of adult life. Rather, it required objectives 'which pupils want to attain because they feel them to be worthwhile . . .'.[6]

Bobbitt's criticism of the scientific curriculum-making movement he had helped establish was not directed at its goal of reorganizing the curriculum along more functional lines. In a letter he wrote to Ralph Tyler in 1946, Bobbitt complained that American schools were still paying too much attention to the goal of 'learning ≃ in the usual sense.' If education was to advance, he went on to say, it would have to aim at 'development of the power to function along needful lines.' What seemed now to be lacking in the view of curriculum selection and organization he once advocated was any emphasis on the changing needs of youth in a changing world. Educational work, he noted, represented a biological road for biological species'.[7]

In an article he wrote in the same year, Bobbitt criticized the lack of truly functional content in the report of the Educational Policy

Commission, *Education of All American Youth*. The Commission had recommended, he argued, a curriculum with a smattering of the content of the natural and social sciences. He thought that their recommendations may have been sufficient for the immediate needs of youth in today's society. They were, however, he pointed out, seriously deficient in providing the more sophisticated scientific knowledge that American youth would need in the future.[8]

When we compare the views expounded by Bobbitt and Peters during the 1920s with those they championed two decades later, we obtain a glimpse of how the thinking of curriculum workers changed after 1930. Gone was their desire to use the schools to simply socialize youth for existing adult work roles. Instead, they talked about how the schools could serve in the cause of social betterment. Gone too was their reliance on the principles of scientific curriculum making. They spoke rather of a curriculum that would enable youth to follow those paths they themselves felt to be worthy. Despite these differences, however, curriculum workers after 1930 remained as strongly committed as did their intellectual forebearers to using the school to reconcile life in an urban, industrial society with liberal democratic ideals. Likewise, they continued to believe as strongly as their predecessors that the curriculum needed to be reorganized along more functional lines. Of those educators who identified themselves professionally with the field of curriculum after 1930, none was more insistent about using the school program to resolve the problems of urbanization and industrialization than was Hollis L. Caswell. It is his work that will occupy our attention in the remainder of this chapter.

II

Caswell was born in 1901 in Woodruff, Kansas, a small town in the north central part of the state near the Nebraska border. Before he began school, the Caswell family relocated to McDonald in Northwest Kansas, where poor farming led his father to become a rural mail carrier and eventually postmaster. Although he was born at the beginning of the twentieth century, the Kansas of Caswell's youth was not terribly different from the rural America in which the other individuals we have already considered in this essay were raised.

Bypassed by the major East-West railroads of the region, the Burlington which ran on the North through Nebraska and the Rock Island which ran on the South through Kansas, life in McDonald existed in isolation from the economic and social transformation that characterized turn-of-the-century America. While most of America during this period faced the transformation from an agrarian to an industrialized economy, McDonald was undergoing the shift from an economy dominated by cattle ranching to one based on wheat farming.

Caswell remained in McDonald through his second year in high school. After finishing high school and completing two years of college at the Kansas State College at Fort Hays, he transferred to the University of Nebraska at Lincoln where he graduated in 1922 with a bachelor's degree in English. During the next four years Caswell served as a high school principal in Aburn, Nebraska and then as superintendent of schools in Syracuse, Nebraska.

Following the similar route of other intellectuals who were concerned with the issues of social control and community, Caswell soon left rural America for the city. Choosing Columbia's Teachers College for his graduate work, he completed his master's and doctorate in educational administration under the direction of George Strayer, one of the founding theorists of the field of educational administration and promoter of the school survey movement. In 1929, Caswell joined the faculty of George Peabody College in Nashville, where he remained for eight years. In 1937, be returned to Teachers College, where he remained until his retirement in 1962. During his years at Teachers College, he served successively as the Chairman of the Department of Curriculum and Teaching, the first such academic department in an American school of education, Associate Dean, Dean, and eventually as President.[9]

The backdrop for Caswell's interest in the curriculum was, as it was for Bobbitt and Charters, America's transition from a rural, agrarian to an urban, industrial society. Writing in 1935 with his colleague from Peabody, Doak Campbell, he argued that any attempt to define an adequate school program had to take into account the social and economic changes that were then taking place:

> An earlier generation lived in an age of scarcity; we live in an age of plenty. They depended upon the use of power from human beings and from animals, we derive our power from the burning of coal and oil and from the harnessing of great rivers. They were compelled to work long hours in order to provide food, clothing, and shelter; we live in a period in which the hours of labor must be restricted in order to provide employment for all our people. They lived in communities in which it was possible to discuss the issues of local government in town meetings. ....
> We live in communities so large and complex that we find it

difficult to act intelligently or effectively in the development of local government.[10]

As a consequence of these changes, Caswell and Campbell noted, America had become an interdependent society. The problems of the day, unemployment, excessive consumerism, and increased crime, to name but a few, were far too complex to be resolved by individuals acting alone or even with the help of their families and local communities. These were problems that were national in scope and could only be addressed through the cooperative efforts of all Americans acting together. It was the task of the schools, they believed, to ensure that all American youth would learn to work together harmoniously for their mutual advantage.[11]

Reflecting on the historical development of the curriculum field in a 1978 speech to the Society of Professors of Curriculum, Caswell offered a number of reasons why after 1930 he and others had abandoned their faith in scientific curriculum-making. First, educators after 1930 were in increasing numbers attracted to the kind of philosophy I have identified with the ideas of Mead. This viewpoint, with its emphasis on the child as an active, creative organism, stood in opposition to the passive view of the child held by the advocates of scientific curriculum-making. Second, during the 1930s Thorndike's connectionism, which provided the psychological underpinnings for scientific curriculum-making, came under attack by many educators who questioned its overly individualistic bias. Third, many educators during the 1930's believed that the Depression required the schools to work actively in the cause of social reform, a view that countered the basic assumptions of scientific curriculum-making.[12]

There was, however, another, and perhaps more important, reason why Caswell and other educators of his day shunned the practices of scientific curriculum-making. During the late 1920s and early 1930s, Taylor's brand of scientific management had come under some disrepute as individuals identified with the emerging fields of industrial psychology and sociology shifted their attention from studying the organization of industrial work to investigating workers themselves.[13] Emphasizing the role that workers' motivation, particularly their sense of participation in decisions about work procedures, played in enhancing productivity, they embraced the same sort of organic view of the group and interactionist psychology that Mead had expounded. Increased productivity was not, according to one of the leading advocates of this position, Mary Parker Follett, simply a matter of adjusting labor to the new and more efficient work procedures designed by management. Rather, she argued, both labor and management had to recognize that they exerted a reciprocal influence over each other and that if productivity were to increase, each party would in part have to meet the expectations of the other.[14] According to Elton Mayo, another promoter of this new approach to industrial relations, it was this kind of cooperation between labor and management that could curb the social dislocations that had accompanied American's transition to an urban, industrialized society.[15] In a sense we might view the transition from scientific curriculum-making to the ideas expounded by Caswell as representing a similar shift of opinion as the transformation we have just seen from Taylorism to the views of Follett and Mayo.

III

Caswell's career encompassed a period in which America faced a number of major threats to the survival of its liberal democratic ethic. He assumed his position at Peabody at the beginning of the Great Depression. Twelve years later, while he was at Teachers College, America entered World War II. His career culminated during the years of the cold war from the late 1940s through the early 1960s. Throughout this period, Caswell seemed continually worried about the prospect of individuals learning to cooperate sufficiently to live in the kind of interdependent society that America had become. Writing in 1932, he warned of the threats to democracy posed by the economic disruptions of the Depression. Other nations facing such problems as unemployment, surplus production, and the shortage of funds for public improvements were abandoning democracy in favor of dictatorial forms of government. Although America remained a democratic society, Caswell believed that a similar fate awaited the nation if its population could not or would not work 'in concert' to solve its problems.[16]

During World War II, he returned again to this theme of cooperation. Americans, Caswell argued, had to do more than seek a military victory to the war. They needed to develop a vision of the kind of world they wished their victory to bring. Caswell's goal was for a world dedicated to the value of cooperation:

> This war is forcing a new conception of values, new ideas of national and world organization. We cannot fight beside the Russians and the Chinese and calmly hold a smug nationalistic ideal unless we deny in the larger interpretation the very thing for which we contend we are fighting; we cannot have our men go to the far corners of the earth without making the world a

neighborhood; we cannot increase our speed of transportation and communication by leaps and bounds and expect old days to return. If there is one thing certain, it is that military victory will plunge us into problems of scope and intensity we have not found before in peace time. Old attitudes must be eradicated. The 'white man's burden' in the Orient! Imperialistic exploitation of the resources of backward nations! Racial differentiation! All such must be modified. New insights, new understandings, new sensitivities are called for now if we are to fight a United Nation's war.[17]

In a 1954 speech Caswell delivered at Michigan State University, he talked about the current criticisms that were being made about American public education. One line of criticism, he noted, was the charge that the schools were promoting such anti-American values as socialism, internationalism and cooperation at the expense of the traditional values of nationalism and competition.[18] At the very moment when these attacks on education were being expressed, Caswell pointed out, Americans were entering a period in which they needed to '. . . develop understanding of other peoples and other cultures, of what it means to live next door to people who are markedly different from us'. He was worried, it seems, lest this accusation about the public schools would prevent them from preparing American youth for the nation's new 'world role' on a planet that was becoming increasingly interdependent.[19]

It was necessary, Caswell believed, for Americans to become more cooperative in their relationships with each other in order to counterbalance the destabilizing influence of the rapid social changes that accompanied urbanization and industrialization. The Depression, he noted, had created a widely felt sense of 'exasperation, desperation, and hatred' within the population which could release 'violent and sudden' social movements.[20] Writing in 1952, he noted a similar threat to social stability in the existing discord between 'labor and management' and 'Catholics and Protestants'.[21]

This instability could, Caswell argued, affect the nation's schools. In a 1937 article, he argued that one of the dangers that seemed to always face the schools in times of social dislocation was that they would fall under the sway of 'selfish business interests' who would use them only to promote their own 'propaganda'.[22] A good example of this threat to public education could be seen, Caswell pointed out in 1943, in the attempt to introduce content about the importance of air power into the curriculum during World War II.[23] Caswell clearly recognized the need to adjust the school program to the demands of the war. He cautioned, however, '... that certain industrial interests have much to gain by 'selling' aviation in a big way to the rank and file of the American people'.[24]

In advancing the value of cooperation, Caswell was in effect attempting to reconcile the ideals of American society with existing social and economic conditions. For him, this was primarily an educational task.[25] It was, then, to the nation's schools and its curriculum that Caswell turned in his effort to promote cooperation among the American population.

IV

Caswell, like Bobbitt and Charters, questioned whether a curriculum organized around the traditional academic disciplines and dedicated to the goal of mental training could prepare youth for their place in modern American society:

> The purpose of schooling is not to develop mastery of certain organized bodies of knowledge. Rather it is to educate the citizen for effective participation in those common undertakings and cooperations which are necessary to sustain our democratic way of life. The common school should be dedicated to educating men and women so that they can work and live together in a complex industrial age and the curriculum should be organized so as to contribute directly to effective participation in solutions of the problems of changing life. It is time to cast out once and for all false concepts of mental discipline and to recognize that study of the traditional school subjects do not result automatically in an understanding of contemporary problems or in ability to contribute to their solution.[26]

In place of the traditional academic curriculum, Caswell advocated, as did Bobbitt and Charters, a more functionally oriented program organized around the problems and concerns of youth in contemporary American society.[27]

During his eight years on the faculty of Peabody College from 1929 to 1937, Caswell had several opportunities to achieve the kind of reorganization of the curriculum he desired. During this period, he served as a consultant for statewide curriculum revision programs in Alabama, Florida, Virginia, Mississippi, and Arkansas and for similar programs involving the city schools of Louisville, Kentucky and Newark, New Jersey. Of these programs, it was in Virginia that Caswell came closest to achieving the more functional curriculum he sought.

In 1931, Sidney Hall, Superintendent of Public Instruction in Virginia and a former faculty member at Peabody, appointed Caswell as the principal consultant for the state's curriculum revision program. During the next six years, Caswell was responsible for directing a complete reorganization of Virginia's elementary and secondary curriculum which involved the participation of over three-quarters of the state's school districts and almost 10,000 teachers. In addition to the preparation of a statewide course of study, the program involved teachers throughout the state in small study groups that examined the nature of curriculum and the process of curriculum planning, developed inservice courses for teachers in curriculum planning, and established curriculum centers on state college and university campuses to provide teachers with assistance in their own work in curriculum development.[28]

In reorganizing the Virginia curriculum, Caswell popularized two concepts, scope and sequence. Scope was Caswell's term for the content included within a curriculum. To achieve a functional curriculum, Caswell chose as his scope those areas of human life in which people typically encounter problems. He located them by examining American culture, much as did the scientific curriculum makers with their job analysis procedure, and identifying certain critical elements which he called 'functional phases of social life.' His analysis yielded eleven such phases, including 'protection and conservation of life', 'production of goods and services', 'recreation', and 'integration of the individual'. It was these eleven problem areas that constituted the content of the Virginia course of study.

Sequence was Caswell's term for the time dimension of the curriculum or what is typically referred to as grade level. To determine the sequence of the Virginia course of study, Caswell identified certain aspects of American culture which he thought to be important in their own right as well as of interest to children. The scope of the Virginia program included eleven such aspects of culture, which Caswell referred to as 'centers of interest', one for each grade level from the first to the eleventh. Among them were 'home and school life' (grade one), 'community life' (grade two), 'social provision for cooperative living' (grade seven), and 'effects of a continuously planning social order upon our living' (grade eleven).[29]

Caswell depicted the Virginia curriculum in the form of a matrix which interrelated the elements of the scope with those of the sequence. Each of the 'functional phases of social life', represented on the vertical dimension of the matrix, was taught at each of the grade levels. represented on the horizontal dimension. The intersection of any element of the scope with any element of the sequence indicated exactly what was taught with respect to a particular 'functional phase' at a given grade level. Caswell referred to these very specific units of content as 'the aspects of centers of interest selected for emphasis'. In the first grade, for example, where the center of interest was 'home and school life', the content included the study of recreation, one of eleven 'functional phases of social life' contained within the curriculum. The emphasis at that grade level was the study of how children learn to enjoy themselves both at home and at school. In grade ten, recreation was also a part of the curriculum. Here, however, the emphasis involved the study of appropriate and inappropriate forms of recreation.[30]

Although Caswell's use of the concepts of scope and sequence enabled him to devise a curriculum organized around contemporary social issues, he did not ignore the traditional academic subjects. The Virginia course of study also included a description of how the curriculum could be used to teach such academic subjects as social studies, language arts, mathematics, and science as well as suggested activities to relate each of these subjects to the various 'functional phases of social life' upon which the curriculum was built.[31]

Cooperation was the center of interest in the Virginia program at the seventh grade level. A major problem of the day, according to the course of study, was the failure of most Americans to realize how the behavior of individuals and small groups affects the entire society. Americans needed to understand '. . . that the selfish demands of one group may destroy the privileges of another, and that the use one generation makes of resources conditions what will be available for future generations'. Resolving this 'maladjustment' in American society required that youth learn to live and work together cooperatively.[32] Throughout grade seven, students examined how various social institutions could enable Americans to cooperatively address the diverse problems they faced in their daily lives.[33]

When it came to defining the guiding principles of the Virginia program, Caswell placed cooperation at the forefront. Industrialization, according to one of these principles, had rendered traditional notions of individualism obsolete. It was necessary instead, Caswell argued in language reminiscent of Mead, that Americans recognize the degree to which they were dependent on each other:

A group exemplifies the democratic ideal when the individuals composing the group understand and are interested in its common purpose, and regulate their activities accordingly. The individual does not exist apart from his social relations. In fact, he is so intimately connected with his environment that he can develop only in relation to it. In reality, social cannot be opposed to individual.[34]

Caswell believed that ideals such as cooperation made their impact on society in so far as they were exhibited in the conduct of its members. Such conduct existed on a broad continuum. At one end was conduct that represented, as he put it, 'definite solutions to specific problems'. At the other end of his continuum was conduct that had wider applicability and would allow individuals to solve any problems they may encounter. Caswell was clearly troubled by the first type of conduct because it taught people in effect not to think but to respond uniformly.[35] In a democratic society, he argued, individuals '... must have command of the means of solving problems rather than of ready-made solutions'. They must, in other words, possess what he referred to as 'generalized controls of conduct', his term for such broadly useful attitudes as those of 'inquiry', 'self integrity', 'open mindedness', and 'tolerence'.[36]

Caswell's starting point for curriculum-making was, as we might expect from his functionalist orientation, the identification of objectives or, as he called them, aims. In selecting aims, he rejected what he saw as the 'mechanistic' approach of the advocates of scientific curriculum-making which resulted in long lists of very narrow and specific abilities. Instead, he favored what he referred to as an 'organismic' viewpoint in which the aims were more inclusive in nature and more broadly applicable.[37] The most appropriate source for these aims, he pointed out, were the 'generalized controls of conduct'.[38]

In developing the Virginia course of study, Caswell used many of these 'generalized controls of conduct' as aims. One such aim was the attitude of harmonious relationships. To illustrate what he meant by this aim, Caswell provided a number of examples of conduct that he thought to be harmonious in nature:

1   The inclination to engage in group activity based upon desirable interests.

2   Tendency to be friendly and approachable.

3   The disposition to engage without friction in work, play, and social intercourse with others.

4   The tendency to adapt one's self to the thought, feeling, and action of his associates.

5   The dispositioin to disagree with another's point of view without personal antagonism.[39]

The purpose of the Virginia course of study in part, then, was to socially control the conduct of the youth of the state so that they would behave more cooperatively. This would be achieved in so far as students acquired from their study the kinds of behavior noted above.

Caswell saw a fundamental difference between his own approach to curriculum development and that of the scientific curriculum-makers. By using very narrow and definite objectives, the scientific curriculum-makers were, he argued, organizing the curriculum around certain specific stimuli that were designed to elicit certain predetermined and uniform behavior in students. Such an approach, he commented, viewed students as passive organisms under the control of the teacher.[40] His approach, on the other hand, viewed students as active creatures whose own actions in the form of interests and goals were the eliciting factors in learning:

> ... this concept of stimuli relatively external to the learner, applied on schedule by the teacher, is not acceptable. Rather, learner and environment are considered one. The learner in the situation becomes the focal point of consideration and his experience the means of education. Educational possibilities are present as felt wants or goals arise from the individual. Activities take on meaning as they are thrown into peculiar relationships as means to the desired goal. Thus, the intent, or goal, or pur-pose of the individual becomes a major point of reference for ongoing instruction.[41]

The distinction Caswell made between his work and that of, say, Bobbitt and Charters, or any scientific curriculum-maker for that matter, was essentially the same distinction I made earlier between Mead and Cooley on the one hand and Ross and Thorndike on the other. Caswell saw the task of social control in much the same way as Mead did as the effort to establish an accord between individual needs and desires and the demands of urban, industrial life. Like Mead, he appeared to see no threat to individuality in the application of techni-ques of social control. In contrast, his description of scientific curriculum-making suggests that those who adhered to this viewpoint were interested simply in fitting individuals to existing social demands.

Throughout this volume, we have argued that American intellectuals were attracted to the idea of social control because it offered them a conceptual framework for explaining how a sense of community could be restored to modern American society. It remains for us in this chapter to consider what kind of community Caswell envisioned for the urban, industrial America of his day.

V

Caswell's social vision did share a common feature with that of Bobbitt and Charters. He believed, as they did, that the solution to the problems of urbanization and industrialization rested on the development of the kind of harmonious and cooperative social relationships I have identified with the concept of community. Caswell, however, had a fundamentally different understanding of cooperation than did Bobbitt and Charters. Bobbitt and Charters argued that with the help of scientific management principles, American society with its present economic and political arrangements could become more cooperative. There was, they believed, nothing inherent in industrial capitalism that would stand in the way of achieving the sense of community they thought to be so important.

Caswell, on the other hand, was less sanguine about industrial capitalism. He appeared, as I have previously noted, to distrust the motivations of those industrialists who were responsible for America's economic growth. There was in fact within the Virginia course of study a clear anti-capitalist bias. One of the objectives of the course of study was that students should understand the workings of industrial capitalism. The description of this aim included the following generalizations about this economic system:

1 The material prosperity of the modern world has been attained under the capitalistic system.

2 Capitalism is based upon the principle of profit to the owner rather than service to the masses of people.

3 The methods of distribution of goods in a capitalistic society tend to direct social products into the hands of the few.

4 Production is based upon the amount of goods purchasers can be induced to consume, rather than upon their needs.

5 The capitalistic system is not planned and lacks direction thus waste and economic cycles result.

6 Natural resources are exploited for profit.

7 The dependence of the laborer upon capital tends to reduce him to a servile status.[42]

Although Caswell recognized the role that industrial capitalism was playing in enhancing the material well being of Americans, he was, unlike Bobbitt and Charters, willing to admit its shortcomings.

What Caswell sought, it seems, was to strike a balance between the forces of change, such as those that brought about America's current economic and social transformation, and the forces of stability. American society, he pointed out in an October 1940 article on the role of the curriculum in national defense, had to be responsive to the need for change, particularly change that would increase individual opportunity:

> But conservation of the values gained by the vision and struggle of our forefathers is not enough to provide the conviction needed for defense at this critical period. Values achieved in earlier times, however important, soon come to be accepted and common place. Inequalities, lack of opportunity, injustices loom large. The future, not the past, is the key to decisive action. There must be perceived in American democracy the promise of a better life in a nation marching forward to progressively greater achievements.[43]

At the same time, however, the nation also required a degree of stability. It was the ability of the schools to make people more cooperative, he noted in a 1953 radio broadcast for the American Broadcasting Company's Town Meeting program, that provided for this stability:

> Our great success in America in avoiding the extremes of religious persecution and class stratification, which were so common in European countries, has resulted I think to no small extent from the understanding and the opportunities gained in the public schools of America... The public schools, however, could serve this great function of fostering national unity and devotion to common ideals so effectively only because the great majority of children attended them.[44]

What ultimately distinguishes the vision of community held by Caswell from that of Bobbitt and Charters was his willingness to allow for social change. Where Bobbitt and Charters saw the America of their day as a stage in the evolutionary development of a more progressive and democratic society, Caswell was less certain. He was less willing than they to accept the goodness of the existing social order. The very survival of American democracy, Caswell believed, depended on the continuing possibility for social improvement:

> Now if American democracy cannot present an opportunity for continuous improvement of living, if we cannot offer the possibility of a future with greater promise than the present, however good the present may be, our shortages will loom larger and larger in the minds of our people. The question will be raised with increasing frequency: Does not some other form of social organization have greater promise than democracy? In France we are told on reliable authority that the recurrence of this question contributed to downfall.[45]

With regard to the issue of change, Caswell seemed more concerned than either Bobbitt or Charters that the curriculum exert an influence in enhancing social equality. In the last chapter, we saw that Bobbitt and Charters, with some reservations, endorsed curriculum differentiation as a means of achieving a more functional curriculum. Caswell, however, was strongly opposed to such a practice. The development of a widespread program for the socially elite and economically favored in contrast to the common man would be a serious blow at the democratizing function of the public school system.[46] Adopting the practice of differentiating the curriculum would, he started in a 1955 speech to the National Association of Secondary School Principals, lead Americans to follow the European practice of using the schools to prepare an elite to lead and the masses of the population to follow.[47]

In 1954, with his appointment to the Presidency of Teachers College Caswell's active career in curriculum work came for all intents and purposes to an end. For the next eight years, until his retirement in 1962, the focus of his attention would be on the administration of what was at the time the nation's most prestigious professional school of education. In his inaugural address as President of Teachers College faculty, Caswell touched briefly on the diverse functions of education in modern society:

> Organized education is of incalculable importance in the modern world. It is a major aid to the individual in achieving a rich and meaningful life; it is a primary means of developing understanding of and devotion to social values; it is a principal

way of fostering good citizenship; and it is the instrumentality which provides much of the knowledge and many of the skills essential to modern technology. Nations which are committed to the achievement of democratic ideals and to the improvement of conditions of living through the use of modern processes of production are completely dependent on organized programs of education.[48]

In 1956, Caswell returned to the same theme in a speech he delivered at the University of Havana. Again, he talked of the many purposes of education, economic growth, social improvement, and the cultivation of values. In nurturing values, Caswell noted, the school had a two-fold task:

> Thus it becomes necessary for education at one and the same time to develop a sense of confidence and assurance in certain values and goals which will serve to unite people and to give them roots in the best things their culture has produced and to foster inquiry and reappraisal of these values and goals.[49]

These two speeches provide, I believe, a good picture of what Caswell sought throughout his career. On the one hand he desired a school curriculum that would prepare youth to take advantage of the opportunities that industrialization offered. On the other hand, however, he desired a school curriculum that would at the same time instill youth with the historic values of liberal democracy thus ensuring their perpetuation. It was this goal of accommodating the conflicting forces of modern life, those promoting change and those maintaining stability, that Caswell hoped to achieve by remaking America in the image of a cooperative community.

VI

In this chapter, our examination of the work of Hollis Caswell has allowed us to continue our treatment of the concept of social control in American curriculum thought to include the years from 1930 through the mid-1950s. Caswell, like Bobbitt and Charters, saw the fundamental task of the curriculum as that of securing social harmony and cooperation in modern American society. What separates Caswell from these two earlier proponents of scientific curriculum-making was his abandonment of the doctrine of social efficiency. By all rights, Caswell should have continued in the tradition established by Bobbitt and

Charters. As a graduate student of Strayer's at Teachers College, Caswell played a important role in championing a favorite efficiency oriented tool of early twentieth century educational administrators, the school survey. Organized at the behest of local boards of education, these surveys typically brought a number of experts in school administration into a school system to study its organization and operation. In his 1929 doctoral dissertation, Caswell defended school surveys on the grounds that they informed school principals 'how efficiently school funds are being expended and how well the children are achieving in their studies'.[50] Although Caswell participated in school surveys throughout his career, he did not carry their efficiency oriented assumptions into his work in curriculum.

Unhampered by the doctrine of efficiency, Caswell was able, unlike Bobbitt and Charters, to take a critical view of industrial capitalism. For Caswell, the schools had to do more than simply fit youth for the work and citizenship roles demanded by a corporate economy. They had to prepare the way for the kind of social change that would correct the abuses industrial capitalism had brought. It was Caswell among the curriculum workers we have considered in this volume who came the closest to achieving the kind of reconciliation between the realities of urban, industrial life and liberal democratic ideals that Mead spelled out in the early years of this century.

Thus far, we have focused our attention on those curriculum workers whose principal contribution was to articulate various proposals for using the curriculum as an instrument of social control. We have said very little about the work of those curriculum workers within the schools who attempted to use these proposals in the selection and organization of the actual school program. It is to this subject that we will now turn in our last chapter. We will consider what occurred in one urban school system, the public schools of Minneapolis, Minnesota, during the first half of this century as administrators responsible for curriculum matters took the ideas of Bobbitt, Charters and Caswell and sought to use them in the development of the actual school program.

Notes

1 FRANKLIN BOBBITT, *The Curriculum of Modern Education*, New York, McGraw-Hill, 1941, pp. 63–4.
2 *Ibid.*, pp. 270–1 and 343–55.
3 *Ibid.*, pp. 66–8.
4 *Ibid.*, pp. 21–2, 228–9, 297–8 and 314–5.
5 CHARLES C. PETERS, *Foundations of Educational Sociology*, New York, Macmillan,

1924, p. vii.

6 CHARLES C. PETERS, *The Curriculum of Democratic Education*, New York, McGraw-Hill, 1942, p. 42.

7 Franklin Bobbitt to Ralph Tyler, 24 August, 1946, *The Ralph Tyler Papers*, University of Chicago Library, Box 4, Folder 13.

8 FRANKLIN BOBBITT, 'The Educational Policy Commission banishes sciences', *The Scientific Monthly*, 63, August, 1946, pp. 117–24.

9 'Interview with Hollis Caswell', Columbia University Oral History Project, *The Caswell Collection*, American Heritage Center, University of Wyoming Library, Box 2, pp. 4–5; 'Biographical file on Hollis Caswell', *The Caswell Collection*, *op. cit*, File B-C279-h1

10 HOLLIS L. CASWELL and DOAK S. CAMPBELL, *Curriculum Development*, New York, American Book Company, 1935, pp. v.-vi.

11 *Ibid.*, chapter 1.

12 HOLLIS L. CASWELL, 'Persistent curriculum problems', address to the Society of Professors of Curriculum, San Francisco, California, 3 March, 1978, *The Caswell Collection*, *op. cit.*, Box 12, pp. 10–13.

13 LOREN BARITZ, *The Servants of Power: A History of the Use of Social Science in American Industry*, Middletown, Wesleyan University Press, 1960, chapters 2 and 4–6.

14 MARY PARKER FOLLETT, 'The psychology of control', in *Dynamic Administration: The Collected Papers of Mary Parker Follett*, edited by HENRY C. METCALF and L. URWICK,, New York, Harper and Brothers, 1941, pp. 183–209.

15 ELTON MAYO, *The Social Problems of an Industrial Civilization*, Boston, Harvard Graduate School of Business Administration, 1945, pp. 3–15.

16 HOLLIS L. CASWELL, 'The schools and social progress', *School Executive Magazine*, 51, June, 1932, pp. 435–6.

17 HOLLIS L. CASWELL, 'How shall a wartime program for schools be developed?' *Teachers College Record*, 44, January, 1943, p. 276.

18 HOLLIS L. CASWELL, 'Current developments in the school curriculum', an address at Michigan State University, East Lansing, Michigan, 14 July, 1954, *The Caswell Collection*, *op. cit.*, Box 11, p. 5.

19 *Ibid.*, pp. 10–11.

20 HOLLIS L. CASWELL, 'The present eductional scene', *Peabody Reflector and Alumni News*, May, 1937, *The Caswell Collection*, Box 1, *op. cit.*, p. 171.

21 HOLLIS L. CASWELL and Associates, *Curriculum Improvement in Public School Systems*, New York, Bureau of Publications, Teachers College, 1950, pp. 26–7.

22 'The present educational scene', *op cit.*, p. 172.

23 For a description of the attempt during World War II to introduce content about the airplane and the air age into the curriculum see MURRAY NELSON and GEORGE MEHAFFY, 'The social studies curriculum during two wars', A paper presented at the annual meeting of the Society for the Study of Curriculum History, New Orleans, Louisiana, April, 1984.

24 'How shall a wartime program for schools be developed?' *op. cit.*, p. 277.

25 HOLLIS L. CASWELL, 'What is the school's responsibility to society?' *The Nation's Schools*, 11, September, 1933, pp. 34–5.

26 HOLLIS L. CASWELL, 'The case against subjects', *Peabody Journal of Education*, 15, January, 1938, p. 180.

27 *Ibid.*, p. 182.

28 Virginia State Board of Education, 'Organization for Virginia State curriculum program', *State Board of Education Bulletin*, Vol. 14, No. 5, Richmond, Division of Purchase and Printing, 1933, p. 39.

29 Virginia State Board of Education, *Tentative Course of Study for Virginia Elementary Schools*, Richmond, Division of Purchase and Printing, 1933, p. 39; Virginia State Board of Education, *Tentative Course of Study for the Core Curriculum of Virginia Secondary Schools, Grade VIII*, Richmond, Division of Purchase and Printing, 1934, pp. 16 and 21–4.

30 *Tentative Course of Study for the Core Curriculum of Virginia Secondary Schools, Grade VIII, ibid.*, pp. 16–19.

31 *Ibid.*, pp. 25–35 and 188–201.

32 *Ibid.*, p. 24.

33 *Ibid.*, p. 17.

34 Virginia State Board of Education, *The Core Curriculum of Secondary Schools*, Richmond, Division of Purchase and Printing, 1933, p. 9.

35 CASWELL and CAMPBELL, *op. cit.*, p. 125.

36 *Ibid*; Virginia State Board of Education, 'Procedures for Virginia State curriculum program', *State Board of Education Bulletin*, Vol. 15, No. 3, Richmond, Division of Purchase and Printing, 1932, pp. 18–19.

37 HOLLIS L. CASWELL, 'Practical application of mechanistic and organismic psychologies to curriculum making', *Journal of Educational Research*, 28, September, 1934, pp. 17–19.

38 CASWELL and CAMPBELL, op. cit., p. 124.

39 *Procedures for Virginia State Curriculum Program, op. cit.*, p. 31.

40 'Practical application of mechanistic and organismic psychologies to curriculum making', *op. cit.*, pp. 21–2.

41 *Ibid.*, pp. 22.

42 *Procedures for Virginia State Curriculum Program, op. cit.*, p. 26.

43 HOLLIS L. CASWELL, 'National defense and the school curriculum', *Curriculum Journal*, 11, October, 1940, p. 250.

44 Transcript of town meeting program of 20 October 1953, *The Caswell Collection, op. cit.*, Box 10, p. 4.

45 'National defense and the school curriculum', *op. cit.*, p. 250.

46 HOLLIS L. CASWELL, 'Curriculum proposals for the future', in *The American High School: Its Responsibility and Opportunity*, edited by HOLLIS L. CASWELL, New York, Harper and Brothers, 1946, p. 137.

47 HOLLIS L. CASWELL, 'The great experiment', a speech delivered to the annual meeting of the National Association of Secondary School Principals, Atlantic City, New Jersey, 22 February, 1955, *The Caswell Collection, op. cit.*, Box 9, pp. 8–9.

48 'The inauguration of Hollis Leland Caswell as President of Teachers College, Columbia University', 21 and 22 March, 1955, *The Caswell Collection, op. cit.*, Box 10, p. 29.

49 HOLLIS L. CASWELL, 'Lecture at the University of Havana', 13 and 14 March, 1956, *The Caswell Collection, op. cit.*, Box 9, p. 11.

50 HOLLIS L. CASWELL, *City School Surveys: An Interpretation and Appraisal*, New York, Bureau of Publications, Teachers College, 1929, pp. 20–1.

6   From Curriculum Thought to School Practice: Minneapolis Educators and the Search for Social Control

I

The individuals we have treated throughout this volume we should not forget, were not solely university scholars. They were, each in their own way, involved in the world of public affairs and policy making. Ross and Mead played major roles in a number of the so-called progressive reforms of the early twentieth century. Cooley began his career and developed the outlines of his social theory while working for the Interstate Commerce Commission and the Census Bureau in Washington. Thorndike lent support to the early twentieth-century eugenics movement and assisted the American Research Council during World War I in seeking wartime applications for the intelligence test.

Similarly, the curriculum workers we have considered in the last two chapters were active in the educational reform efforts of the day. Bobbitt spent a year as Assistant Superintendent of Schools in Los Angeles developing the approach to curriculum making he spelled out in his most popular book, *How to Make a Curriculum*. Throughout his career, Charters participated in a number of curriculum development projects in a variety of vocational areas including retail sales, secretarial work and pharmacy. Caswell developed his approach to curriculum planning while serving as a consultant to curriculum reorganization projects in several Southern States, the most important of which was in Virginia. These educators were initially attracted to the idea of social control not so much out of a theoretical or philosophical interest but out of a desire to reform the actual program of the nation's schools.

Considering the involvement of Bobbitt, Charters and Caswell in attempts at curriculum reform, this volume would be incomplete if we did not address the impact their ideas had on the actual program of American schools. In contemplating how we might assess this impact, we are struck almost immediately by the absence of historical research on the subject. There have been very few investigations of the efforts of twentieth-century school people to reform the actual curriculum. It seems that if we are to reach any conclusions about this influence, we will have to undertake our own study. The limitations of space in this study would make it difficult for us to examine the nation as a whole. A more promising strategy, I think, would be for us to examine one school system in depth during the first half of this century to see what influence, if any, the ideas promoted by Bobbitt, Charters and Caswell had on its curriculum. Such a study might serve as a model for the necessary further research required to assess the actual influence of curriculum ideas on efforts during this century to reorganize the curriculum along more functional lines. In this chapter, we will follow this approach by examining the attempts at curriculum change which took place in the public schools of Minneapolis, Minnesota from 1917 to 1954. Our concern will be two-fold. First, we shall look to see if Minneapolis educators sought as did Bobbitt, Charters and Caswell to make their curriculum more functional. Second, we shall investigate whether educators in Minneapolis attempted to use the curriculum in the manner suggested by the founding theorists of the curriculum field as an instrument of social control for the restoration of an American community.

The Minneapolis public schools offer an ideal case for the kind of investigation we are undertaking. Throughout the first half of this century, Minneapolis educators were involved, under the leadership of Prudence Cutright, Assistant Superintendent and Head of the Division of Instruction, in an attempt to create a more functional school curriculum. In pursuing this effort at curriculum reform, Cutright and others in Minneapolis promoted changes that were quite similar to those advocated by Bobbitt, Charters and Caswell. They even at times spoke as did these formative theorists of the curriculum field of the need for the American people to become more cooperative in their relationships with each other.

II

In 1914, the Minneapolis Board of Education appointed the leading spokesman for administrative efficiency of the day, Frank Spaulding, to the superintendency. During his three year incumbency in Minneapolis, Spaulding secured the establishment of two vocational high schools, one for females and one for males, reorganized the Attendance Department into a Department of Attendance and Vocational Guidance, conducted a vocational survey, and promoted a favorite efficiency reform of the day, the junior high school. In 1917, the year Spaulding left Minneapolis for the superintendency in Cleveland, Ohio, the Board of Education established the city's first junior high schools.[1]

In 1923, Minneapolis replaced the existing course in ninth-grade ancient history with a course entitled Community Life Problems. W.H. Shepard, a Minneapolis teacher, proposed the new course to aid the adjustment of students to changes in 'industrial life in Minneapolis' by providing them with the opportunity to study occupations and vocations that were potentially avilable to them. Such a course, according to Shepard, would bring 'students into direct contact with the business world in its own province', while at the same time 'associating the business man with the schoolroom'.[2] Three years later, as a further means of aiding students' vocational adjustment, the high school visiting teachers, whose task had been to supervise attendance, were reclassified as vocational guidance counselors.[3]

The earliest effort to make the Minneapolis course of study more functional was the introduction of curriculum differentiation into the high schools. In 1912, the high school curriculum was composed of seven programs. Two of the programs, the Latin and modern languages courses of study, were distinctly college preparatory in purpose and similar to programs recommended by the National Education Association's Committee of Ten in its 1894 report. The other five programs, art, commercial, general, home economics and manual training were designed to prepare students for immediate employment after graduation. Despite the existence of several alternative curricula, the Minneapolis school administration followed the recommendation of the Committee of Ten that any high school program should contain sufficient flexibility to enable students to prepare for college. Minneapolis high school students could, then, select any one of the five vocationally oriented programs and modify it to meet college entrance requirements.[4]

The first attempt to provide a more functional differentiation occurred in 1914, when a technical course was introduced for males at the city's Central High School and when Girls' Vocational High School was established to provide training in such areas as needlework, catering and stenography. This distinctiveness among the high school programs was reinforced in 1920 with the introduction of three programs, college preparatory, commercial and industrial arts-music, to replace the existing seven course curriculum. Despite the fact that this new secondary program seemed to sharpen the distinction between what was college preparatory and what was vocational, Minneapolis continued the practice of allowing students in the vocational programs to modify their courses of study to meet college entrance requirements.[5]

In 1925, when we would have expected the influence of the social efficiency movement to be at its height, Minneapolis shifted directions and abandoned its differentiated curriculum in favor of a system of constants and electives. Under this scheme, all students in the city's high schools were required to take the same courses in English, social studies and physical education. Students were allowed to complete the remainder of their three-year program by selecting from elective courses, some designed to meet college entrance requirements and the remainder designed to prepare for immediate employment after graduation. The published course of study listed a number of possible groupings of electives to provide for a 'purely academic' program as well as vocationally oriented programs in manual training, home economics, stenography and bookkeeping. The policy of allowing students to meet college entrance requirements no matter what their vocational interests continued. Printed in capital letters on the last page of the course of study was the following statement: 'It is always possible at the discretion of the principal to make such minor changes in the selection of courses as will fit pupils for specific college entrance requirements.'[6]

A similar flexibility existed in the vocational high schools. Students enrolled in any vocational training program not only met the occupational training standards set by the Federal Government but were prepared also for college admission. Such an arrangement was defended in a 1933 description of vocational education in Minneapolis on the grounds that it provided 'greater adaptability upon the part of the graduates than would result from purely vocational training'.[7]

Notwithstanding the existence, at least for a time, of a differentiated secondary curriculum, Minneapolis educators were hostile toward the practice of ability grouping. Throughout the 1920s and 1930s, Minneapolis junior high schools employed ability grouping on an experimental basis.[8] Although teachers discussed the question of ability grouping during these years, they never seemed to embrace the practice.[9] In a series of city wide teacher forums held in 1937, teachers accepted the practice of differentiation but rejected ability grouping on the grounds that it would not in fact create homogeneous classrooms and because they believed that it was inherently an 'anti-democratic practice'.[10]

The interest in differentiation lost its appeal during the 1940s. In a 1941 paper, Assistant Superintendent Prudence Cutright, the architect of Minneapolis's efforts from the mid-1920s onward to make the curriculum more functional, raised the question of whether in fact a college preparatory curriculum should be different from a curriculum that prepares students for immediate employment after graduation. Her reply was no. 'What is good for pupils planning to enter college', she remarked, 'is good for the group planning to go to work'.[11]

The result of Minneapolis' first major effort to make the school program more functional, curriculum differentiation, was a mixed one. Whatever influence curriculum differentiation had on Minneapolis was muted by three factors. First, there was the practice of allowing all students, notwithstanding their course of study, to meet college entrance requirements. Second, there was the replacement in 1925 of a differentiated high school curriculum by a system of constants and electives. Third, there was the unwillingness of Minneapolis educators throughout this period to accept the idea of ability grouping.

It seems that efforts to introduce efficiency ideas during the 1920s were only partially successful. In 1925, two years after the ninth grade Community Life Problems course was introduced, the twelfth grade sociology course was reorganized and its academic content enhanced. According to Superintendent W.F. Webster, 'the results were salutary, and Minneapolis now offers a course in sociology that would do credit to a junior college, The text used is in fact a college text'.[12]

For most of the decade, efficiency values and more traditional disciplinary values appeared to coexist almost side by side. The elementary reading curriculum is illustrative. Reading was defined in the *Course of Study in Work Reading* in the particularistic terms favored by efficiency minded educators as a 'complex of abilities' required by students to meet the demands and problems of daily living. Teachers were urged to 'break this ability into its elements and develop one element after another....'.[13] In the companion syllabus, the *Course of Study in Recreational Reading*, however, the reason given for teaching reading was to develop in children 'a love for good literature'. Using reading to meet practical, every day needs was thought to be a secondary consideration.[14]

III

If there was any particular event that marked the beginning of Minneapolis' wholehearted conversion to the doctrine of social efficiency, it was the Great Depression. Although school enrollments remained relatively stable during the early years of the Depression, Minneapolis educators were forced to provide for their students with increasingly less money. In 1931, the City's Board of Estimate and Taxation ordered a 10 percent decrease in the school budget. In 1932, school expenditures were again reduced by 10 percent. In 1933, another budget reduction took place, this time amounting to 17 percent.[15] To meet the demands of a restricted budget, Minneapolis educators sought to run the schools more economically. Each year between 1931 and 1935, the teaching staff was reduced anywhere from 14 to 26 percent.[16] Economy was such an all-embracing concern that Superintendent Caroll Reed, upon hearing of the death of one of his elementary teachers, was reported to have remarked that 'every vacancy furnishes the opportunity to make a saving'.[17] It was a concern that was to have its effect on the school curriculum.

The guiding force behind the efficiency-oriented changes that took place in Minneapolis during the 1930s was Prudence Cutright. Cutright came to Minneapolis in 1924 from the La Crosse, Wisconsin Public Schools, where she served as Assistant Superintendent, to head the city's new Bureau of Research and Curriculum Construction. Ten years later, she would be promoted to Assistant Superintendent, first for Instruction and then for Elementary Education. Cutright's educational background placed her clearly within the social efficiency tradition. She completed her undergraduate degree at the University of Chicago, where she took Bobbitt's curriculum course.[18] During her first three years in Minneapolis, she completed her master's degree at the University of Minnesota. Her thesis, which she wrote under the direction of Leo Brueckner, an expert of the day in mental testing, was a study of the relative efficiency of different types of dictation exercises in improving students' use of correct punctuation.[19]

Cutright approached the task of curriculum construction from what she called the 'scientific point of view'. Her method, which was similar to that advanced by Bobbitt, saw the first task of the curriculum worker as that of establishing the aims or objectives of education.[20] There were, she noted, again mirroring Bobbitt's viewpoint, two basic ways of identifying these objectives. A curriculum committee could undertake a 'community survey' of how individuals used a particular subject 'in their everyday activities'. The survey would reveal the most appropriate objectives for the study of that subject. Second, a committee could by 'consensus' select a number of objectives from a larger pool of available objectives, which themselves were identified by an examination of certain 'authoritative writings'.[21]

Cutright's early work in curriculum development in Minneapolis indicated her devotion to the ideas of Bobbitt. In one early project, she developed the objectives for an elementary citizenship curriculum by having teachers identify the 'faulty behaviors' of students in light of correct, adult citizenship practices. In another, she used Bobbitt's ten classes of human activities as a source for developing composition topics which were to be used to identify the common spelling errors of elementary school children.[22]

Cutright not only embraced the methodology of scientific curriculum making, she accepted its efficiency goals. At the beginning of the Depression in 1929, about 8 percent of the high school graduating class was unemployed. By 1933, the figure had reached 22 percent.[23] This unemployment, Cutright suggested in a paper she authored in 1941, had led many students of 'limited academic abilities', who typically would have left school before graduation to seek employment, to remain in the high schools. The existing course of study, which she labelled as the 'old subject matter preparatory curriculum', was not appropriate for the more diverse student body that was coming to populate the schools.[24] In the 1937 report of the Division of Instruction, which she headed, Cutright attacked the historic disciplinary emphasis of the school curriculum on the grounds that it did not prepare students for life:

> Experiments have shown that while a child may be very accurate in solving mathematical problems, that his accuracy did not carry over to practical affairs and other matters to any great extent. Therefore, a teacher who still teaches as if the thing she was trying to do was to train the mind as we train muscles of the body is to a large extent, wasting a child's time and effort.[25]

What was needed was a new curriculum for all students that would develop 'a generation of boys and girls who will be able to use facts, knowledge and skills to meet life problems and life situations with increasing effectiveness'.[26]

Cutright's viewpoint was reflected throughout the 1930s as Minneapolis educators addressed the issue of curriculum change. Early in the decade, the city's junior high school principals organized a committee to review the course of study for each subject taught in grades seven through nine. Each topic taught was to be examined for its potential value in preparing students for particular 'life situations'. 'All subject matter topics', the principals announced, 'which fail to relate to life situations or which fail to relate to the needs of junior high school pupils shall be eliminated'.[27] Similarly, the *School Bulletin*, the Minneapolis schools staff newsletter, of 7 November 1935 urged the city's English teachers in planning their courses of study to first 'survey life, noting what experiences most people have and what desirable personal experiences they miss'.[28]

Social adjustment became the byword of the day in Minneapolis. In

1934, the topic outline for elementary mathematics was revised to take into account 'the life situations confronting children both in and out of the school which require counting, adding, subtraction, etc'. The resulting curriculum was designed to emphasize 'the practical application of arithmetic to life situations such as arise in spending money for food and clothing . . .'.[29] In the following year a junior high school mathematics committee called for a mathematics curriculum related to the existing 'social and economic situation'.[30]

In this climate, many teachers took pains to justify how their courses of study aided the social adjustment of youth. The city's art teachers began to talk about the value of their subject in teaching 'creative planning and craftsmanship' rather than 'simple training in artistic skills'.[31] In a similar vein, Minneapolis' foreign language teachers argued that their subject had 'practical' and 'commercial' value as American business expanded its operations to international markets where the ability to speak a foreign language might enhance one's competitive edge.[32]

One measure of the impact that efficiency-minded thinking had on Minneapolis during the 1930s was to be found in a series of articles which a reporter by the name of Bess Wilson prepared for the *Minneapolis Journal*. During the early months of 1935 Wilson visited a number of Minneapolis classrooms. The reports of these visits appeared first in the *Journal* and were later republished as a book. The point of her visits, Wilson announced in the lead article, was to investigate the charge that Minneapolis schools devoted a large amount of time to the 'fads and frills' of education. What she found, she informed her readers, was that in fact the schools devoted significant time to '. . . that practical application which makes education a first aid to living'.[33]

In several classrooms she visited, students were required to serve as hosts or hostesses to greet guests. The purpose of this task, Wilson reported, was to expose students to possible future occupations by giving them the chance to 'perform one of the important duties of a secretary, usher or attendant in a business house'. It was training that would assist the student, she pointed out, 'when he conducts an office or shop for himself'.[34] A similar objective guided the physical education class she visited. An important purpose of the course, Wilson noted, was '. . . to add a good personal appearance and manner to any other qualifications the pupil should have when he becomes a job seeker'.[35]

Finally, Wilson visited a ninth grade Community Life Problems class in which students learned about the city by visiting Minneapolis's major government agencies and business establishments. One student, she observed, had visited the Minneapolis Retail Credit Association and reported to the class on how individuals obtained credit and the functioning of the Assocation. These field trips, Wilson stated, were designed 'to help pupils towards possible success in his biggest job — that of making himself into a useful and intelligent citizen'.[36] It was, in fact, the desire of Minneapolis educators to make citizenship training a more central part of the social studies curriculum that led to their most concerted effort during the 1930s and 1940s to make the school program more functional, the Modern Problems course.

IV

In 1925, Minneapolis had undertaken a revision of its high school curriculum. As part of that revision, the social studies curriculum had been changed to reflect the efficiency-oriented recommendations of the 1916 Social Studies Committee of the National Education Association's Commission on the Reorganization of Secondary Education.[37] For the senior year, the Committee had recommended the introduction of courses organized around the social problems of secondary age youth. They suggested either the introduction of courses in political science, economics, or sociology that dealt with these problems or the development of a single, integrated social science course with the same focus on social problems, which they called Problems of Democracy.[38] Minneapolis followed the Committee's first recommendation and instituted a one semester required course in American government and semester electives in economics, sociology and commercial law.[39]

This twelfth grade social studies program had, however, only partially met Cutright's goal for a curriculum to prepare students for the demands of adult society. The sociology course that was added, we have already stated, emphasized the study of sociology as an academic discipline. The very reason for introducing the course had been to enhance the academic content of what had been a course in contemporary social problems. Similarly, the new course in American government involved the study of the organization and operation of the Federal and state government, which the Commission's Social Studies Committee had warned in its 1913 preliminary report stood in direct opposition to the goals of social efficiency.[40]

What seemed to have prevented Minneapolis from fully embracing the recommendations of the Social Studies Committee was the view of some of the city's educators that the social studies included a number of distinct disciplines. In an October 1939 memorandum to the city's high school principals, Cutright questioned the practice of appointing separate department chairmen in each high school for geography, history and government. She was concerned that this practice might indicate that teachers held what she believed to be the erroneous view that the social studies were 'three separate and distinct subjects'. There should be, she felt, a 'minimum of sharp breaks in the curriculum'.[41] Treating the social studies as a number of separate subjects was incompatible, she argued, with the goal of establishing a more functionally oriented curriculum:

> Since the purpose of education is to develop the ability to meet problems and situations with increasing effectiveness, it is obvious that the curriculum must give more prominent place to *actual* experiences in dealing with situations and problems. There are no problems that fall neatly into one subject-matter division. Real problems override subject-matter boundary lines ...[42]

To deal with this problem, Earl Peckham, the Supervisor of Secondary Education in Cutright's Division of Instruction, recommended to a 1937 city-wide social studies committee the development of a senior level contemporary problems course.[43] Peckham forward two proposals for such a course to this committee. One was composed of three suggested units: 'taxation and the common man', 'world wars and who pays for them', and 'making a living'. The second proposal, developed by Milton Schadegg, a social studies teacher at Minneapolis's Central High School, was a complete course of seventeen units, including such topics as 'sobriety', 'social inadequacy', and 'social misfits'.[44] What Peckham was in effect proposing was a course similar to the Problems of Democracy course recommended by the Commission on the Reorganization of Secondary Education twenty-one years earlier.

In 1939, a new integrated twelfth-grade social studies course, known as Modern Problems, was introduced. During the next five years, Modern Problems was offered as an alternative to the existing senior level social studies courses. Students were allowed to take Modern Problems I in lieu of taking the required course in American Government. Modern Problems II was an elective which students could select instead of existing courses in sociology, economics or commercial law.[45]

Despite Cutright's hope for this new course, it did not as implemented appear all that different from the existing twelfth-grade social studies offerings. The course description for Modern Problems I was virtually the same as the description of the course in American government. The only difference was that this course was, unlike the government course, to include a unit on occupational adjustment. This unit, however, never seems to have actually been added. In 1944, five years after Modern Problems was first introduced, the Senior High School Social Studies Committee recommended that a unit on vocational guidance needed to be added to the course. The description of Modern Problems II included the study of such issues as 'population, labor, housing, family life and consumer needs'. Similar issues were already a part of the sociology, economics and commercial law courses.[46]

Some Minneapolis teachers evidently saw little difference between Modern Problems, or American Government'. The name of the course West High School history faculty, for example, viewed Modern Problems as just another course in government. Modern Problems, they pointed out at their October 1940 department meeting, was ' ... a full year subject using American government as the core subject and about a semester for Modern Problems. The subject could be named Civics, Modern Problems, or American Government'. The name of the course had more to do with meeting 'the credit requirements of the state department [of education]' than with its content.[47]

Why might it be that these teachers at West High School saw so little change as a result of this addition to the curriculum? To understand this, we need to look further at the events surrounding the introduction of Modern Problems. In April 1940, Barbara Wright, Head of the Counseling Division, informed Assistant Superintendent Cutright that the University of Minnesota might not accept Modern Problems for its social science entrance requirement, which called for courses in history, American government, commercial geography, economics and sociology. Wright went on to suggest that perhaps the State Department of Education could assist Minneapolis in obtaining the University's approval of Modern Problems for meeting this requirement.[48]

That same month, Superintendent Reed wrote to State Commissioner of Education John Rockwell to inform him that in his opinion Modern Problems met state high school graduation requirements for a course in the social sciences that included the study of American government. This requirement is met, he noted, 'by intensive study in a one semester course required of all seniors'. He requested Rockwell's assistance in obtaining University approval of the course.[49] Rockwell, in turn, wrote to Royal Shumway, Assistant Dean of the University's College of Letters, Sciences and Arts, to notify him that Modern Problems appeared to meet state requirements for a senior year

'Introduction to Social Science' course. Minneapolis, he stated, did not have to offer a specific course in either economics or sociology to meet this requirement because these disciplines '... may be involved in the various problems considered in this course'.[50] A week later, Shumway wrote back to Rockwell to tell him that the University would abide by his interpretation and accept Modern Problems as meeting its social science entrance requirements.[51]

The following month, A.B. Caldwell, Deputy State Commissioner of Education, wrote to Cutright to ask if the difficulty involving Modern Problems had been resolved. Cutright replied that the matter was 'cleared up'. 'It will', she added, 'simplify bookkeeping on credit in high school enormously'.[52] For the next four years, Minneapolis continued to offer both semester courses in American government, sociology, economics and commercial law as well as the new, two semester Modern problems course. In 1944, the separate social science courses were dropped from the curriculum and a one-year Modern Problems course, involving one semester devoted to the study of American government and one semester for the consideration of contemporary problems, became the required senior year social studies course.[53]

Why, however, was the study of American government confined to one semester, thereby limiting the possibility of curriculum integration? The State Department of Education and the University were only interested in ensuring that government was taught, not how that instruction was organized. All Minneapolis students, as it turned out, were not able to take both semesters of Modern Problems. Students enrolled in the city's vocational schools only had enough room in their programs to take one semester of social studies during their senior year. If they were to meet the state graduation requirement in government, it was necessary that the subject be taught in one semester. There was not, then, sufficient time in this one semester course to complete the required work in government and to treat contemporary problems.[54]

Minneapolis educators were not, it seems, completely successful during the 1940s in using Modern Problems to achieve the kind of functional reorganization of the curriculum that Bobbitt and Charters had advocated. As an effort at curriculum reform, Modern Problems had mixed results. Mary Lou Nelson, who took Modern Problems at Minneapolis' South High School in 1940, noted that despite the official name of the course, students of the day called it 'civics'. Her recollection of the course was that no attention was paid to the contemporary problems of youth.[55] Bob Ansel, who took Modern Problems eight years later at North High School, reported a different experience. The social studies courses he had taken in high school prior to his senior year had all concentrated on historical issues. Modern Problems was 'the only one I can remember that had a focus on contemporary social issues'. Ansel took the course during the 1948 Presidential election. A major assignment, he reported, was for students to hold a mock political party convention.[56]

Students who took the Modern Problems a decade later noted a similar diversity of classroom practices. Roger Ryberg, a 1956 graduate of North High School, saw Modern Problems as being 'much more relevant and useful' than other social studies courses he had taken. Its content included material, he commented, that 'nobody had addressed before'.[57] Kathleen Kunzman took Modern Problems four years later at Edison High School. She, however, did not 'remember dealing with any social issues'. Except for a discussion of Communism, which was a favorite topic of the teacher, the Modern Problems course that she took was devoted to the study of government and economics.[58]

What stood in the way of the school administration's attempt to use Modern Problems to realize a more functional curriculum was the impact of certain local factors. First, for Modern Problems to be a viable course it needed to be accepted by the University of Minnesota in fulfillment of its social science entrance requirement. Second, the course, again to be viable, had to be accepted by the State Department of Education as satisfying its high school graduation requirement for the study of American government. Third, the study of American government to be accessible to all of the city's high school seniors had to be offered in a one semester course. Taken together, these three factors necessitated the development of a Modern Problems course in which one semester was devoted to the study of American government and the other to the integration of sociology and economics around the social problems of high school youth. The result was a new course that was not very different from the courses it was designed to replace. It was this anomaly between the goal the school administration had hoped to achieve by the introduction of Modern Problems and what actually was accomplished that apparently caught the attention of the West High School history faculty and accounted for their skeptical view of this new addition to the curriculum.

Modern Problems never became a successful vehicle for achieving a more functionally oriented school curriculum. In December of 1946, the city's senior high school principals recommended that Modern Problems be made into an elective course. They noted that while the state only required two years of social studies, Minneapolis offered a three-year program, an elective in world history in the tenth grade and required courses in American history and Modern Problems in the eleventh and twelfth grades. Students who took the entire program, they pointed out, had little opportunity to take electives in other areas. No action, however, was taken by the school administration on this recommendation.[59] Two years later, the city-wide Social Studies Steering Committee considered abandoning the course altogether. What prevented them from making this recommendation was the mistaken belief of the Committee's Chairman that the state required Modern Problems for high school graduation.[60]

At the heart of this dissatisfaction with Modern Problems was the difficulty that Minneapolis teachers experienced in actually achieving the integration of the various social science disciplines around certain so-called problems of youth. In the same year that Modern Problems became the required senior level social studies course, Laurel Burkle, an assistant to Cutright, had recommended that the schools may need to have some experience with Modern Problems before 'they evolve a successful approach to the course and discover how the social and economic problems may be integrated'.[61]

This realization, it appears, was never actually achieved. By the mid-1950s, Minneapolis began to move away from this effort at curriculum integration. In 1956, the administration introduced an alternative senior year social studies program in several of the city's high schools made up of six year-long courses, referred to as 'equivalent courses'. They included Problems of Government, Current World Problems, Economics in Everyday Life, Social Problems and Community Study, Psychology of Daily Living and Occupational Relations. In each of these 'equivalents', thirty weeks were devoted to the same core content, which was similar to but less extensive than the content of Modern Problems. The remaining eight weeks of each course was devoted to a specific study of the particular subject emphasized by each 'equivalent'.[62]

Further modifications in Modern Problems occurred throughout the next two decades. By the mid-1960s Modern Prolems had disappeared from many of the city's high schools in favor of courses in government, economics, geography, psychology and sociology. By 1976, the course was offically dropped from the city's secondary school curriculum.[63]

Throughout the history of Modern Problems, teachers were particularly dissatisfied with the course. Their major criticism was that they did not know how to bring about the kind of functional integration of content that Modern Problems was designed to achieve. In 1963, two of the city's high school principals reported that their teachers had given up on the idea of integration and were using Modern Problems to teach American and world history.[64] A year earlier, Kopple Friedman, the Supervisor of Secondary Social Studies, who had supported the place of Modern Problems in the curriculum throughout the 1950's, noted that he now had doubts about the suitability of an integrated, problems oriented course. 'I continually observe the inability of some teachers to handle curriculums that represent any departure from textbooks. I often question the handling of general courses, such as the typical twelfth grade problems course, even by teachers who have social studies majors.'[65]

Thus far in our examination of curriculum change in Minneapolis, we have seen that the school administration shared the belief of Bobbitt, Charters and Caswell about the need to have a more functional curriculum. Although their first major attempt to introduce such a program, the Modern Problems course, was not completely successful, they did not abandon their effort. In 1945, the school administration introduced a new program to integrate the curriculum around the concerns of American youth, the Common Learnings Program. In examining this program, we will not only see another example of the continuing commitment of Minneapolis educators to the goal of making the curriculum more functional. We will also see how Minneapolis educators, following the lead of Bobbitt, Charters and Caswell, sought to use the curriculum as an instrument of social control for restoring a sense of community to twentieth-century urban, industrial America.

V

America's entry into World War II provided a conducive climate in Minneapolis for the continuation of the functionally oriented curriculum changes of the 1930s. In the *School Bulletin* of 29 May 1941, issued under the masthead 'Minneapolis Schools Defend the American Way of Life', Cutright defended the study of history in the city's elementary schools on the grounds that it instilled '. . . in the mind of these children a deep and abiding loyalty for their native land'.[66] Similarly, in a 'Defense Bulletin' prepared by the Division of Elementary Education in 1942, Cutright commented that 'the new curriculum must be geared to place major effort on the aims and activities which will strengthen and support the war effort of every loyal American'.[67]

A similar commitment prevailed throughout the war years. In 1943, for example, the Senior High School Social Studies Policies Committee recommended that social studies teachers devote time to the discussion of such topics as 'manpower, rationing and civil defense'.[68] In 1944, however, noting that the war would soon be over, Minneapolis educators shifted the focus of their concern for social adjustment somewhat and called for curriculum changes that would aid the retraining of those who had served in the military or in other war related work.[69]

Even with the end of the war, Minneapolis educators remained devoted to the task of reorganizing the curriculum along more functional lines. Cutright writing about the need for postwar 'curriculum reconstruction' defined the process of curriculum design in the same 'scientific' terms that she had used for the previous two decades. The only noticeable change is that where in her earlier writings she had noted the contribution of Bobbitt to her work, she now identified her approach to curriculum planning with one of Bobbitt's intellectual heirs, Hilda Taba.[70]

At a city-wide workshop held in the summer of 1946, Superintendent Willard Goslin called for a new effort at curriculum reform. 'Education', he argued, 'is at the present time further removed from realities of life than has been the case formerly'. He then turned to the theme of cooperation that had played such a central role in the writings of Bobbitt, Charters and Caswell. 'We need a greater shift in emphasis from the concern for the development of the individual as an individual to the concern for the development of the general welfare.'[71]

The major recommendation of the workshop was the development of a program in Common Learnings. Common Learnings, a term coined by the National Education Association's Educational Policies Commission in its 1944 Yearbook, referred to the use of curriculum integration to make the school program more functional.[72] The Common Learnings Program that was introduced in Minneapolis was a two-hour class in the junior and senior high schools which students took in lieu of their required courses in English and social studies. Much like the Modern Problems course, it was organized around 'the personal and social problems common to the young people of the school'.[73]

The intent of Common Learnings was to enhance the efficiency of the curriculum in adjusting students to the day-to-day demands of social life. A discussion among English teachers from Minneapolis and its twin city of St. Paul about the objectives of the program is illustrative. English was to be taught in Common Learnings classrooms. They argued, however, that:

> ... there must be a relaxing of standards. We must learn to distinguish between everyday, utilitarian English and profes-

sional, scholarly English. Most high school students will use only the first, and the whole school program cannot be geared to meet the needs of the few who expect to enter college.[74]

These teachers evidently felt that the existing emphasis in teaching English in Minneapolis and St. Paul needed to be changed. The focus should be on the teaching of those rules of grammar which 'have become socially acceptable' and on the teaching of written English which students 'need in their life work', primarily the writing of social and business letters and reports.[75]

It is difficult to tell, however, whether the intent of the Common Learnings Program was actually realized in Minneapolis classrooms. The *School Bulletin* of 20 February 1947, reported the apparently successful attempt of one teacher, Elizabeth Scheaffer, at Nokomis Junior High School to integrate English and mathematics around the functional theme of money management. During the course of the year, the students studied such topics as bank accounts, discounts, installment buying and buying on credit. To find out about how banks operated, the students visited a local bank where some of them opened up savings accounts. To keep accurate records of their accounts, students had to know about interest. Their arithmetic work was thus devoted to learning about interest and learning how to calculate the interest they had earned on their accounts using percents. These activities in turn led to other work in arithmetic, such as the multiplication of decimals. Written English was also taught incidentally when the students wrote letters to thank bank officals for allowing them to visit their bank and when students had to write reports on the various aspects of money management which they had studied.[76]

Two Common Learnings teachers at Roosevelt High School, however, tell a different story about the changes brought by this program. Edward Haynes, who taught in Roosevelt's Common Learnings Program from 1945 to 1950, maintained that he taught the same college preparatory material in his Common Learnings classes which he had always taught in his history courses.[77] Dorothy Heath, who taught Common Learnings from 1945 to 1948, claimed to have taught precisely 'what the other students were getting'. To ensure this for instruction in English, she reported that she followed the lesson plans of the English Department Chairwoman.[78]

What appears to have happened was that a variety of practices, some that embraced functional themes and some that were more traditionally academic in nature, went on in Common Learnings classrooms. In March 1950, Geri Hoffner, a reporter for the *Minneapolis*

Tribune, visited a number of Common Learnings classrooms through-out the city. In a ninth-grade classroom, she observed students working on a unit entitled 'Making the Most of Myself'. The students themselves had suggested this area of study, which included such topics as earning better grades, making better friends and enjoying a happier home life.[79] In a tenth-grade Common Learnings classroom, however, she listened to student reports for a unit entitled 'Our Heritage from the Past'. Here, the reports included such traditional academic topics as the British vs. the American system of government, the reign of Charles I, and the life of Oliver Cormwell. Following their reports, Hoffner noted that the students broke into small groups and undertook a variety of activities. One group began an oral reading of *Hamlet*; another group visited the library; and a third group began working on a unit entitled 'The World in which We Live'.[80]

The existence of a variety of different and perhaps conflicting types of activities in Common Learnings classrooms can be explained by two factors. First, Common Learnings teachers, who had come from the ranks of the city's social studies and English teachers, received little in the way of training for this new program. Dorothy Heath reported that she learned 'just by plunging into this thing with a week or two preparation'.[81] Second, the principal resources given to the teachers, a series of curriculum guides, did not specify precisely what should take place in a Common Learnings classroom. Instead, the guides offered numerous suggestions, some that were suitable for a functionally oriented class and others that better fit a more traditional college preparatory class. The suggested activities for the seventh grade unit entitled 'Understanding People of Other Countries' is illustrative of the diversity of the recommendations. For this unit, students could, accord-ing to the guide, list the occupations of residents of the countries which they studied, collect stamps and coins from other countries, report on the history of countries which they studied, and list the contributions of different cultures to the lives of the people of Minneapolis.[82]

The Common Learnings Program was first offered in Minneapolis in 1945. During the next four years, Common Learnings was gradually introduced as a required course in both the junior and senior high schools until by 1950 it was offered in seven of Minneapolis's ten high schools and all eleven junior high schools. In February of 1950, a month before Cutright retired, a controversy arose over the Common Learn-ings Programs which will, as we shall see, tell us much about the role the school curriculum played in Minneapolis as an instrument of social control.

VI

In February 1950, eight Minneapolis residents organized a Parents Council to challenge the Common Learnings requirement.[83] At the February meeting of the Minneapolis Board of Education, the Council presented a petition signed by 861 city residents requesting, among other things, that the Common Learnings Program should be made optional and that a program 'of teaching the basic subjects separately' should be offered to all students and be staffed by 'teachers fully trained in their subject fields'.[84]

The brunt of the Parents Council attack on the Common Learnings Program was directed at the practice of curriculum integration. Mrs R.J. Heidelberger, speaking to the Board at its February meeting, complained that the traditional academic disciplines were not taught in the Common Learnings Program. Both of her daughters, she pointed out, had been enrolled in junior high school Common Learnings courses and were not taught 'the basic subjects'. One spent the year, Mrs Heidelberger claimed, studying about farming, while the other examined the 'community life' of the block on which she lived.[85] Gladys Peterson objected to the fact that her daughter received an 'A' grade in her ninth-grade Common Leanings course but failed the high school English diagnostic test and continued to earn poor grades in English after being transferred to a private school. Peterson went on to claim that it was not possible to teach English 'incidently' as she felt was being attempted in the Common Learnings Program.[86] Another parent, who was upset that the Common Learnings Program ignored the basic subjects, pointed out that her son entered junior high school with a reading comprehension score of 7.1 and after half a semester in the Common Learnings Program had a score of 5.9.[87]

What worried these parents was that their children might be learning less in the Common Learnings Program than they had in a more traditional curriculum. As one parent wrote to Superintendent Herbert Bruner:

> You are no doubt as interested in your school curriculum as I, who have only two children, ages 13 and 16, in the schools. In noting the development of my children, they appear to have less reading, less English grammar, less basic arithmetic and less ability to study than children in other schools in other cities. I have been greatly disappointed in the Minneapolis Schools. If progressive education means less of these basic subjects and more casual teaching of subjects like common learnings, I object very much to this trend.[88]

Of particular concern to these parents was their belief that if their children were enrolled in Common Learnings, they would not be prepared for, or even admitted to, college.[89]

Parents Council members were probably overly and unnecessarily troubled about the academic quality of the Common Learnings Program. What was taught under the rubric of Common Learnings was, as we have seen, not that different from what was taught in traditional, college preparatory courses. Luella Cook, Curriculum Consultant for the Minneapolis Schools, pointed out that the city's high school graduates would not be denied admission to the University of Minnesota simply because they had gone through the Common Learnings Program.[90] In fact, Common Learnings had not been in existence long enough for there to have been many graduates of the program applying for admission to the University.[91] Several members of the school administration did speak directly at the February meeting to the question of the academic soundness of Common Learnings. Both Wilmer Menge, Assistant Superintendent of Secondary Education, and Mercedes Nelson, Assistant Principal at Roosevelt High School, pointed out that the study of history was a state graduation requirement and thus included in Common Learnings classes. Menge also noted that all Common Learnings instructors were fully certified teachers.[92]

Superintendent Bruner noted that at Folwell Junior High School the students who completed one year of the Common Learnings Program performed above grade level in reading comprehension and arithmetic.[93] Two years earlier, a comparative study had been conducted at Roosevelt High School of the achievement of graduates with identical intelligence test scores who had been enrolled in Common Learnings and in the regular program. The mean grade point average of both groups was virtually the same as were their scores on the Cooperative English Test. On the American Council on Education Test, the mean score of the graduates of the Common Learnings Program was 35.78, while the mean score for the graduates of the regular program ws 31.64.[94]

Administrative assurances about the quality of the Common Learnings Program did not, however, affect the opposition of the Parents Council. This was no doubt the case because the Council was interested in more than just the academic quality of Common Learnings. Its members were equally concerned about the values and attitudes which they believed their children were being taught in Common Learnings classrooms. One parent at the February Board meeting complained about the lack of discipline in the Common Learnings classrooms which she visited. Children were 'wandering around the room' at will, and there was 'so much talking' that she could not hear what the teacher was saying. Wright Brooks, who helped draft the Parents Council petition, criticized the practice of teacher-student planning that took place in Common Learnings classrooms. When both teachers and students were involved in discussing what should be taught, the result was, he believed, that the students obtained 'a disjointed, disconnected view of the field of learning'.[95]

Mrs Stanley Berglund, the Head of the Council, suggested to the Board of Education that there was in the program 'too much emphasis on the child's interest rather than on what is best for him'. She also objected to the method of grading used in the program because she claimed that the student was evaluated '. . . on how well he is utilizing his own ability, not on where he stands in comparison with his class'. Such a view, she argued, was inconsistent with the real world which was 'dominated by competition and compulsions'. 'The parents', she pointed out, 'do not want a child indoctrinated with the theory that he is in competition with only himself'.[96]

Underlying these complaints about the values supposedly taught in Common Learnings classrooms was the belief, expressed by one parent, that the program was a system of 'thought control in the classroom' which threatened traditional American values. According to this one parent, the development of a similar program in Des Moines, Iowa had led 'many Protestant parents' to remove their children from the public schools and to place them instead in parochial schools.[97] What seemed to bother Parent Council members in this regard was their fear that the Common Learnings Program would supplant what they saw as the traditional role of the family in moral instruction.

As part of their duties, Common Learnings teachers were expected to spend part of each week visiting the homes of their students.[98] These visits, according to Elizabeth Scheaffer, who taught at Nokomis Junior High School, were designed to enable teachers to become better acquainted with their students. Teachers, she noted, would be able to use the information they obtained from these home visits to aid the adjustment of their students to the demands of school life.[99] Some parents were, however, skeptical about the soundness of this practice. Mrs Irving Gerald pointed out to the Board at the February meeting that it was not the job of the teachers to 'take on psychological and family problems'.[100] 'The parents', noted Mrs Berglund, 'would like the privilege of teaching their own children at home, such things as: When should we go steady? How to plan a party. How can we become popular? The merits of boys doing dishes, doing beds, preparing meals'.[101]

The fears of the Parents Council on this score were probably well taken. In a newspaper article that he wrote in defense of Common Learnings, Superintendent Bruner argued that the schools had to respond to the new realities of the postwar world:

> The air age and the atomic age are already upon us, before the problems of the automobile age have fully been solved; yet the need to keep pace with technological advance gives rise to a new set of problems with which we must also cope. The schools, too, as well as the community, must concern themselves with mental health, and·in a confused world create an environment conducive to wholesome learning.[102]

Bruner went on to claim that the 'traditional curriculum' had failed to meet 'modern needs'. What was called for, he noted, echoing the beliefs of Bobbitt, Charters and Caswell, was a curriculum that promoted the values of cooperation and interdependence:

> Children need the actual experience of working with their classmates on a project whose importance they recognize. They need to feel the pride of shared accomplishment and to feel spurred to their best efforts by the needs of the group. . . . Out of such experiences, which involve the reading of books, as well as discussion with their classmates, they will develop, if well-planned, right attitudes, and from right attitudes will come right behaviors.[103]

The task of the school and its curriculum for Bruner, it seems, was to build the same kind of cooperative community to which the founding theorists of the curriculum field were dedicated. The Parents Council, then, was correct to worry that the school administration was with the introduction of Common Learnings about to turn the curriculum into an instrument of social control for promoting values which Council members saw in conflict with their own. By attacking the Common Learnings Program, the Parents Council was fighting to preserve a very different view of American society from that of the school administration as well as to preserve their ability to pass that view on to their children.

The Council's petition was referred by the Board to the school administration for study. After two months of study, the administration offered a compromise. Common Learnings should remain a required course in the junior high schools but should be made optional in the senior high schools. Superintendent Bruner went to the Board of Education meeting of 23 May 1950, fully expecting to receive Board support. This was, as he called it a 'technical matter' in which the Board should not act without first consulting the school administration. The Board, however, felt differently. School Board Director Fabianke argued that the Board had never fully authorized the Common Learnings Program but had only approved funds for administrators 'to study new ways of learning'. The effectiveness of Common Learnings, she argued, had not been proved. Because of its 'controversial nature', she felt that it should be an optional program until its superiority over more traditional programs had been demonstrated.[104]

Beyond the nature of the program itself, the Board was troubled by the controversy that Common Learnings had created within the community. School Board President Rustad argued that although she was in favor of Common Learnings, she did not think it should be compulsory 'in areas were there were strong objections to the program'. Curriculum change, she believed, 'should progress at a rate which would be acceptable to parents'. School Board Director Cunningham concurred. He too supported the idea of Common Learnings but felt that before the course was made a requirement, 'parents should be consulted'.

School Board Secretary Ramberg then took issue with Superintendent Bruner about the seeming prerogative of school administrators in this matter. The Board of Education, Ramberg argued, was elected to resolve matters of this type. School Board Director Fabianke agreed. The Board, she pointed out, had referred the matter to the school administration, but administrators were not able to reach a solution that would be acceptable to the Parents Council. The Board, she concluded, should resolve the controversy. By a vote of four to two, the Board decided to make Common Learnings optional in both the junior and senior high schools.[105]

In September 1950, Superintendent Bruner resigned to accept a faculty position at New York University and was replaced by Rufus Putnam.[106] According to the *Minneapolis Review*, a local labor newspaper, the Board of Education, disturbed at Bruner's handling of the Common Learnings controversy, had forced him to resign.[107]

Seeking to avoid any further misunderstandings with the community, Putnam appointed a thirty-eight member Lay Advisory Committee on matters of curriculum. He even went so far as to appoint several of the leaders of the Parents Council to this new committee, including Mrs Stanley Berglund and Don Raihle.[108] The task of the Committee, Putnam noted in a letter to the President of the Minneapolis PTA, Herbert Parker, was, first, to keep members of the community informed about the school curriculum and, second, to make the school administration aware of public criticism of the school program.[109] The

Committee, Putnam evidently believed, could be used to deflect the kind of popular criticism that had led to the conflict over Common Learnings. At the October 1951 meeting of the Board of Education, Putnam stated that in return for their consultative role, members of the Advisory Committee would have to agree that 'criticism and comment which are made at meetings should not be discussed outside the meeting'.[110]

Putnam also established a more cautious policy than had been the case earlier with respect to the introduction of innovative changes. The schools would, he commented in the *Minneapolis Tribune,* continue to experiment with new programs. He went on to state, however, that 'an experiment in a given subject would be confined to one school or a few schools. These schools will watch it closely before it is expanded to other schools'.[111]

Despite Putnam's efforts, Common Learnings, although it was an optional course, continued to engender controversy. In November 1951, Putnam arranged for members of the Lay Advisory Committee to visit a number of city schools as a means of informing them about the existing curriculum. The Committee's members were divided into several small groups, each escorted on their visit by an administrator selected by Putnam. Putnam, it seems, was also interested in gauging the views of the Committee's members about the curriculum and instructed each of his administrators to prepare a report detailing the reactions and comments of the Lay Advisory Committee members.

From the reports, it appears that Common Learnings remained a potential source of dissatisfaction. Ruth Scribner, an elementary school Principal, noted that in her group which visited Ramsey Junior High School, 'Mrs Berglund was very critical of Miss Barron's Common Learnings class. No definite statement was offered [by Mrs Berglund] except that no leadership was possible with small group discussion'.[112] Similarly, Luella Cook reported that her group, which included Don Raihle, did not like the Common Learnings class they saw at Edison High School. The teacher, unlike others they saw at Edison, did not give her class clear directions. Cook warned Putnam that 'Common Learnings classes are still under scrutiny. We need to understand better where we are vulnerable. It was unfortunate in this particular tour that observers found (I fear) what they were looking for'.[113]

Throughout the decade of the 1950s, Common Learnings continued to cause difficulties for the school administration. At the May 1953 meeting of the Lay Advisory Committee, Putnam and his administrative staff went to great pains to show that Common Learnings did not represent the radical change that some had claimed. He stated that

English and social studies were still taught in Common Learnings classes. The only effect of integrating the two subjects, he noted, was that 'it enables a teacher to make use of English in social studies and social studies in English'.[114] Luella Cook pointed out that in the junior high schools, where Common Learnings was most likely to be found, there was a curriculum guide for the teaching of English and social studies that regulated instruction whether these subjects were taught separately or integrated into the Common Learnings Program. Common Learnings was, she went on to say, a 'loaded word' that possessed all kinds of negative connotations. A far more accurate description of what was occurring in Minneapolis was what she called the 'double period class'. Arthur Lewis, another member of Putnam's staff, stated that Common Learnings was neither a course in which content was selected in accord with student interest nor a course organized around current problems in society.[115]

The meeting seemed to be successful in winning over at least one former opponent of Common Learnings. Wright Brooks, who had been a member of the Parents Council three years earlier, pointed out that while Common Learnings had once been a course organized around the problems of youth, it was now simply a course in English and social studies.[116] Don Raihle, on the other hand, continued to remain unconvinced that the schools had retreated from their attempt to make the curriculum more functional. In March 1954, he wrote a letter to the editor of the *Minneapolis Star* in which he attacked the support given to Common Learnings by the Principal of Ramsey Junior High School, Russell Brackett. Brackett's support for this program had, according to Raihle, undermined both learning and respect for authority at Ramsey. Raihle went on to point out that Brackett:

> ... had the 'roudies' under his wing most of their waking hours for three years. He has made school for them one huge 'play pen' of fun, enjoyment and easy living. His students were passed from one grade to the next with their age group regardless of whether or not they had done well in class. They were pumped full of what Brackett calls 'world understanding' but apparently little was taught about 'understanding' and 'respect' here at home.[117]

To offset this kind of criticism, the school administration began to talk less about Common Learnings and more about a so-called 'double period program'. In April 1954, a letter was sent to parents of junior high school students by Assistant Superintendent Harry Cooper indicating that the same curriculum was followed either in the 'double period program' or in separate classes in English and social studies. In both instances, he pointed out, the students studied geography, history and basic communication skills. Further, in both instances the students had the opportunity to engage in group activities that would teach them the skills of 'living and working together effectively'. What distinguished the two approaches from each other, Cooper believed, was that teachers in the 'double period program' had more opportunity than those who taught either English or social studies alone to get to know their students.[118]

In 1957, the term Common Learnings was officially dropped in favor of the term 'double period'.[119] A memorandum describing the 'double period' issued two years later pointed out that the program has 'the same objectives and includes the same material' as does English and social studies when taught separately and that 'each subject retains its identity.'[120] In 1960, the city's junior high school principals made their final break with the tradition of Common Learnings and voted unanimously to change the name of the 'double period program' to that of 'English-Social Studies'.[121] During the next ten years these combined courses were gradually eliminated. By 1962, they had disappeared from the city's high schools, and by 1970 they were discontinued in Minneapolis' junior high schools.[122]

When the Minneapolis school administration introduced the Common Learnings Program in 1945, Bobbitt had already retired, Charters was just about to retire, and Caswell was midway through his career. Nevertheless, in establishing Common Learnings, Minneapolis educators seemed to share the outlook of these leaders of the American curriculum field. Although Minneapolis educators did not speak specifically about a spirit of community, they did believe as did Bobbitt, Charters and Caswell that the ongoing functioning of American society required a more cooperative citizenry. The Common Learnings Program represented the effort of Minneapolis educators to use the curriculum as an instrument of social control to achieve this goal for succeeding generations of American youth.

In the end, however, Common Learnings was no more successful than the Modern Problems course in making the curriculum more functional. As was the case with Modern Problems, the impact of day to day local events interfered with the ability of the school administration to use Common Learnings to fundamentally change the school curriculum. Community pressure from the Parents Council forced the school administration to retreat from its initial goal of replacing separate courses in English and social studies with a single, integrated course in Common Learnings. Continuing community pressure forced the school administration to deemphasize the very characteristics of Common Learnings that distinguished it from existing courses. The demise of Common Learnings in fact preceded that of Modern Problems by six years.

There is some evidence to suggest that what occurred in Minneapolis may be representative of what happened throughout the nation's school systems during this period. Investigations of curriculum reform in several American cities, Atlanta, Georgia, Fitchburg, Massachusetts, and Scarsdale, New York, also point to the role of what I have called local factors in limiting the success of these efforts.[123] What we are lacking, however, are specific studies that look directly, as does my study of Minneapolis, at the issue of social control. Without such investigations, we must for the present conclude that the twentieth-century effort to use the curriculum as an instrument of social control was hardly the success its proponents hoped that it would be.

VII

By the mid-1950s, the understanding of the school curriculum that had dominated turn-of-the-century educational thinking had undergone a fundamental transformation. At the beginning of the twentieth century when educators talked about the curriculum, they were for the most part referring to a sequence of separate subjects or disciplines which students completed during their years of schooling in order to develop their mental faculties. Fifty years later, the emergence of a field of curriculum, both as an academic discipline in the university and an occupational role in the public schools, had brought about a change in this viewpoint. Now when educators talked about the curriculum, they were usually referring to a collection of experiences and activities which integrated together what were once thought of as separate subjects and which served as a vehicle for adjusting students to the demands of adult life. At the root of this transformation was the effort of the founding theorists of the American curriculum field to use the school program to resolve the tension between the nation's liberal democratic ethic and the realities of twentieth-century urban industrial life.

Our examination of the development of the American curriculum field closes with Caswell's appointment to the Presidency of Teachers College in 1954. Although curriculum theorists had by that time proposed how the school program might be used to enhance liberal democratic values, our study of Minneapolis suggests that those who were responsible for curriculum selection and organization in the public schools were only marginally successful in actually implementing these proposals. Our study of Minneapolis indicates that the actual American school curriculum never really became the instrument of social control that the founding theorists of the curriculum field sought.

The following thirty years have for the most part been a replay of the past. New educational movements have appeared to replace those that we have considered in this essay. The idea of mental disciplines gave way in the late 1950s and early 1960s to the structure of the disciplines movement. Since 1970, such proposals as those for career education and competency based education have supplanted the social efficiency movement in the effort to model education after the practices of industrial capitalism. And during the same period such movements as those for open education and humanistic education have appeared to take up the cause once advanced by Caswell. The struggle, however, between a so-called academically oriented school program and a more functional one has continued with little sign of resolution. If the criticisms of American education that have appeared in such reports as *A Nation at Risk* are indicative of current educational thinking, we are, it appears, about to return something akin to the idea of mental disciplines to the primacy it enjoyed in educational thought at the turn of this century.[124]

There is, however, a critical difference between the curriculum thinking that we have examined in this essay and the thinking of the last thirty years. Somewhere along the way, the great social purpose of reconciling liberal democracy with twentieth century life that appeared in Mead's social psychology and which was carried into curriculum thought with varying degrees of success by Bobbitt, Charters and Caswell has become lost. There have been many educators during the last thirty years who have in the name of a more functional curriculum promoted the various educational movements that I mentioned above. There have been few, if any, however, who have like Caswell, and even like Bobbitt and Charters, recognized why this is so important for the life of our country and its liberal democratic heritage.

Notes

1 Minneapolis Public Schools, *A Million a Year*, Monograph No. 1, Series 1916–1917, Minneapolis, Board of Education, 1917; FRANK E. SPAULDING, *School Superintendent in Action in Five Cities*, Rindge, New Hampshire, Richard R. Smith Publishers, 1955, pp. 476–85.
2 WILLIAM F. WEBSTER, *Minneapolis Public Schools Annual Report, 1928–1929*, Minneapolis, Board of Education, 1929, pp. 41 and 260.

3 *Ibid.*, p. 49.

4 *Senior High School Course of Study, Minneapolis, Minnesota*, Minneapolis, Board of Education, 1912–1913; National Education Association of the United States, *Report of the Committee of Ten on Secondary School Studies*, New York, American Book Company, 1894, p. 45.

5 *Senior High School Course of Study, Minneapolis, Minnesota*, Minneapolis, Board of Education, 1919–1920; *Senior High School Course of Study, Minneapolis, Minnesota*, Minneapolis, Board of Education, 1920–1924.

6 *Senior High School Course of Study, Minneapolis, Minnesota*, Minneapolis, Board of Education, 1925–1931.

7 Minneapolis Public Schools, *Presenting Glimpses of Minneapolis Public Schools*, Minneapolis, Board of Education, 1937, p. 17.

8 Minneapolis Public Schools, *Distribution of Ability Groups in 6A Grades*, Minneapolis, Board of Education, 1924, p. 1; CARROLL REED, *Care of the Individual Child in the Minneapolis Public Schools*, Report of the Superintendent of Schools to the Board of Education, Minneapolis, Board of Education, 1937, p. 12.

9 *Minneapolis School Bulletin*, 1 February, 1934, p. 3; *Minneapolis School Bulletin*, 23 September, 1937, pp. 1–3; *Minneapolis School Bulletin*, 19 May, 1938, pp. 1–3.

10 'Teacher forums', 9, 10, 16, 17 March, 1937, General Files of the Minneapolis Public Schools, Minneapolis Public Schools Information Service Center.

11 Prudence Cutright, 'The curriculum and the world today', General Files, *op. cit.*, p. 9.

12 Webster, *op. cit.*, p. 43.

13 Minneapolis Public Schools, *Course of Study in Work Reading*, Minneapolis, Board of Education, 1928, pp. 1 and 3.

14 Minneapolis Public Schools, *Course of Study in Recreational Reading*, Minneapolis, Board of Education, 1929, p. 13.

15 CARROLL REED, *The Years of the Depression, 1930–1935*, Report of the Superintendent of Schools to the Board of Education, Minneapolis, Board of Education, 1935, pp. 13–20 and 156–7.

16 *Ibid.*, pp. 158–9.

17 WILLIAM C. PHILLIPS, 'The reaction of the Minneapolis public schools to the great depression, 1929–1941', unpublished masters thesis, University of Minnesota, 1966, p. 85.

18 MAXINE SULLIVAN, University of Chicago Registrar, private interview held at the University of Chicago, 18 July, 1984; University of Chicago, *Bulletin of Information-School of Education, 1918–1919*, Vol. 18, No. 3, Chicago, University of Chicago, 1918, pp. 36–7.

19 PRUDENCE CUTRIGHT, 'What effect has the systematic use of dictation exercises on the ability of children to use selected marks of punctuation', unpublished masters thesis, University of Minnesota, 1927.

20 PRUDENCE CUTRIGHT, 'How to use the scientific method in curriculum studies', in *Seventh Yearbook of the Department of Supervisors and Directors of Instruction*, edited by Paul Rankin, New York, Teachers College, 1934, p. 120; PRUDENCE CUTRIGHT, 'Biographical, sketch of curriculum study and construction in the Minneapolis public schools', General Files, 6 January, 1940, *op. cit.*, p. 2.

21 Minneapolis Public Schools, 'Curriculum bulletin No. 277,' General Files, 29 February, 1936, *op. cit.*, p. 2.

22 PRUDENCE CUTRIGHT, 'The use of research in supervision and curriculum con-

struction', in *First Yearbook of the National Conference on Educational Method*, edited by JAMES HOSIC, New York, Teachers College, 1928, pp. 158–9 and 163.

23 REED, *op. cit.*, p. 21.

24 'The curriculum and the world today', *op. cit.*, p. 5.

25 PRUDENCE CUTRIGHT, 'Report of the Division of Instruction', General Files, 1937, *op. cit.*, p. 20.

26 'The curriculum and the world today', *op. cit.*, p. 4.

27 Minneapolis Public Schools, 'A study of curriculum values in the junior high school', General Files, *op. cit.*, n.d.

28 *Minneapolis School Bulletin*, 7 November, 1935, p. 1.

29 *Minneapolis School Buttetin*, 4 October, 1934, p. 3.

30 *Minneapolis School Bulletin*, 21 November, 1935, pp. 1 and 4.

31 *Minneapolis School Bulletin*, 5 January, 1939, pp. 1 and 4.

32 *Minneapolis School Bulletin*, 28 April, 1938, p. 3.

33 BESS WILSON, *The Three R's Plus: A Study of Minneapolis Public Schools*, Minneapolis, Minneapolis Journal, 1935, pp. 22.

34 *Ibid.*, p. 20.

35 *Ibid.*, p. 65.

36 *Ibid.*, pp. 63–4.

37 Commission on the Reorganization of Secondary Education, *The Social Studies in Secondary Education*, Bulletin No. 28, Washington, D.C., U.S. Government Printing Office, 1916, p. 12; *Senior High School Course of Study, Minneapolis, Minnesota*, Minneapolis, Board of Education, 1925–1931, pp. 4–5.

38 Commission on the Reorganization of Secondary Education, *ibid.*, p. 52.

39 *Senior High School Course of Study*, *op. cit.*, p. 5.

40 Minneapolis Public Schools, *The Scope of the Senior High School*, Minneapolis, Board of Education, 1935, pp. 13–14; Commission on the Reorganization of Secondary Education, *Preliminary Statement by Chairmen of Committees of the National Education Association on the Reorganization of Secondary Education*, Bulletin No. 41, Washington, D.C., U.S. Government Printing Office, 1913, p. 17.

41 Cutright to high school principals, 26 October, 1939, General Files, *op. cit.*

42 PRUDENCE CUTRIGHT, 'Some guiding principles for teaching and for curriculum development', General Files, 31 October, 1938, *op. cit.*, p. 2.

43 Minneapolis Public Schools, 'Curriculum bulletin No. 400', General Files, 8 November, 1937, *op. cit.*

44 Minneapolis Public Schools, 'Curriculum bulletin No. 424', General Files, 8 December, 1937, *op. cit.*

45 Minneapolis Public Schools, 'Curriculum bulletin No. 701', General Files, October, 1939, *op. cit.*

46 Minneapolis Public Schools, 'Curriculum bulletin No. 198', General Files, 29 March, 1944, *op. cit.; Senior High School Course of Study, Minneapolis, Minnesota*, Minneapolis, Board of Education, 1938–1939, p. 11; *Senior High School Course of Study, Minneapolis, Minnesota*, Minneapolis, Board of Education, 1941–1942, pp. 11–12; *Senior High School Course of Study, Minneapolis, Minnesota*, Minneapolis, Board of Education, 1943–1944, pp. 12–3.

47 Minutes, Department of History, West High School, General Files, 19 October, 1940, *op. cit.*

48 Wright to Cutright, 4 April, 1940, General Files, *op. cit.*

49 Reed to Rockwell, 29 April, 1940, General Files, *op. cit.*

50 Rockwell to Shumway, 6 May, 1940, General Files, *op. cit.*

51 Shumway to Rockwell, 14 May, 1940, General Files, *op. cit.*

52 Caldwell to Cutright, 5 June, 1940, General Files, *op. cit.;* Cutright to Caldwell, 11 June, 1940, General Files, *op. cit.*

53 Minneapolis Public Schools, 'Curriculum bulletin No. S–201', 13 April, 1944, General Files, *op. cit.*

54 Minneapolis Public Schools, 'Report to the teachers of social studies grades 7–12' General Files, *op. cit.*, p. 6.

55 Mary Lou Nelson, private interview held in Minneapolis, Minnesota, 22 May, 1984.

56 Bob Ansel, private interview held in Minneapolis, Minnesota, 25 May, 1984.

57 Roger Ryberg, private interview held in Minneapolis, Minnesota, 3 June, 1984.

58 Kathleen Kunzman, private interview held in Minneapolis, Minnesota, 20 May, 1984.

59 Minutes, Senior High School Principals, 10 December, 1946, General Files, *op. cit.*

60 Minutes, Social Studies Steering Committee, 21 October, 1948, General Files, *op. cit.*

61 Minneapolis Public Schools, 'Report to the teachers of social studies in grades 7–12', February–June, 1944, General Files, *op. cit.*, p. 7.

62 Minneapolis Public Schools, 'Report to principals of senior high schools on social studies curriculum study', 2 March, 1955, General Files, *op. cit.*, pp. 2–3; Minneapolis Public Schools, 'Illustrative material from the social studies curriculum study', August, 1956, General Files, *op. cit.*, p. 13.

63 For a complete history of the Modern Problems course in Minneapolis see, BARRY M. FRANKLIN, 'The social efficiency movement and curriculum change, 1939 –1976', in *Social Histories of the Secondary Curriculum: Subjects for Study*, edited by IVOR F. GOODSON, Lewes, England, Falmer Press, 1984, pp. 239–68.

64 Minutes, Senior High Schools Principals, 17 April, 1963, General Files, *op. cit.*, p. 2.

65 Friedman to National Council for the Social Studies' Committee on the Social Studies and National Interest, 7 December, 1962, General Files, *op. cit.*

66 *Minneapolis School Bulletin*, 29 May, 1941, p. 3.

67 *Minneapolis School Bulletin*, 26 February, 1942, p. 4.

68 Minneapolis Public Schools, 'Report of the senior high school social studies policies committee', February, 1943, General Files, *op. cit.*

69 *Minneapolis School Bulletin*, 23 March, 1944, p. 1; *Minneapolis School Bulletin*, 13 April, 1944, p. 3.

70 PRUDENCE CUTRIGHT, 'Practices in curriculum development', in *American Education in the Postwar Period, Forty-fourth Year-book of the National Society for the Study of Education,* Part I, edited by NELSON HENRY, Chicago, University of Chicago Press, 1945, pp. 267–88.

71 *Minneapolis Workshop News*, 21 June, 1946, p. 4.

72 Educational Policies Commission, *Education for All American Youth*, Washington, D.C., National Education Association, 1944, pp. 234–40 and 248–52.

73 Minneapolis Public Schools, *A Primer for Common Learnings*, Minneapolis, Board of Education, 1948, pp. 7–8.

74 *Minneapolis Workshop News*, September, 1949, p. 12.

75 *Ibid.*, p. 13.

76 *Minneapolis School Bulletin*, 20 February, 1947, p. 6.

77 Edward Haynes, private interview held in Minneapolis, Minnesota, 22 November, 1980.
78 Dorothy Heath, private interview held in Minneapolis, Minnesota, 22 November, 1980.
79 *Minneapolis Tribune*, 22 March, 1950, p. 13.
80 *Minneapolis Tribune*, 27 March, 1950, p. 9.
81 HEATH, *op. cit.*
82 Minneapolis Public Schools, *World Citizenship: A Resource Guide for Teacher Use*, Minneapolis, Board of Education, 1949, p. 13.
83 *Minneapolis Star*, 10 February, 1950, p. 25.
84 Minneapolis Public Schools, *Board of Education Minutes*, 14 February, 1950, p. 1.
85 *Ibid.*, p. 3.
86 *Ibid.*, pp. 9–10.
87 *Ibid.*, p. 15.
88 Moore to Bruner, 6 February, 1950, General Files, *op. cit.*
89 *Board of Education Minutes*, *op. cit.*, pp. 3, 10 and 13.
90 *Ibid.*, p. 4.
91 *Minneapolis Tribune*, 10 March, 1950, p. 11.
92 *Board of Education Minutes*, *op. cit.*, pp. 6, 7 and 13.
93 *Ibid.*, p. 15.
94 *Minneapolis School Bulletin*, 27 May, 1948, p. 11.
95 *Board of Education Minutes*, *op. cit.*, pp. 3, 5.
96 *Ibid.*, p. 2.
97 *Minneapolis Tribune*, 11 March, 1950, p. 9.
98 HAYNES, *op. cit.*
99 *Minneapolis School Bulletin*, 20 February, 1947, p. 6.
100 *Board of Education Minutes*, *op. cit.*, p. 9.
101 *Ibid.*, p. 2.
102 *Minneapolis Tribune*, 13 April, 1950, p. 10.
103 *Ibid.*
104 Minneapolis Public Schools, *Board of Education Minutes*, 23 May, 1950, pp. 88–9.
105 *Ibid.*, pp. 89–90.
106 Bruner to Board of Education, 14 September, 1950, General Files, *op. cit.*
107 *Minneapolis Labor Review*, 28 September, 1950, p. 1.
108 *Minneapolis Tribune*, 14 August, 1951, p. 1.
109 Putnam to Parker, 1 October, 1951, General Files, *op. cit.*
110 Minneapolis Public Schools, *Board of Education Minutes*, 30 October, 1951, p. 252.
111 *Minneapolis Tribune*, *op. cit.*, p. 1.
112 Ruth Scribner, 'Report of tour # 1 for Lay Advisory Committee', 6 November, 1951, General Files, *op. cit.*
113 Luella Cook, 'Report of tour # 3 for Lay Advisory Committee', 6 November, 1951, General Files, *op. cit.*
114 Minutes, Lay Advisory Committee, 7 May, 1953, General Files, *op. cit.*, p. 4.
115 *Ibid.*, p. 5.
116 *Ibid.*
117 Raihle to Editor, *Minneapolis Star*, 4 March, 1954, General Files, *op. cit.*
118 Cooper to junior high school parents, 5 April, 1954, General Files, *op. cit.*
119 Memorandum, 4 March, 1957, General Files, *op. cit.*

120 Minneapolis public schools, 'What is the double period', 14 December, 1959, General Files, *op cit.*

121 Minutes, Junior High School Principals, 12 October, 1960, General Files, *op. cit.*

122 Minneapolis Public Schools, *Directory*, 1950–1970.

123 CAROL A. O'CONNOR, 'Setting a standard for suburbia: Innovation in the Scarsdale schools, 1920–1930', *History of Education Quarterly*, 20, Fall, 1980, pp. 295–311; PAUL RINGEL, 'Cooperative industrial education: The Fitchburg plan', a paper presented at the annual meeting of the American Educational Research Association, Los Angeles, California, April 1981; WAYNE URBAN, 'Educational reform in a new south city: Atlanta, 1890–1925', in *Education and the Rise of the New South*, edited by RONALD GOODENOW and ARTHUR O. WHITE, Boston; G.K. Hall and Company, 1981, chapter 6.

124 National Commission on Excellence in Education, *A Nation at Risk*, Washington, D.C. U.S. Government Printing Office, 1983.

Index

Index